FINDING ONESELF IN THE OTHER

FINDING ONESELF IN THE OTHER

G. A. Cohen

Edited by Michael Otsuka

PRINCETON UNIVERSITY PRESS

PRINCETON AND OXFORD

Published by Princeton University Press,
41 William Street, Princeton, New Jersey 08540
In the United Kingdom: Princeton University Press,
6 Oxford Street, Woodstock, Oxfordshire OX20 1TW

press.princeton.edu

Cover photograph taken by Derek Parfit

Library of Congress Cataloging-in-Publication Data

Cohen, G. A. (Gerald Allan), 1941–2009.
Finding oneself in the other / G.A. Cohen ; edited by Michael Otsuka.
p. cm.
Includes bibliographical references and index.
ISBN 978-0-691-14880-9 (hardcover : alk. paper) — ISBN 978-0-691-14881-6 (pbk. : alk. paper)
1. Cohen, G. A. (Gerald Allan), 1941–2009. 2. Philosophers—Great Britain.
3. Political science—Philosophy. 4. Social sciences—Philosophy. I. Otsuka, Michael. II. Title.

B1618.C648A5 2013
320—dc23
2012001073

British Library Cataloging-in-Publication Data is available
This book has been composed in Minion Pro
Printed on acid-free paper. ∞

Printed in the United States of America

10 9 8 7 6 5 4 3 2 1

Contents

Editor's Preface vii

Acknowledgments xiii

Chapter 1 Isaiah's Marx, and Mine 1

Chapter 2 Prague Preamble to "Why Not Socialism?" 16

Chapter 3 A Black and White Issue 20

Chapter 4 Two Weeks in India 26

Chapter 5 Complete Bullshit 94

Chapter 6 Casting the First Stone: Who Can, and Who Can't, Condemn the Terrorists? 115

Chapter 7 Ways of Silencing Critics 134

Chapter 8 Rescuing Conservatism: A Defense of Existing Value (All Souls version) 143

Chapter 9 Valedictory Lecture: My Philosophical Development (and impressions of philosophers whom I met along the way) 175

Chapter 10 Notes on Regarding People as Equals 193

Chapter 11 One Kind of Spirituality: Come Back, Feuerbach, All Is Forgiven! 201

Works Cited 209

Index 213

Editor's Preface

This is the second of three volumes of writings by G. A. (Jerry) Cohen that have been collected and edited after his death in 2009. The first brought together previously uncollected essays in political philosophy,[1] and the third will include lectures and other writings on the history of moral and political philosophy.[2] This one combines philosophical and nonphilosophical writings of a more personal nature, which depart from the strictures of formal academic prose.

As a consequence of this departure, every chapter of this book should be accessible to nonphilosophers as well as philosophers and should engage nonacademics as well as academics. There are extended stretches of first-person narration—of, for example, Cohen's first trip to India, his time as a student at McGill and Oxford, and his interrogation of his apparatchik Uncle Norman during a visit to Prague as a young man. They make it clear what prompted Thomas Nagel to describe Cohen as a "wonderful raconteur" in a review of his earlier, narration-rich book, *If You're an Egalitarian, How Come You're So Rich?*[3] The more philosophical writings collected here are also unforbidding. The topics are of general interest: on the truth in conservatism, on who can condemn terrorists, and on the essence of bullshit. Moreover, rather than being enmeshed in the intricacies of highly developed academic controversies, these writings explore relatively uncharted territory, as in the case of his essays on conservatism and terrorism, or follow the trail of a single pioneer, as in the case of his essay on bullshit.

The book opens, in Chapter 1 ("Isaiah's Marx, and Mine"), with a tribute to his teacher and mentor Isaiah Berlin, written for a festschrift that was published in 1991. Cohen provides an account of his time at Oxford as a B.Phil. student under Berlin's guidance in the early 1960s. He also describes their differing views on the person and convictions of Karl Marx.

Chapter 2 ("Prague Preamble to 'Why Not Socialism?'") was written for delivery as introductory remarks to a lecture on socialism in Prague in 2001.[4] It traces Cohen's loss of belief during the 1960s in the actually existing communism of the Soviet Union and the rest of the Eastern Bloc and offers an apology, in both senses of the word, for the earlier persistence of that belief.

[1] *On the Currency of Egalitarian Justice.*

[2] *Lectures on the History of Moral and Political Philosophy.*

[3] Nagel, "Getting Personal," p. 6.

[4] Visa difficulties prevented Cohen from making it to the Czech Republic to deliver this lecture.

Chapter 3 ("A Black and White Issue") provides a terse, dispassionate defense of the academic boycott of apartheid South Africa. It was originally published in 1989 in a periodical for faculty and students at the University of Oxford.

Chapter 4 ("Two Weeks in India") is a slightly abridged version of Cohen's nearly contemporaneous reflections on a journey through India in 1993. Fifteen years later, Cohen wrote to some editors at university presses to express an interest in publishing this:

> I attach a peculiar item, being the travel diary (or whatever you want to call it) that I wrote about my first trip to India, which was in January 1993. I originally circulated it privately, around that time, and many people urged me to try to have it published, because they found the narration gripping. I suppose the most illustrious person who thought it should be published was Amartya Sen. But I was firm in my mind that I did not want to publish it, because there's so much stuff in it about other people that they might not want known.
>
> The years go by, things sink into people's past, and I have changed my mind about publication. I'm now very keen to publish it. ... I would make not many changes: just eliminate the most egregious bits, people's-sensitivities-wise, and add a few explanatory footnotes and an epilogue.

Cohen's account of India is the nonphilosophical highlight of this volume. His remarks on poverty and begging are unforgettable, as are various vignettes of encounters with strangers. Upon my first reading shortly after it was written, I was struck by the way it gave me a wonderful vicarious sense of what it is like to be Jerry Cohen: the blooming, buzzing insights and perceptions; the empathy, intensity, and fascination; his sense of the ridiculous; the joie de vivre. At the time of his death, Cohen had not yet found a publisher for this manuscript and therefore had not yet made the changes he mentioned in the above correspondence. In preparing this manuscript for publication here, I have tried to eliminate passages that people he encountered on this trip might find upsetting to discover in print.

Chapter 5 divides into two parts. The first part, entitled "Deeper into Bullshit," was originally published in a festschrift for Harry Frankfurt in 2002.[5] Having declared it "too speculative," but I suspect also for reasons of space, Cohen withheld publication there of the second part, entitled "Why One Kind of Bullshit Flourishes in France," which I am pleased to have the opportunity to publish here. The overarching title of this chapter—"Complete Bullshit"—is the name Cohen chose for his computer file that brought Parts I and II together.

[5] In his "Reply to G. A. Cohen" in the same festschrift, Frankfurt remarks that "Cohen's essay is, so far as I am aware, the first significant attempt either to criticize or to extend my work on bullshit" (Sarah Buss and Lee Overton, eds., *Contours of Agency*, p. 340). This work of Frankfurt's was later repackaged as a little book, *On Bullshit*.

Chapters 6 ("Casting the First Stone") and 7 ("Ways of Silencing Critics") ask who does and who does not have standing to condemn those who commit acts of terrorism and other apparent wrongs, where this question is not meant to be settled simply by a determination of whether the acts under investigation are in fact morally justified. Rather, the answer will also depend on such things as whether those who condemn terrorism are themselves responsible for the injustice that provides the terrorists with their cause, or whether they have committed atrocities as bad as those of the terrorists whom they condemn. Chapter 6 is the published version of a lecture to the Royal Institute of Philosophy in London in 2005, and Chapter 7 consists of previously unpublished further reflections that were prompted by the writing of that lecture.

Chapter 8 ("Rescuing Conservatism") is the most outstanding philosophical essay of this collection: an original, rich, and finely wrought set of meditations. It offers a defense of the "small-c conservatism" of valuable and valued things.[6] This was the last work of philosophy that Cohen brought to a sufficiently finished state to publish. In late March of 2009, he sent it to the editors of a festschrift for T. M. Scanlon.[7] The version published here differs from the festschrift version insofar as it restores his references to All Souls College that were present in several earlier drafts but replaced, at a late stage, with references to a fictional liberal arts college.[8] As a consequence of his elimination of these references to All Souls, Cohen also omitted a brief section entitled "Identity and Tradition" from the festschrift version. That discussion is published here, for the first time, as Section 5 of Chapter 8.

Cohen was prompted to articulate the case for conservatism in response to a proposal that his college accept outside sources of funding. He was later persuaded to eliminate references in the paper to the imperative to preserve All Souls unchanged. The fear was that such talk would expose his defense of conservatism to ad hominem mockery as a parochial concern bound up with an elite establishment of which he was a member. I have nevertheless chosen to restore the references to All Souls here in order to reproduce the paper as Cohen had conceived it throughout most of its gestation and to convey some of the personal roots of his conviction. My decision to do so has been made less difficult by the realization that I am thereby preserving a thing of value that might otherwise be lost. It is also made easier by the availability of the alternative festschrift version, which advances the more disinterested case.

Chapter 9 is Cohen's Valedictory Lecture, which marked his retirement in 2008 from his Chichele Chair in Social and Political Theory at All Souls. It re-

[6] As he makes clear in this essay, Cohen remained adamantly opposed to the "large-C Conservatism" of the British Conservative Party and the political Right more generally.

[7] R. Jay Wallace, Rahul Kumar, and Samuel Freeman, eds., *Reasons and Recognition*.

[8] Almost all of these changes occur in Section 2, which is entitled "Keeping Valuable and Valued Things As They Are, and Accepting the Given."

turns to the Chapter 1 narration of his philosophical development and fills out the chronology in both directions—back to his first encounter with philosophy as a child in Montreal, and forward to his time as a lecturer at University College London. The prepared text of that lecture is published here. The only known recording of that lecture, by Maris Kopcke Tinture as a member of the audience, has been posted on Princeton University Press's Web page.[9] Cohen shared a CD of this recording, plus the text, with some friends who had been unable to attend the lecture itself. These came with the following cover letter:

> I am sending you a CD that records most of my May 1, 2008 Valedictory Lecture.
>
> Some points:
>
> 1. Eight minutes in the middle of the lecture were not recorded. So the second major track of the CD presents material that begins eight minutes later than the material at the end of the first track. The missing words are in the Valedictory Lecture text, which I am also sending. But PLEASE don't read the text, apart from that unrecorded part, except when listening to the CD, because the text is much less funny unspoken. And there are also ad-libs away from the text on the CD.
> 2. On the other hand, if I may continue in instructional mode, please don't listen to the CD without following it in the text. I say that because the CD audio is not always clear, and the text makes clear what's being said.

The last two chapters of this book are embryonic drafts of two unfinished papers, which I include in this volume after consultation with the family. Please bear in mind while reading these papers that neither is close to what it would have been if Cohen had been able to bring it to completion.

Chapter 10 ("Notes on Regarding People as Equals"), which Cohen drafted in 2006 and revised in 2008–9, contains, in his words, "preliminary reflections, many of them barely half-baked," on the question of what it is to regard another as one's equal. He sketches a Hegelian answer to this question. These are, as his own title indicates, notes rather than an essay in more finished form.

Chapter 11 ("One Kind of Spirituality"), which Cohen began to write three months before his death, is even less finished. In correspondence, he described it as so "raw" that he "would never dream of giving it" as a talk in its present form. Cohen also wrote that he "would not publish this without further explanation of what is meant." In conversation he mentioned that he was not sure that the word "spirituality" was the appropriate one to capture the notion he was trying to express, which was that one can feel blessed in a manner that should be understood as neither deity-affirming nor merely metaphorical.

[9] http://press.princeton.edu/titles/9886.html.

Even in their unfinished state, however, these two papers shed light on Cohen's "Hegelian Prelude" to Chapter 8, on conservatism.

The title of this book is drawn from the second sentence of that prelude, which opens as follows:

> Hegel says that "Spirit" achieves freedom when the subject finds itself in its own object, so that "it is at home with itself in its own otherness as such."
>
> This essay explores modes of finding oneself in the other. I am not here interested in the characterization of that condition as freedom, not because that is an unimportant aspect of Hegel's claim—it *is*, after all, his claim—but just because I fry other fish here. The conservatism that I defend is Hegelian to this extent: in each of three cases that I shall distinguish, namely, that of accepting the given, of valuing the valuable, and of valuing the valued, the subject is at peace with the object.

The title also resonates with a sentence in "One Kind of Spirituality": "Since there is no God for the relation of celebrating (or sacrificing and so on) to be in relation *to*, but it is a sentiment fraught with relationality, it can find its completion only in relation to the world and to other human beings." The theme of finding completion in relation to the world of other human beings recurs in many of the other essays in this volume: for example, in the focus on interpersonal justifiability in "Casting the First Stone" and "Ways of Silencing Critics," in his Hegelian understanding of what it is to regard another as one's equal, and in his encounters with various others that he conveys in his account of his two weeks in India. This theme is also captured in the very title of Chapter 1: "Isaiah's Marx, and Mine." And of course, in his philosophical writings outside the four corners of this book, Cohen found himself—his philosophical bearings, his theoretical commitments, and his distinctive voice—through a remarkable series of engagements with the thoughts of others: not only Marx, but also his contemporaries Nozick, Dworkin, and Rawls. Through his engagement with them, he reached the same heights.

Acknowledgments

The following works by G. A. Cohen, which constitute all or part of the chapters numbered below, have been reprinted, with gratefully acknowledged permission where appropriate:

1. “Isaiah’s Marx, and Mine.” In Avishai Margalit and Edna Ullmann-Margalit, eds. *Isaiah Berlin: A Celebration*. London: Hogarth Press; Chicago: University of Chicago Press, 1991. Copyright © 1991 G. A. Cohen. Reprinted with the permission of University of Chicago Press.
3. “A Black and White Issue.” *Oxford Magazine*, No. 42, Second Week, Hilary Term, 1989, pp. 5–7. Reprinted in part.
5. “Deeper into Bullshit.” In Sarah Buss and Lee Overton, eds. *Contours of Agency: Essays on Themes from Harry Frankfurt*. Cambridge, Mass.: MIT Press, 2002. Reprinted with the permission of MIT Press.
6. “Casting the First Stone: Who Can, and Who Can’t, Condemn the Terrorists?” In Anthony O’Hear, ed. *Political Philosophy*. Royal Institute of Philosophy Supplement. Vol. 58. Cambridge: Cambridge University Press, 2006. Copyright © 2006 The Royal Institute of Philosophy and the Contributors. Reprinted with the permission of Cambridge University Press.
8. “Rescuing Conservatism: A Defense of Existing Value.” In R. Jay Wallace, Rahul Kumar, and Samuel Freeman, eds. *Reasons and Recognition: Essays on the Philosophy of T. M. Scanlon*. New York: Oxford University Press, 2011. Reprinted in revised form with the permission of Oxford University Press.

Thanks to Ian Malcolm, Ben Tate, and Lauren Lepow at Princeton University Press, who were exemplary editors in their different roles, and to Tom Broughton-Willett, for preparing the Index. I have benefited throughout from the guidance of Hillel Steiner and Andrew Williams, who served as readers for the Press. Of the many who knew Jerry to whom I turned for advice, Annette Barnes, Rajeev Bhargava, and Cécile Fabre were especially generous with their time. Finally, I’m very grateful to Jerry’s family—Gideon, Maggie, Michael, Michèle, Miriam, and Sarah—for their inspiration and support.

FINDING ONESELF IN THE OTHER

Chapter One

ISAIAH'S MARX, AND MINE

1. Isaiah says that nothing is historically inevitable. Maybe he is wrong to think that nothing is, but it is surely true that many things are not. If, for example, I had not happened to attend—I was not required to be there—the seminar on "Identity and Individuation" given by David Wiggins and Michael Woods in New College, Oxford, on October 9, 1961, then I might never have come to know Isaiah Berlin. Although he was not at the seminar himself, my presence there was the first link in a loose causal chain that led to our friendship.

I had arrived in Oxford on September 14 of that year, having boarded ship eight days earlier in my native Montreal, in fresh possession of a McGill University Bachelor of Arts degree in Philosophy and Political Science. At McGill I was educated well in the history of European political theory, and in parts of the history of European philosophy, but I had not learned how to handle philosophical issues in their own right. I could expound, quite effectively, what Descartes and Hobbes and Hume said, but I was not well placed to comment on whether what they said was true. I was, moreover, almost entirely untouched by the philosophy then current in Oxford, a philosophy which my McGill teacher Raymond Klibansky had described, without derision, as "talk about talk." I was not arrogant. Although I had satisfied my teachers at McGill, I did not expect to shine at Oxford, nor did I feel any need to do so. But I was also not terrified at the prospect of having to master something quite new. I expected to get by, and to come away with a B.Phil. The seminar meeting on "Identity and Individuation" dissolved that expectation.

At the time, I hardly knew what identity and individuation were, and I was going to the seminar to learn about them, and also to learn about Oxford seminars, since this was to be my first one, on the first day of my first Oxford term. At the head of the table sat Wiggins and Woods, and Woods proceeded to read a paper to the meeting. He began by saying that he would call a criterion of identity a "CI" and a principle of individuation a "PI." He then said that his purpose was to investigate how CIs and PIs were related to one another.

This was not a good beginning, as far as I was concerned. Since I did not really know what identity and individuation were, reflection about the relationship between the criterion of the first and the principle of the second was, for me, premature, I did not understand what Woods went on to say. I could not construe particular sentences, nor did I get the general drift. Woods was and is a lucid expositor, but he reasonably took himself to be addressing graduates who were accustomed to high-powered argument, and that did not include me.

In the discussion following Woods's paper, things got worse. A young man began to examine Woods's claims, using (what I would learn was) the touchstone of Oxford philosophy, a particular example. The young man was Willie Charlton, who went on to become a professional philosopher. The particular example concerned a character called a "pursuivant." The word sounded French, and, for a Montrealer, that was, initially, reassuring. I thought it must mean *something that follows*, and, although I had not followed Woods's paper, I had noticed that whether or not this followed from that seemed in these parts to be an important issue. But if we had words in Montreal which sounded like 'pursuivant' (such as the word *'poursuivant'*), we did not, in my recollection, have any pursuivants there, and before long I realized that I was, once again, lost. I could not achieve control over Willie Charlton's example.

I left the seminar in a state of apprehension. The big frog from the small pond was at sea, and likely to sink without trace. As I have said, I did not need to excel at Oxford, but I did need to get the B.Phil. degree: for self-esteem, for the sake of making a living, for the old folks at home. And now I was confident that I could not master this difficult thing, Oxford philosophy, in the two years available to me. Or, if that statement is a misremembering overdramatization of the sense I then had of my plight, what is certainly true is that I was not confident that I would be able to pass the B.Phil. examination. Feeling threatened, I sought a risk-reducing strategy, a way of meeting the B.Phil. requirements which was consonant with my unpromising undergraduate preparation.

Those requirements, then as now, were a thesis of thirty thousand words and three written examinations: two on selected branches of philosophy, and one on a great dead philosopher or great superseded school of philosophy, a list of these being provided. With respect to the branches, almost all B.Phil. candidates chose at least one of Epistemology and Metaphysics and Logic and Scientific Method, since those subjects were thought to constitute the center of philosophy, and they were, moreover, ones in which Oxford was preeminent. They were also, and not only as far as I was concerned, the hardest options, and the Wiggins/Woods seminar had convinced me that they were too hard for me. Moral Philosophy and Political Philosophy were also available, and they were less redoubtable, but few chose more than one of them, and almost no one chose Political Philosophy. That was partly because Oxford then participated in the neglect of political philosophy which characterized the Anglophone philosophical scene generally. In 1961, the "sixties," which were to put many political topics on the philosophical agenda, had not yet occurred, and there was no commanding work in political philosophy[1] to inspire the student: John Rawls's *Theory of Justice* had begun to

[1] In "Does Political Theory Still Exist?"—which first appeared [in French, as "La théorie politique existe-t-elle?"—Ed.] in 1961—Isaiah Berlin remarked that "no commanding work of political philosophy has appeared in the twentieth century" (p. 143).

germinate in the fifties, but it did not appear until 1971. Moral philosophy was in better shape, locally, with Richard Hare and Philippa Foot locked in fierce illuminating controversy, and Alan Montefiore looking on nearby and ruminating wisely. But moral philosophy was nevertheless thought to be relatively easy to master, a softish option; and political philosophy was thought soft to the point of viscidity, held in contempt (not entirely unfairly, considering the quality of most of the very little that was then produced within the field) if not by the paid professionals then certainly by most of my B.Phil. cohort. It was regarded, at best, as a byway or curio. As for the dead thinkers and schools, they were Plato, Aristotle, Kant, the Rationalists, the Empiricists, Medieval Philosophers, and the Original Authorities for the Rise of Mathematical Logic. But candidates could also choose alternative philosophers, provided that they had "special permission."

My first decision, which I thought cowardly but to which I was resolved to stick, was to do Moral Philosophy and Political Philosophy: the combination was, after all, allowed, even if it was not encouraged. The problem of the historical paper was thornier. Of medieval philosophers I had only a smattering of Aquinas; as for the Rationalists and the Empiricists, there were, in each case, too many of them for either paper to be a prudent option; Kant was also out because, although I had read his *Groundwork* and *Prolegomena*, his formidable *Critiques* were unexplored territory; I knew quite a bit of Plato and Aristotle, but I also knew that, to study them seriously in Oxford, I would need to know (what I did not) Greek; and, since I had not done even unmathematical logic, the Rise of Mathematical Logic could not be contemplated.

I decided that I would be well advised to sue for "special permission" to do something else. Yet I could not think of a philosopher whom Oxford would regard as appropriately major and whom I thought I might master in an Oxford way in the available time. Marx might be regarded as major, but certainly not as a philosopher. Hegel might be regarded as major, and even (albeit with some reluctance) as a philosopher, but I had not read much Hegel and I did not think that two years would be enough time for me to be able to absorb his forbidding texts, let alone for me to be able to present and criticize their content at the required level of competence.

Anxiously examining the *Regulations*, I noticed that there existed a B.Phil. (later to be renamed "M.Phil." so that Americans might realize that it was a higher degree) in Politics, and that one of its papers was the Political (and so, presumably, not the other) Theories of Hegel and Marx. Those theories I felt pretty sure I could manage.

In the wake of these reflections, I approached my supervisor, Gilbert Ryle, and I asked him whether I could do Moral Philosophy, Political Philosophy, and, in place of a historical paper in Philosophy, the Politics paper on Hegel and Marx, and a thesis on some aspect of Marxism. "Yes," he said, "as long as you keep your ears open for other noises." I made (and kept) a promise to do so. The frog from the small pond was now treading water.

2. Halfway into that first Michaelmas Term, Ryle decided that it was time for me to address the Hegel and Marx side of my program. He announced that he would arrange a meeting with Isaiah Berlin. I gulped, and looked forward to the occasion.

It was, however, deferred. I received one of Ryle's little notes, famous for their brevity, often saying just "yes" or "no" to would-be contributors to his journal, *Mind*. The note I got was a bit longer, and more mischievous. It read: "There will be a delay, since Isaiah is in India, helping to celebrate—as who would not?—the death of Rabindranath Tagore." (Tagore was born in 1861 and he died in 1941, so probably it was the centennial of his birth, rather than the vigesimal of his death, that Isaiah was helping to celebrate.)

For me, at that time, Isaiah was the author of three works which I had admired as an undergraduate: *Karl Marx*, *Historical Inevitability*, and *The Hedgehog and the Fox*. I had no quarrel with the last of these, but I was hostile to the message of each of the others. I believed in Marx, and in the historical inevitability in which he believed. Isaiah was negative both about my hero's personality and about his doctrine. My attitude to Isaiah's negativity was not, like that of some other young leftists, contemptuous. I thought of his books as weighty challenges.

Eventually, the Tagore engagement over, Isaiah summoned me, and I turned up at his comfortable All Souls room with its superlarge armchairs and sofa. There ensued our first interview, and it was rather a trial, as far as I was concerned. For Isaiah was tough, even severe; the only time, indeed, that I have known him to be so, whether towards me or about anybody else, across twenty-nine years of an otherwise consistently giving attitude towards people and their projects. I do not know why he presented himself sternly on that first occasion.

I said that I wanted to do a thesis on Marx. Isaiah said that that was a bad idea, that so much had been written about Marx that there was little interesting left to say. With some trepidation I said that, even so, I wanted to work on Marx. Isaiah yielded. He then said that if I wanted to work on Marx, I would have to start with Hegel, and that Baillie's translation of the *Phenomenology* was abominable. Next, he asked a question: "Do you read German?"

The frog from the small pond was at sea again, for I did not. "No," I croaked. A moment's silence, then, "Well, do you read French?" "Yes," said the drowning frog, grasping the *bouée de sauvetage*, and feeling suddenly grateful to the pond from whence he came. "Very well: then, read Hyppolite's translation of the *Phenomenology*. It's not at all bad." "Yes," I said, "I will."

That afternoon my friend Marshall Berman and I went to Parker's bookstore and I bought Hyppolite's two-volume translation of Hegel, and, for good measure, his two-volume commentary, *Genèse et structure de la Phénoménologie de l'esprit*. I am afraid that I have not yet cut the pages of any of those four volumes, and that I never read *The Phenomenology*, in any language, while at Oxford: it was not required for the Hegel and Marx paper, and I did not, in the end, do a thesis on Marx anyway. (Some years later, I read vast stretches of *The Phenomenology*, though not, thank God, the whole thing, in A. V. Miller's translation, which is not easier, even if it is, as they claim, more faithful, than Baillie's.)

3. At my second meeting with Isaiah, we talked not about Marx but about a character invented by Isaiah to make a point about morality. This character enjoys sticking pins into people. When you ask what the pleasure of that is, he says that it is the way the skin first resists and then gives way: it is the puncturing of the skin that supplies the fun. When you ask whether he can get the same pleasure in any other way, he says that he can, by sticking pins into tennis balls: they are just as good. When you then ask why he does not concentrate on tennis balls and leave people alone, he looks puzzled. Tennis balls are not *more* enjoyable than people are, he explains.

The pin-pusher knows that he causes pain, and he knows what pain is, but he fails to see in the fact that people suffer pain, and tennis balls (which are easy to get) do not, a reason for leaving people alone. The pin-pusher is blind to its being a reason against doing something that it causes a person pain. And, since he is not mistaken about any pertinent facts, his blindness shows that there is such a thing as a specifically moral perception (which he lacks).

I was fascinated by Isaiah's construction, and persuaded of its point, and, for our third meeting, I prepared a short essay called "Brave New World and the Pin Pusher." I do not remember how I used Isaiah's fable. In any case, Isaiah listened attentively to my effort and he responded to something I said by reflecting that, although he thought that Jews should either assimilate or go to Israel, he could do neither himself. He began to talk about being Jewish, about Weizmann and Namier and Disraeli and other Jews, about Marx *as* a Jew, about the Holocaust, about great rabbis, about the Zionist movement, and about the Bund in Russia, whose attitude to "the Jewish question" was comparable to the one I had been taught growing up in a communist Jewish community in Montreal. He went on and on and I found it riveting and hugely instructive. Our common Jewishness, and not a shared interest in Marx, connected us in that third session of supervision.

According to Isaiah, "all Jews who are at all conscious of their identity as Jews are steeped in history."[2] I was very conscious of my Jewish identity, from an upbringing which gave me near fluency in Yiddish and a certain familiarity with its literature, even while I was taught to reject Jewish (and all other) religion and also, after Israel's initial honeymoon with the Soviet Union, the claims of Zionism. But I was not "steeped in history," if that implies knowing a lot about it, and here I was, getting steeped (or, at least, dipped) in it by Isaiah, in so engaging a way.

[2] "Benjamin Disraeli," p. 252.

That afternoon, so I felt, and I basked in the thought of it, Isaiah accepted me. I saw him frequently as a student at Oxford, and he told me about many things, and we talked very little about Marx. One thing which we did talk about was Oxford philosophy, about whose claims I had developed some doubts, partly as a result of an unsettling reading of Ernest Gellner's *Words and Things*, which said that Oxford philosophy was terrible. Isaiah helped me to negotiate and contain the Gellner challenge. He defended a posture towards Oxford philosophy which was, characteristically, neither fanatically pro nor obstructively anti.

One doctrine then still sovereign in Oxford was the *Wienerkreis* tenet, brought to Britain by A. J. Ayer, that all *a priori* truths (ones that can be known by thinking about their content, without empirical research) are analytic (true by virtue of the meanings of the terms used to express them). I could see that synthetic *a priori* truths would be peculiar things, but, so it then seemed to me, the true sentence "nothing can be red and green all over" was undoubtedly synthetic, and yet not something we know to be true just because we have not found a counterinstance to it. Isaiah said that I might be right, but joked that in the reigning climate one should perhaps not *call* the thing "synthetic *a priori*." That might be too provocative, and some sort of Marrano[3] strategy was wiser.

I have continued to see Isaiah regularly over the ensuing years, and I learn from him on every single occasion. As is widely recognized, his erudition is deep, and it covers an immense range. Less well known are the ingenuity and resourcefulness with which he is able to justify his claims, for they become evident only in his responses to the relentless questioning which not everyone will have had the opportunity of directing at him.

But I am supposed to be saying something about Marx, and I must make my way back to that.

4. In June of 1963 I left Oxford, B.Phil. in hand, to lecture in philosophy at University College London. In my first couple of years at UCL I worked little on Marx, being more occupied with trying to reduce my persisting ignorance of central areas of contemporary philosophy. But in the autumn of 1965 I went back to Marx, having sailed to Montreal to teach for a term at McGill University. There I taught a lot of Marxism, and, as a result, I conceived the idea of writing a defense of Marx's theory of history. On my return in January to UCL, I set to work.

My meetings with Isaiah continued, in London cafés and clubs, but, despite my new preoccupation, they were not burdened by extensive discussion of Marx. For I judged that Isaiah would not be interested in the theoretical problems of historical materialism which were exercising me: what are relations of

[3] Marranos were Spanish Jews who pretended to be Christians in order not to be targets of the Spanish Inquisition.

production? how, exactly, are they explained by productive forces? what belongs in the superstructure, and what falls outside it? and so on. For Isaiah, Marx was a brilliant but dislocated personality, whose theory was an expression of both of those properties. It was a theory destined to produce great fruit for social science and disastrous results for humanity. Isaiah has never belittled Marx's achievement. He describes historical materialism as "without parallel" in its "clarity … rigour … and [intellectual] power," and Marx as "the true father of modern economic history, and, indeed, of modern sociology."[4] But for all its fertility for future intellectual developments, it was, in its consuming ambition, fundamentally misconceived; and, since I knew that Isaiah thought that, I could not expect him to share my interest in making it precise.

While I worked on *Karl Marx's Theory of History*, Isaiah took a warm and supportive interest, but not a close one, in what I was doing, and we did not argue about it very much. His confidence meant a great deal to me, and I could bear the lack of criticism. Occasionally, of course, a dispute erupted, and often I felt that I was fighting a rearguard battle. I would protest that Marx was not antidemocratic, and I would furnish forth chapter and verse. I would protest, also with documentation, that he was not a fanatical Utopian. Isaiah would acknowledge the scriptural premise but reject the interpretive conclusion, and he would offer me a wry smile which said that in my heart I could not accept it either. We disagreed profoundly about historical materialism, but, while now and then briefly airing our disagreement, we did not pursue it with vigor, not because we feared conflict, but because we wanted to avoid predictable grooves.

5. Isaiah's antipathy to Marxist theory reflects more than his belief that it has had baneful political effects and his disagreement with its distinctive claims. For there is in Isaiah a certain empiricist resistance to the project of grand theory as such, a conviction that it is bound to be one-sided. He is wary of the desire for formula and system, and of the need, by which some are seized, to find a dramatic, roundly plotted "libretto"[5] in history. Isaiah's opposition is excited by any sign of a propensity to the regimentation of fact by self-driving reason.

Though skeptical about general theories of society, Isaiah is not their philistine opponent. He did much to secure a place for sociology in Oxford studies, and no one has done more to promote an interest in the history of large conceptions of humanity and politics. Isaiah is attracted to the theater of theory, but he cannot help remembering what is concealed backstage, all the spoiling qualifications and complications which grand theorists conceal from themselves. So he writes, tellingly, that Marx found "moorings" for himself "only at the price of ignoring a good deal of reality seen by less agonized, more ordinary, but saner,

[4] *Karl Marx*, p. 116.

[5] "Herzen and Bakunin," p. 86.

men."[6] Yet Isaiah would surely agree that if people like Marx did not press forward with unsober zeal, then saner people would be possessed of less that is worth reckoning with.

The reckoning in Isaiah's *Karl Marx* must be judged a remarkable achievement, particularly when one reflects that its author was not yet thirty when he completed it, and that it rests on an enormous knowledge of nineteenth-century European history. The book manifests what Peter Strawson has called Isaiah's power to "breathe life into the history of ideas"[7] and, too, his capacity to show how ideas grow out of circumstances: for a compelling illustration, see his ravishing characterization of the politics of Paris at the midcentury.[8] There are also splendidly vivid and subtle expositions of central Marxist ideas, such as the claim that social being determines consciousness.[9] And, beginning with the third (1963) edition, there is Isaiah's agile response to the then recent extensive discussion of Marx on alienation. His rendering of the connection between the alienation problematic and historical materialism proper, though lightly carried off, would be difficult to surpass.[10]

Yet it is not, in the first instance, a theory that Isaiah expounds, but a thinker, a human being, a mental temper displayed not only in a theory but in life.[11] Isaiah goes for what animates the person, for his governing passion and consequent bent. But what makes a person tick, what drives him, is not a sure guide to the structure of his theory, for theories are abstract objects, sets of sentences subject to logical laws, which impose themselves on the theorist and consequently force his theory to take unexpected turns which may not be noticed when the existential meaning of the theory for the thinker is always in prime focus. For my part, I can only admire and not emulate the work of figuring forth the phenomenology of a great thinker's experience. Propositions, not people, are my academic material, and for me Karl Marx is more a set of writings than he is a man.

That generates a difference between Isaiah and me which, unlike some other ones, is not rooted in discrepant political attitudes. And this difference of approach made it difficult for me to discharge the commission which the editors

[6] "Benjamin Disraeli," p. 284.

[7] In conversation with Ved Mehta, as reported by the latter in *Fly and the Fly-Bottle*. For an unnervingly effective demonstration of that power, see Berlin's exposition of the views of Joseph de Maistre in "The Counter-Enlightenment," pp. 62–63. In the course of reading it you have to remind yourself of where you stand in order not to be recruited to de Maistre's view.

[8] *Karl Marx*, pp. 62–63.

[9] Ibid., p. 98.

[10] Ibid., p. 99.

[11] For Berlin, "every thought belongs, not just somewhere, but to someone, and is at home in a context of other thoughts, a context which is not purely formally prescribed. Thoughts are present to Berlin not just, or primarily, as systematic possibilities, but as historically and psychologically actual, and as something to be known and understood in these concrete terms" (Bernard Williams, introduction to Berlin, *Concepts and Categories*, p. xii).

of this volume laid on me, which was to write about "Isaiah's Marx." My difficulty is that I am not equipped to comment shrewdly on Isaiah's portrait of Marx the man, and although I might be able to take apart some things he says about Marx's theory, it would show lack of proportion to bang on unduly on that particular drum. But, having said that, I shall now express some disagreements with Isaiah. I shall start with a few dissenting observations about Marx's personality (Section 6), and I shall then criticize Isaiah's contentions (a) that Marx did not condemn capitalism at the bar of moral principle (Sections 6, 8); (b) that he thought that communism would realize, completely, all worthwhile values (Section 7); (c) that his commitment to the working class was a by-product of his inevitabilitarian view of history (Section 8); and (d) that, more generally, he regarded the course of history, and not moral principles, as the right guide to political choice (Section 8).

6. To respond fully to Isaiah's vision of Marx I would have to measure it against my own, but I have never formed a clear image of Marx's character. I lack what Isaiah has: a feeling for the nature of the man, a strong sense of what he was like, of a sort that I can have of people only if I have actually met them, or if they have revealed themselves in diaries or in letters. (There is no Marx journal, and he does not expose himself, as opposed to his theoretical and political views, in his letters.)

I do, of course, have some idea of Marx's character, and it does overlap with Isaiah's, unflattering though the latter is. I do not think that Marx was a man on whom one could rely for genial companionship. I agree that he could be precipitately aggressive, that he was richly endowed with spleen, that he was sometimes ungenerously impatient with what he thought were mediocre minds, and I do not think that can all be put down to the rigor of his circumstances. I also have to say that I am ashamed of Marx's anti-Semitic strain, which Isaiah documents unanswerably.[12]

My sense of Marx is that on a good day he would be expansive, sidesplittingly funny, happy to acknowledge his own limitations, even, for part of the time, courteously attentive to what one had to say oneself, and full of incisive questions. On a bad day, he would be intolerable: dogmatic, bitter, scornful, and dismissive. I cannot put a probability on the proposition that a random Marx day would be a good one, so, if I wanted relaxed company, rather than spectacle, my preference would be to spend the day with the gracious and gallant Engels. One thing we could do is talk about Marx, in the safety of his absence.

That said, it strikes me that Isaiah forsakes nuance and balance and goes overboard when he takes Marx's spleen as emblematic of his entire (including political) personality and describes him as "a grim and poverty-stricken sub-

[12] "Benjamin Disraeli," pp. 276–78.

versive pamphleteer, a bitter, lonely and fanatical exile [etc.],"[13] "an isolated and bitterly hostile figure."[14] "Pamphleteer" is hardly a fair summary of Marx's literary achievement, and "isolated" leaves out of account his reassuring awareness of a large and growing international socialist movement which looked to him for inspiration. There is too much denigration in the quoted phrases, and it gets worse in the allegation that there is in Marx "an unmistakable note of sardonic, gloating joy in the very thought of ... the coming holocaust of all the innocents and the fools and the contemptible philistines, so little aware of their terrible fate"[15] and a "savage exultation" at the "approaching cataclysm."[16] These characterizations are not documented, and they are not, in my view, sustainable. They imply that Marx felt disappointment when he concluded that in Britain and the Netherlands there might be a peaceful parliamentary dissolution of capitalism,[17] whereas I think that he was unambivalently satisfied with that conclusion. I also think that he was expressing heavy regret and no exultation at all when he somberly reflected that presocialist history (to which, of course, the socialist revolution itself belongs) resembles "that hideous pagan idol, who would not drink the nectar but from the skulls of the slain."[18]

If Isaiah overplays Marx's savagery and vindictiveness, he also, and curiously—because then the picture begins to look self-contradictory—overstates his imperturbability. I do not agree with Isaiah that, despite the outer adversity and (partly consequent) inner turmoil of Marx's life, "it is a singularly unbroken, positive and self-confident figure that faces us during forty years of illness, poverty and unceasing warfare."[19] Were that so, Marx's bitterness (for I do not question the bitterness, as opposed to its unremitting pervasiveness) would be inexplicable. It is inconceivable to me that Marx's "inner life" was "uncomplicated and secure."[20] The only evidence for that is that he did not express insecurity (as such), but that is not strong evidence, since it is readily counterexplained by his towering pride.

I believe that Marx must often have been broken and depressed and that he deserves, among other reactions, a measure of compassion. Had he possessed the confidence and control attributed to him in Isaiah's depiction, he would

[13] Ibid., p. 260.

[14] *Karl Marx*, p. 15.

[15] "Herzen and Bakunin," p. 99.

[16] "Alexander Herzen," p. 209.

[17] "Speech on the Hague Congress," p. 324. Marx also said, a year earlier, that "insurrection would be madness where peaceful agitation would move swiftly and surely do the work." I see no warrant for the judgment of Jon Elster, from whose *Making Sense of Marx* (p. 445) I draw the latter quotation, that such comments "may not have corresponded to [Marx's] inner beliefs" (ibid., p. 446).

[18] "The Future Results of British Rule in India," p. 222.

[19] *Karl Marx*, p. 24.

[20] Ibid., p. 206.

surely have done more towards finishing *Capital*, the jungle-like condition of which shocked Engels when he confronted Marx's *Nachlass*. Anyone who has plowed through, or even just peered at, the fragmented and neurotically repetitive voluminous writing which Marx spidered out in the late 1850s and the 1860s will recognize a personality more vulnerable and more self-flagellating than Isaiah's description suggests. (How, anyway, is Isaiah's attribution to Marx of unbroken self-confidence consistent with his recording elsewhere that he was "haunted by a perpetual feeling of insecurity?"[21])

The sheer mass and detail of what Marx wrote about the capitalist and other economies prompts a further disagreement with Isaiah. I cannot accept that the supposed absence from *Capital* of "appeals to conscience or to principle" and of "detailed prediction" of the socialist future "follow[s] from the concentration of attention on the practical problems of action,"[22] for such concentration would be incompatible with the presence in the *Capital* manuscripts of thousands of pages of abstract theory[23] and (what is from a practical point of view even less urgent) of the history of abstract theory. I would, moreover, deny that *Capital* lacks "appeals to … principle": there is an extensive, even if usually only implied, appeal to principle in the hundreds of pages of description of the exploitation and misery of the working class. When Marx exclaims that "capitalist justice is truly to be wondered at!",[24] when he calls the capitalist a "robber"[25] and an "embezzler"[26] he must be understood to be voicing a (fully justified) moral condemnation.

7. It is unacceptably paradoxical to represent Marx as unconcerned with values. To do so is to take too seriously those *macho* moments when he disparaged them in the name of class militancy. Isaiah has, of course, offered us persuasive reflections on the structure of value, and it is appropriate to test Marx against the truths about values which Isaiah has stressed.

A number of Enlightenment thinkers claimed that all human values would be realized, once reason was at the helm of society. Isaiah regards that as a dangerous delusion, and he has indefatigably insisted that the values which have in fact and with good reason attracted human beings are incapable of full joint realization, in some cases for reasons of logic, and in others because of general truths of human nature and social organization. There are different things to admire in different forms of society, and not all the admirable things can be had

[21] Ibid., p. 76.

[22] Ibid., p. 6.

[23] The nature of all that arduous theory construction also makes it impossible for me to accept that Marx was "scarcely interested" in truth in the ordinary sense of correspondence of proposition to fact (ibid., p. 114).

[24] *Capital*, vol. 1, p. 815.

[25] Ibid., vol. 1, p. 728.

[26] Ibid., vol. 1, p. 761.

together. Accordingly, we must reject the "ancient faith … that all the positive values in which men have believed must, in the end, be compatible, and perhaps even entail one another."[27] The chief problem, in politics as in personal life, is a sound choice of sacrifices, and there is damage to both thought and practice when people imagine that sacrifice is avoidable.

Isaiah construes Marx as an apostle of the myth "of a final harmony in which all riddles are solved, all contradictions reconciled."[28] He thinks Marx believed that communism would deliver everything that is worthwhile in a perfect synthesis, and that such a belief underlay his supposed willingness to countenance any kind of savagery in the service of achieving that communism.

Now Marx did not, of course, expressly deny that fundamental human values are compatible. Few have: Isaiah's affirmation of value incompatibility is a strikingly original contribution. But I do not think that Marx offended against the truth about values as much as Isaiah supposes, partly because Marx's canvas displayed not human life as a whole but only the part of it that (more or less) immediately reflects social division. The historical materialist prediction of an end to specifically *class* conflict is not a forecast of heaven on earth. There remains, after all, "individual [nonclass] antagonism,"[29] and consequent room for the persistence of "human misery"[30] and even "tragedy."[31]

Although I agree with Isaiah that significant values are seriously incompatible,[32] I think that the particular disvalues which Marx hated most, to wit, social injustice and socially generated restriction on the development of the faculties of the individual, can both be defeated, and, moreover, that each is likely to be defeated only when and because the other has been. (In saying that Marx hated injustice, I am mindful of the fact that he sometimes disparaged justice as a value. But that is because he was confused about justice, and he mistakenly thought that he did not believe that capitalism was unjust.)[33]

I also cannot endorse Isaiah's statement that there is an incompatibility between "unlimited personal liberty" and "social equality,"[34] not because I believe that social equality is compatible with unlimited personal liberty, but because I think that unlimited personal liberty for all is itself impossible. I think, moreover, that social equality, if truly achieved,[35] would greatly increase the liberty

[27] "Two Concepts of Liberty," p. 167.

[28] Ibid., p. 168.

[29] Karl Marx, preface to *Contribution*, p. 21.

[30] *Karl Marx*, p. 179.

[31] "Two Concepts of Liberty," p. 169.

[32] I have, indeed, defended him on that score, against the late Gerald McCallum, in "A Note on Values and Sacrifices."

[33] See my review of *Karl Marx* by Allen Wood, p. 444.

[34] "Herzen and Bakunin," p. 105.

[35] For it is a distinct contention, and one on which I do not here comment, that it is unachievable and that the attempt to achieve it has disastrous consequences for liberty.

of those individuals who have little of it, even if it reduces (in some ways drastically) the liberty of very rich people. So while there is indeed a conflict between social equality and the liberty of some people, that is no reason for moderating the pursuit of social equality, since a humane concern for liberty must first of all direct itself to the condition of those who enjoy hardly any of it.

I should add that Isaiah does not himself believe that unlimited personal liberty is possible: he denies, in effect, that it is possible in the very sentence in which he asserts its incompatibility with social equality. Nor does he assign to liberty absolute priority over equality. He thinks that liberty may, to a degree, yield to equality: hence his commendation of Roosevelt's New Deal as "the most constructive compromise between individual liberty and economic security which our own time has witnessed."[36]

8. In my judgment, nothing was more fundamental to Marx's motivation than his perception of the misery which the capitalism of his day imposed upon the working class. I therefore strongly disagree with Isaiah's view of the relationship in Marx's thought between the march of history and the cause of the proletariat.

In Isaiah's presentation, Marx held that "those men alone are rational who identify themselves with the ... ascendant class in their society ... Accordingly Marx, having identified the rising class in the struggles of his own time with the proletariat, devoted the rest of his own life to planning victory for those at whose head he had decided to place himself."[37] Setting aside the separate question of whether Marx indeed conceived quite so leading a role for himself, my principal objection to the foregoing representation is that Marx's condemnation of the exploitation and alienation of the proletariat preceded his invention of historical materialism and thoroughly sufficed to determine his commitment to the proletariat's cause. In tracing that commitment to a special view about rational life-choices—one which, in any case, I do not think Marx held—Isaiah makes Marx out to be less soundly motivated than he was in fact.

This induces me to express a reservation about an aspect of Isaiah's arresting comparison between the psychologies of Karl Marx and Benjamin Disraeli. Each, he says, was a precariously marginal Jew who moved towards the center of things by allying himself with a social class distant from his own origins: in Disraeli's case, the British aristocracy, in Marx's, the proletariat.[38] But the proletariat were a fitter object of solidarity than were the Tory nobility, and an outsider's sympathy for them need not be explained by peculiarities of his psychology. In fact, Marx cared greatly in an ordinary human way about the workers' suffering, whatever other motives that care might have mingled with, and whatever other

[36] "Political Ideas in the Twentieth Century," p. 31. (I have criticized the phrasing of this praise of Roosevelt in "Capitalism, Freedom, and the Proletariat," p. 13.) See, too, "Two Concepts of Liberty," pp. 169–70.

[37] *Karl Marx*, p. 6.

[38] "Benjamin Disraeli," pp. 280–81.

attitudes, including the contempt Isaiah would allege and emphasize, he might also have had.

In my view, Isaiah sharply exaggerates the strength of vindictive personal motivation in Marx's embrace of the proletarian cause. I cannot agree that, when Marx "speaks of the proletariat," he speaks less "of real workers" and more "of his own indignant self," that "the insults he is avenging and the enemies he is pulverising are, as often as not, his own," and that "*this* it is that lends passion and reality to his words."[39] The accusation that Marx dealt only with an abstract "humanity in general"[40] and lacked strong concern for real people is, I believe, refuted by (to take just one example) his masterful and compassionate use of the British government Blue Books' description of the plight of very particular worker human beings, a use which, elsewhere,[41] Isaiah respectfully commends.

Nor do I think that "Marx denounces the existing order by appealing not to ideals but to history:." What follows the colon in that sentence of Isaiah's is hard to reconcile with what precedes it: ": he denounces [the existing order] … as being the effect of laws of social development which make it inevitable that at a certain stage of history one class … should dispossess and exploit another, and so lead to the repression and crippling of men."[42] To say that there was no appeal to ideals in Marx is to say, incredibly, that dispossession, exploitation, repression, and crippling played no part in generating Marx's condemnation of the system.

To be sure, Marx did not think, and he was right not to, that *simply* denouncing the system for its manifest injustice would suffice to spirit it away. And it is also true that, for Marx, there is a task which capitalism must perform before it will be either possible or desirable to overturn it. For capitalism serves to develop "the productive forces of social labour": that is its "historic mission and justification."[43] Only when that development has been accomplished, is its "historical destiny … fulfilled,"[44] and then it is time for it to go. Capitalism is tolerable while it is carrying out its progressive task, but humane ideals declare that there is not a shred of justification for it once it has done so.

It scarcely follows that, for Marx, "the only sense in which it is possible to show that something is good or bad, right or wrong, is by demonstrating that it accords or discords with the historical process."[45] Not a single text of Marx demands

[39] Ibid., pp. 281–82, my emphasis.

[40] Ibid., p. 281.

[41] See *Karl Marx*, pp. 135, 183.

[42] Ibid., p. 5.

[43] *Capital*, vol. 3, p. 368.

[44] *The Grundrisse*, p. 325: for a number of other relevant texts, see the citations in sections 5 and 6 of chapter 7 of my *Karl Marx's Theory of History*.

[45] *Karl Marx*, p. 113.

that strange restriction on the scope of social criticism.[46] A famous sentence in the *Critique of the Gotha Programme* which is frequently cited in substantiation of some such attribution to him in fact subverts it. The sentence is preceded by a morally informed critique of the norm of distributive justice ("to each according to his contribution") which Marx thought would perforce govern the initial, immediately postcapitalist, stage of communism. Having displayed the "defects" of that norm, Marx says that they are unsurprising, since "right can never be higher than the economic structure of society and its cultural development conditioned thereby."[47] The sentence presupposes—it is amazing that in the vast realms of Marxology this is never, to my knowledge, remarked—an antirelativist contrast between lower and higher forms of right or justice. One page before Isaiah writes what I quoted at the top of this paragraph he says, in similar vein, that, for Marx, "the only real rights are those conferred by history, the right to act the part which is historically imposed on one's class."[48] That statement, and the one quoted above, appear to me to be contradicted by Isaiah's recognition, nearby, that, in Marx's view, the proletariat's "destitution causes it to represent human beings as such—what it is entitled to is the minimum to which all men are entitled."[49]

Far from dismissing ideals as mere instruments of history, Marx saw the realization of an ideal of freedom from subordination as history's highest purpose, and he measured historical epochs according to their contribution to the achievement of that ideal. I think it fitting to close this countercase with the following pregnant quotation:

> The recognition [by labor] of the products as its own, and the judgment that its separation from the conditions of its realization is unjust—forcibly imposed—is an enormous awareness, itself the product of the mode of production resting on capital, and as much the knell to its doom as, with the slave's awareness that he *cannot be the property of another*, with his consciousness of himself as a person, the existence of slavery becomes a merely artificial, vegetative existence and ceases to be able to prevail as the basis of production. [50,51]

[46] For further discussion, including an attempt to explain why there is a tendency to misinterpret Marx in the way just quoted, see my *History, Labour, and Freedom*, Oxford University Press, 1988, ch. 4, section 8.

[47] *The Critique of the Gotha Programme*, p. 24.

[48] *Karl Marx*, p. 112.

[49] Ibid., p. 113.

[50] *Zur Kritik der Politischen Ökonomie* (manuscript 1861–63), p. 2287. As Jon Elster points out (*Making Sense of Marx*, p. 106), the same passage appears in the earlier *Grundrisse* manuscript of 1857–58, with the very significant difference that Marx replaced "*ungehörig*" (improper) by "*ein Unrecht*" (an injustice) in the revised version of his manuscript.

[51] I am grateful to Arnold Zuboff for incisive criticism of drafts of this piece. And, for constructive suggestions, I thank Charlotte Brewer, Maggie Cohen, Jon Elster, Ted Honderich, Will Kymlicka, John McMurtry, Avishai Margalit, Mike Otsuka, Bill Shaw, Seana Shiffrin, and Jo Wolff.

Chapter Two

PRAGUE PREAMBLE TO "WHY NOT SOCIALISM?"

The real title of this lecture is "Why Not Socialism?": that is what I have called it whenever I have not given it in Prague. But, here, in Prague, in the city of Franz Kafka, disguises are sometimes necessary, and it seemed wise not to use my real title, "Why Not Socialism?", as my title, but rather the advertised one, "Are Equality and Community Possible?" As far as I'm concerned, the meanings of the two titles are pretty similar, but the difference between them might sound bigger to you than it does to me.

I believe that most Czechs would have reacted to the "Why Not Socialism?" title with anger, or with amusement, or with both. Czechoslovakia underwent savage tyranny and monumental crimes in the *name* of socialism. And, what is worse, from the point of view of a socialist, the country suffered that fate *partly* as a result of an absolutely sincere attempt to create a genuinely socialist society. There was, in the communist years, a totally cynical manipulation of the name and ideal of socialism in the interest of personal gain and power and self-advancement, but there was *also*, alongside that, and please forgive me for repeating this, there was also an absolutely sincere dedication to the socialist ideal. If the now mercifully defunct experiment had had nothing to do with real socialist commitment, but had merely been made to bear the *name* "socialism," then we socialists—I say "we" because I remain a socialist—would have less reason than we actually have to be disheartened by the fact that the experiment was a disaster.

As a child and as a youth, growing up in a Communist Party working-class home in Montreal, I was a member of the international communist movement. I was one of the millions who believed with all my mind and all my heart and with everything good and life-affirming in me that the Soviet Union and what we called the People's Democracies and People's China were creating societies devoted to social justice and human fulfillment. I gained that belief when I was about five or six years old, in 1946 or 1947, as a result of my upbringing, in a communist working-class family in Montreal. I *began* to lose that belief in the early 1960s, which were my early twenties, and I lost the belief comprehensively no later than August 21, 1968, on which day I said to my then wife, "For the first time in my life I am *anti*-Soviet." It is not that I had remained naive about the Soviet Union and Eastern Europe before the tanks rolled in. On the contrary: I already thought of myself as an extreme critic of actually existing communism.

But until that day there was, at least in concept, a "thou" to whom my criticism and my anger could be addressed. The Soviet Union lost its "thou" status for me, and became a monstrous "it," when the 8:00 A.M. BBC news began: "Soviet, Polish, East German, Hungarian, and Bulgarian troops this morning entered . . ."

I know that what I had believed was paradise, or on the road to paradise, was for you and your forebears a form of hell. I don't think I can be *blamed* for not having realized that, for having thought the very opposite.[1] My false belief was borne up by noble sentiments. But, rationally or otherwise, I nevertheless feel a need to apologize, and I hereby do.

My Soviet allegiance came from an upbringing in which I was raised as a Marxist (and Stalinist communist) the way other people are raised Roman Catholic or Muslim. My parents and most of my relatives were working-class communists, and several of them had served years in Canadian jails for their convictions. One of those who had been jailed was my Uncle Norman: he was married to my father's sister Jenny, who, I can tell you, once danced with Joseph Stalin. In August 1964, I spent two weeks in Czechoslovakia, in Prague, on Lermontova in Podbaba, in what was then Norman and Jenny's home. They were there because Norman was at the time an editor of *World Marxist Review*, the now defunct Prague-based theoretical journal of the also now defunct international communist movement. Daytimes I wandered around Prague, speaking with whoever would speak to me. I spoke some Russian and some German, and Norman and Jenny were both very busy so I had lots of time to wander around this glorious city and to talk to people, and, in the evening, to argue with Jenny and Norman about what I thought I had discovered.

Going out and about the town, I found no one with a good word for the regime. I returned that first evening and said so to Uncle Norman, perhaps a bit sadistically. I was punishing him for my disappointment: didn't his total identification with the regime make him a suitable object for that punishment? But Norman had a reply. "Gosh," he exclaimed, "you must have met some really weird people!" So I went out the next day and, when my polling produced the same results, I presented them, once again, to Uncle Norman. This time his response was graver. "You have to understand that before the revolution there was a considerable middle class in Prague, and they have lost a lot from the workers' revolution." And the response to the findings of day three was: "You have to understand, Prague had a *huge* middle class." After day three I ceased to seek enlightenment from Uncle Norman: I didn't want to be told that the middle class had been even *bigger* than *huge*.

What did I believe about Czechoslovakia *before* I made the ambulations and inquiries whose fruit I presented to Norman on those August evenings in 1964?

[1] [Cohen provides his grounds for such exculpation in the penultimate paragraph of this essay.—Ed.]

I believed that Czechoslovakia was doing tolerably with respect to material provision, but that it suffered from an unjustifiable lack of freedom of speech and other civil freedoms. I refer to freedom of speech in particular because that issue was the focus of the biggest lesson that I learned in Prague in August 1964. Before I say what the lesson was, some background is necessary.

The communists of my childhood responded in three different ways to the charge that the communist countries denied freedom of speech, and the three responses were of different degrees of sophistication. First, and crudest, there was the response that consisted in simply denying that there *were* restrictions on freedom of speech: I shall explain how it was possible for people to believe such a huge falsehood in a moment. A second and more sophisticated response acknowledged the restrictions, with an expression of regret, followed by a justification of the restrictions that referred to the enemy without and within: there could not, alas, be freedom of speech, because the capitalist world would exploit freedom of speech, for counterrevolutionary purposes. There were different variants of this response. You could make it but also think, for example, that the authorities were going too far. You could think *some* restrictions of freedom of speech were justified, but that the restrictions *actually* in force were more extensive than could be justified: you could show how daring, how *free* you were by saying so. And, finally, there was the most sophisticated response, which was what I believed, namely, that, contrary to the first response, there *was* extensive restriction on freedom, and, contrary to the second response, (virtually) *none* of it was justified, *but* it was something that only or largely affected intellectuals, and one should therefore not get it out of perspective. It *was* an evil, but a limited evil: one should take care not to conclude that it was a larger evil than it in fact was.[2]

And in August 1964 I learned that that belief of mine was a patronizing view, because lack of freedom of speech cuts *everyone* off from the truth. If all you've got is *Rudé právo*, and you know it lies, you cannot really know what's happening in the world around you, and you know your information is controlled by liars, even if you have no wish to express anything *yourself*. Freedom of speech is imperative not only because no human being has the right to silence another, but also because human beings have not only a right to express *themselves* but a right of access to the views of others, and to the truth, rights which go beyond the right not to be unjustifiably interfered with (which includes a right to freedom of expression), rights which are more positive, but no less urgent for that. In the absence of freedom of speech, not only are those who would otherwise speak muzzled, but everybody lives in a prison.

Now, I promised to say how it was possible for people to believe that European communism was fulfilling socialist ideals. How, for example, could anyone believe

[2] Perhaps Uncle Norman believed all three inconsistent things: I can only speculate. But I can *report* that he often said, of friendly critics of communism, "They make a *fetish* of freedom," however that was to be interpreted.

the first and crude reply to the charge that freedom of speech was suppressed, the reply that simply *denied* that? How could anyone close his eyes to such an evident thing? Did that belief not reflect self-serving interests, or, at any rate, wishful thinking? Well, it certainly *was* what those who believed it wanted to believe. But that says why they were *motivated* to believe it, and not how it was *possible* for them to believe it. I am motivated to believe that my wife is faithful to me, but it would not be possible for me to believe that if I saw her in another's arms.

Here we have to distinguish between those who had visited the Soviet Union, or some other communist country, and those who had not. I shall speak only of the majority that had not. How could we[3] fail to believe what the press reported, and what the great majority of the people who surrounded us thought? Well, we thought that that great majority got their opinions from the bourgeois press, so all that needs explanation is why we didn't believe that press. And the answer is that we *knew*—I say *knew*, not *believed*—that the bourgeois press lied. I do not mean that we knew that it lied about the character of life in the Soviet Union, since, for the most part, it didn't lie about that, because it didn't have to. I mean that we knew that it lied about capitalism, that it misreported strikes, for example, that it covered up poverty. The press was owned by capitalists and reported everything from a capitalist point of view. It was motivated to lie about capitalist Quebec and capitalist Canada, and we knew that it did, so why should it not for the same reasons lie about the rival, socialist, society? How could we know that it had no need to lie about actually existing socialism in order to paint it in those dark colors?

We thought equality and community were good, we tried to achieve them, and we produced a disaster. Should we conclude that what we thought good, equality and community, are not, in fact, good? That conclusion, though frequently drawn, is crazy. The grapes may indeed be sour, but the fox's failure to reach them doesn't show that they are. Should we conclude, instead, that *any* attempt to produce this particular good *must* fail? Only if we think we know either that this was the only possible way to try to produce it, *or* that what made this attempt fail would make any attempt fail, *or* that, for some other reason, any attempt must fail. I believe that we know none of those things. In my view, the correct conclusions are that we must try *differently*, in some sense and degree of "differently," and that we must be much more cautious. It is in that spirit, one of continued but chastened dedication, that the paper "Why Not Socialism?", to which these remarks are a preamble, was written.[4]

[3] As explained, *I did* believe that there was extensive restriction on speech, but there were other things I believed, or failed to believe, that would surprise you.

[4] I thank Michèle Cohen for helpful discussion.

Chapter Three

A BLACK AND WHITE ISSUE

In September 1985, the Executive Committee of the World Archaeological Congress (WAC) decided to bar participants from South Africa and Namibia from their gathering at Southampton in the following year. The vote was unanimous: everyone was persuaded by the pragmatic argument that the congress would otherwise be unviable, certainly as (anything approaching) a *world* congress, and possibly completely. But some committee members also thought that the ban was "morally correct."

Many archaeologists strongly opposed the decision to exclude South Africa. Very few of them, and this applies to the banned scholars themselves, sympathized with the apartheid regime. The principal grounds of opposition to boycott were a commitment to honoring academic freedom *and* a desire to maximize academic exchange. Those considerations tend not to be distinguished, on either side of the debate, but they are substantially different. A concern to maximize academic exchange should have induced support for the ban, since there was a choice between exchange with South Africans and exchange with academics from a far larger part of the world. If the organizers had regarded the irreversible decision of much of the Third World to boycott a nonboycotting congress as wayward, they might have decided in favor of South African participation, but it would have been hard for them to justify such a decision by invoking the desirability of sustaining international academic exchange.

The value of that exchange will constitute a decreasingly appropriate reason for admitting South Africans, as the international academic boycott increases its hold. But the issue of denying academic freedom is different, and it is wrong to suggest that the WAC organizers had to choose between denying the academic freedom of South Africans and denying the academic freedom of Third World scholars. Third World scholars who would have decided not to attend a nonbanning congress could not have complained that their freedom was denied, and those forbidden by their governments to come, or deprived of government funding, would not have suffered a denial of academic freedom at the hands of congress organizers. The only freedom the Executive Committee ever contemplated denying was the freedom it did deny: of South African and Namibian academics.

In considering the question of international restriction on the freedom of South African academics, it bears emphasizing that they perforce accept limitations on their academic freedom at home, and that, while they may not personally favor apartheid, some of them belong to institutions which are known to furnish the military and intelligence branches of the apartheid regime with material and intellectual support, and few to ones that are known not to. Many South African scholars courageously resist implication in the structure of privilege and its murderous techniques of defense, and those who do so would be exempted from any boycott that I would wish to endorse. But I think that they should be excepted not primarily because of their (unquestionable) personal desert, but because it seems to me that an appropriately *selective* boycott, of the sort now favored by the African National Congress, is the best way forward from a strategic point of view.

I recently received an application to pursue graduate work at Oxford from a South African student (whom I took to be white). The student acknowledged with sympathy the policy of selective boycott and duly presented his credentials as an adherent of various resistance organizations. It seems to me not unsuitable that he should have done so. Our facilities are scarce, and I do not think that we should extend them to people who, through inaction, accept complicity with the oppression their privileges presuppose, whatever their *beliefs* about apartheid may be: we sustain their complicity when we offer to accommodate them. But that is entirely consistent with providing encouragement and support to white South Africans who do not merely deplore apartheid but give their opposition to it an active form.

A policy of selective academic boycott expresses condemnation of the apartheid regime. For some people, that fact itself, together with the desirability of showing where we stand, of not condoning apartheid through silence, justifies a boycott policy. But I would not advocate boycott on those self-regarding grounds. I believe that the only responsible way to assess any policy towards South Africa is strategically: that is, with reference to the policy's probable impact on the struggle for liberation. The stakes are too high for us to treat our own purity of stance as a major concern.

The expressive dimension of boycott is, nevertheless, highly relevant from the strategic point of view itself. That is because the political effect of boycott operates not only through its consequences for particular academics and institutions, but also through what it says about South Africa, and through the reaction to that statement both within South Africa and in the world outside.

What is the right strategic perspective within which to evaluate the wisdom of academic boycott? If you think that there exist conditions under which Pretoria would yield power because of an increase in humane understanding, then you might oppose boycott on the ground that it threatens to steel the regime's present antidemocratic resolve: you might think that boycott is destructive because it reinforces the "*laager* mentality." But I believe that so great is the scale of unjust power and advantage in South Africa that there will not be progress towards democracy unless and until the regime is placed under extreme duress: the white power structure has too much to lose for any contrary view to be credible. It needs to be not won round, but defeated, through the creation of intolerable levels of internal and external pressure. It needs to be weakened, and part of the process of weakening it is to deepen lines of division within the privileged community. The academic boycott helps to do that, by bringing international indignation more saliently to bear, and by forcing harder choices on a subcommunity capable of resistance, advocacy, and influence.

An evil as profound, and as solidly protected, as apartheid is, cannot be overcome by entirely attractive means. Unattractive though it is, academic boycott is a far cry from terror, and we are obliged to hope that the more nonviolent pressure is applied, the less the pressure of terror will be necessary. We cannot be sure that nonviolent pressure will have a telling effect. But we can be sure that there will be no liberation without severe pressure.

That is the main part of the case for an academic boycott of South Africa. There is also an important subsidiary part, which I shall describe after I have first distinguished kinds of grounds on which an academic boycott might be opposed.

The most obvious ground has to do with the value of academic freedom, and with the related imperative of not denying it. But that consideration plays a role in antiboycott argument in two rather different ways. It appears, first, in the position that academic freedom should never be restricted, or not, at any rate, by academics themselves. But, while academic freedom is undoubtedly a precious value, and while one might well think that academics in particular have a special duty to honor it, it is surely perverse to think that it must be honored at any cost, including the one which boycott-supporters claim that honoring it imposes here: forgoing an instrument of progress towards democracy and the freedom which is more than merely academic. In face of the contention that a selective suspension of academic freedom would promote the liberation of brutally treated people, an absolute attitude to academic freedom appears lacking in moral balance. The same cannot, however, be said about the distinct position that, although there are conditions which would justify denying academic freedom, the inherent wrongness of doing so is not compensated for by good political consequences in the present instance, because they are too insubstantial. And that view must in turn be distinguished from the more purely pragmatic one which says that denying academic freedom would, in the South African case, actually be counterproductive, because, for example, it would reduce the quality of the higher education which is needed by Africans in the run-up to majority rule.

It seems to me that opponents of apartheid who disapprove of academic boycott must affirm one or more of the following propositions:

1. Academics should never deny anyone's academic freedom (whether or not other agents, such as states, are ever justified in doing so).
2. There are circumstances under which Pretoria would yield to benign persuasion.
3. The regime will yield only under pressure, but academics have no obligation to contribute to that pressure.
4. Pressure is indeed necessary, but only military force and terror will have any effect.
5. Nonviolent pressure is (also) desirable, but an academic boycott could not form an effective part of it.
6. While academic boycott might have some desirable political effects, they are unlikely to be large enough to justify the violation of academic freedom which boycott entails.
7. An academic boycott would be counterproductive.

Some selection of (5), (6), and (7) is, I believe, the only position which is not (like (2)) immediately implausible, or (like (1) and (3)) morally perverse, or (like (4)) unlikely to be embraced by boycott opponents. It is not a disreputable position, and, although I think that it is incorrect, it is difficult to prove that it is. But one thing is certain: in the judgment of those who stand on the front line in South Africa, such as the African National Congress and Archbishop Desmond Tutu, an academic boycott *is* strategically desirable. (Tutu applauded the WAC ban, and called for its generalization.)

Now, it is not necessarily a decisive argument in favor of academic boycott that Tutu and the ANC and the United Democratic Front and the South West African People's Organization and the South African National Students' Congress (which is the largest union of black students in South Africa) all advocate it. The fact that the liberation movement advocates boycott cannot be *its* reason for supporting boycott. Necessarily, it must have independent reasons, and they might, in principle, be such bad ones that their insufficiency could undermine the consideration, which must play a part in *our* deliberation, that the movement advocates a boycott.

For although the latter consideration is, as I said, not necessarily decisive, it is also not irrelevant. It is *an* argument in favor of boycott, and potentially a very strong one. This is so for at least three reasons.

First, the people who face the enemy are better placed than we are to judge what tactics are required. It is evidence for the desirability of boycott that they think that the evidence supports its desirability.

Secondly, and quite independently, given that they have in fact called for a boycott, we extend a strengthening solidarity by responding to their call, and we weaken them by ignoring it. We reduce their self-confidence when we reject policies which they favor.

Finally, there is the consideration of coordination. The commander might have chosen the wrong hill, but that does not show that we should not join the struggle to take it. The decision whether or not to enter a particular battleground must partly depend on whether effort is already actually converging there. It can be a strategic mistake to withhold support from an (antecedently misconceived) campaign which has in fact been launched.

Because of the strategic perspective outlined earlier, and for the foregoing movement-supporting reasons, I favor an academic boycott of South Africa. Its precise nature and forms of implementation require considerable discussion. I have not thought enough, or heard enough, to have, at this date, settled beliefs about important details. But my provisional view is that a university like Oxford should publicly record its recognition of the just demand of the oppressed majority in South Africa for elementary political rights, and restrict admission of South African students and other scholarly exchange to members of that majority and to those others who tangibly support their struggle for political rights.

Such selectivity raises difficult criteria questions, and there is probably no practical way for those who want to apply a boycott to concert a response to them. Decisions on boycott will have to be decentralized, and, often, taken with imperfect information.[1] That will lead to injustice, both formal (the same sort of cases being accorded different treatment) and substantive (committed opponents of the regime will sometimes be denied access, and complicit benefactors will sometimes get it). Analogous injustice is unavoidable in war. As Professor Thurstan Shaw pointed out when supporting the WAC boycott in a letter of response to the presidents of the Royal Society and the British Academy who had condemned it: "in the last war underground resistance fighters were sometimes killed by the British and American bombs supporting them."

The size of the South African injustice makes it appropriate to invoke the grim ethics of war. Apartheid fails to honor equality of civic standing, which is a first principle of modern civilization, observed by otherwise reprehensible governments. To say that South Africa practices racial discrimination fails to express what makes it unique: the society is *founded* on racial exclusion and oppression. That is the fundamental and generative evil. And the consequent further evil is a murderous repression of those who struggle for elementary rights. In the judg-

[1] This article is about who should come from South Africa, not who should go. But a discriminating policy (as opposed to one of comprehensive prohibition) is surely also appropriate with respect to the latter question. It offers embattled locals desired support, and it enables foreign opponents of apartheid to enrich the stock of information which they need to run a selective boycott on would-be visitors from South Africa in an intelligent way.

ment of the Commonwealth Eminent Persons Group, the apartheid regime "is awesome in its cruelty. It is achieved and sustained only through force, creating human misery and deprivation and blighting the lives of millions."

An academic boycott would help to raise political consciousness outside South Africa. As Neal Ascherson says, it would be part of a process of "training the world to act towards South Africa in a coordinated way, getting the international community used to joint decision and action" in respect of a situation which calls for an internationally unified response. Even if within South Africa there were—as there could not, of course, conceivably be—widespread unawareness of an academic boycott, knowledge of it outside South Africa would have marshaling effects, and would lend emphasis to the judgment that apartheid is a moral barbarity.

Chapter Four

TWO WEEKS IN INDIA

> To know Indians was to take a delight in people as people; every encounter was an adventure.
>
> —V. S. Naipaul, *An Area of Darkness*, p. 243.

In the first twenty-four hours of my trip to India, I made a few notes, filling a page or two with a record of what was happening. Then I stopped doing that. It seemed artificial, to step back from the flow of experience and describe. But, now that I am once again in England, having returned five days ago, I do want to record as much as I can remember of what happened.[1]

I'll mostly go in chronological order. Now and then, a general theme will obtrude, and I'll break the narrative to address the general theme, and resume the chronicle when I'm done.

I was scheduled to leave Heathrow on Air India on January 1 and to arrive in Bombay (with stops in Paris and Delhi) on January 2. I would spend part of the day and one night in Bombay in the care of V. K. Ramachandran (Ram), an economist friend whom I had come to know and like in Helsinki in July of 1988, and I would leave Bombay for Goa (on Indian Airlines, an outfit distinct from Air India) on January 3. Goa was my first official engagement: I was due to lecture there on January 4 under the title "Is There Still a Case for Socialism?"

Things didn't happen that way. London fog and a go-slow by Indian Airlines pilots (protesting for more money and more airport safety) disrupted my schedule.

The fog on the evening of January 1 was heavy. Michèle,[2] who had driven me to the airport, reported on my return from India that driving back to Oxford that evening had been hair-raising. We sat in the plane, from about 6:00 P.M., waiting to take off. Most of the passengers were Indian. I had an aisle seat. On

[1] [Cohen returned from his two weeks in India on January 15, 1993. He composed the following account of the trip in January, February, and March of that year.—Ed.]

[2] [Cohen's second wife—Ed.]

my left was an Indian granny with a one-year-old (or so) in her arms. She was a gruff, commanding type, the man in the window seat to her left, the presumptive father of the baby. He was semishaven, with virtually no English (it turned out), and with a craving for free beer (unavailable: you had to pay). The baby was beautiful and sociable. He reached for my fingers with his. Being a sociable person, I gladly reciprocated. Granny didn't like that. It was pretty plain that she regarded me as not to be touched by the baby. And not, I think, out of solicitude towards me, for she could see that I was genuinely available and she never said or implied anything apologetic. My first experience on this trip of the Indian preoccupation with contamination?

Well, we sat there for two and a half hours, waiting for clearance to take off. It didn't come. At 8:30 P.M. the pilot announced that we would not take off that evening. We'd stay on the plane and have a meal, we'd afterwards be shepherded to a hotel, and we'd take off the next morning. Fair enough, I thought, having shed my usual disposition to anxiety when traveling. I had something to regret, but nothing to worry about. After all, I had my money, my credit card, my lectures in my black bag, and I could ring India from the hotel and tell somebody I might be late. That is, that I might not make Goa on time, might have to take a later Bombay-Goa flight.

Then the meal came. For me it was vegetarian Indian: that's what I had been allowed to specify at the Air India office when settling my flights. The meal was amazingly good, the best vegetarian meal I had had in my life, and now still the best, even though I've now eaten in India itself. (Mr. Zibell, who pops up at the end of this narrative, on the plane back to London from Delhi, had the same high opinion of the fare.) So I thought as I ecstasied my way through the delicate flavors and textures and delicious tongue-stings: Jerry, you are going to enjoy eating in India.

I was worried that the hotel they were to take us to would be back in London itself (what do I know about how airlines cope in such crises?). But we stayed at *The Edwardian*, within or near the airport precincts, overdecorated but comfortable. That evening, after 10:30, I rang Michèle but not Mim and Chris, in *case* they weren't awake.[3]

Before retiring, I took two small single malts (Talisker) in the hotel bar with some codelayed people, specifically a very small Indian engineer from Delhi and a burly Norwegian international businessman of some kind from Oslo. At the bar the seats were huge horse-saddles (real ones), and you had to spread your thighs in an ungainly way. The Indian engineer preferred to stand. He said that he didn't want to be taken for a ride. I looked forward to good food and good jokes.

[3] ["Mim" is Cohen's daughter Miriam, and Chris is her husband.—Ed.]

Heathrow, 6:30 a.m., Saturday, January 2

I pulled the curtain back across the large window of my *Edwardian* room. A few clouds, but the fog had gone. A clear(-ish) London sky meant Bombay that night/next morning.

The Air India crowd were supposed to wait to eat at 8:00 a.m. in a special place in the hotel. I was hungry and ambitious for a breakfast, so I played the role of a higher-caste (than what we were) guest and took a splendid breakfast surrounded by Spanish women servers in the proper breakfast room. My imposture was in due course detected, but nobody cared.

I had hoped that we'd have new seats on the plane, because the baby had cried a lot during our three-hour stationary sit the previous evening, and because Granny had seemed so disapproving. But we were not reseated, despite the fact that many rows of seats were now nearly empty, because the Paris-bound part of the original cohort of passengers had been packed onto another airline. Nobody complained that our section was dense while another was nearly empty, and I settled in next to Granny.

She remained obdurately uncommunicative, saying nothing even when rising to make her way to the back of the plane (remarkably infrequently: I was impressed). Her son or son-in-law (indiscernible which, if either, he was: they never chatted, so you could not pick up signs) eventually found a fellow beerophile and sat far away, near a door, for the sake of the leg room. Once or twice both Granny and Daddy were absent, and the sleeping baby was abandoned to my unrequested care. I made sure it didn't slip off the chair.

The first eight and a half hours of this flight to Bombay were spent flying to Delhi. Baby slept through all of them. Not a peep. The whole flight was smooth and uneventful. They showed lots of films and filmettes. One or two Indian "mainstream" films, that is, not the arty type that reach the Western intellectual classes, but of a melodramatic and predictable character that you could not have imagined, produced in Bollywood. The sometimes beautiful heroine's lips may not touch the man's (that is banned), so she winds around him to sinuous music as he tries and fails to plant his lips on hers. I am sure there are those who would say that it's all the sexier for the prohibition on kissing. Personally, I would have preferred less sex and more kissing.

At length, we reach Delhi. And there I began my aborted diary, as follows:

12.45 a.m. January 3 Indian Time

> I write as we land in Delhi. I will not get off here, but I am overwhelmed, tears in my eyes. I am here. I am in India, this infinitely fascinating country of sorrow. I am embarrassed to go on writing, lest someone see. So I will stop … But my neighbours are all getting off. So I have now resituated myself, at the window seat. India seems to be fog and a few airport lights. And people happy to be coming home.

We touched down at 5:50 A.M. in Bombay. The air was hot and wet, like a sultry New York August midday, but without the sun. But, before I continue with January 3, a general theme obtrudes.

When Rajeev Bhargava and I were planning my India tour, I said that I did not want to go to Calcutta. For I did not think that I could bear to face all the misery and mendicancy. I thought I would find it too harrowing.

That was a mistake. As I shall chronicle later, I did not find it very difficult to negotiate what poverty I saw. Maybe that is in part explained by my being less humane than I thought I was. But, however that may be, it is also explained by the poor being more human than I implicitly thought they were, and by their lives being more active, and more meaningful, than I had realized.

The mendicant poor have a tough time, and I don't. They know that, and they know that I know that. But they don't want my pity, and if I project pity at them, I am demeaning them, because they don't want it. (They pretend to want it. They tell sob stories that are sometimes true and sometimes false, and never told *because* they are true. The text is always the same, except for some flairfully inventive Delhi kids to be described later, whose text is an evident tissue of lies. But this is just the language of beggary, not an appeal for sympathy.) What they want is a little money. They are right to ask for it, and I am happy to give it. And there is not only no desire for pity from me when I give, but also, so it seemed, no smolder behind their eyes that I could give ten times as much and still not notice it. The moving thing is that our eyes meet with a certain mutual understanding and with unexaggerated gratitude from them. You can open to each other. You can open to a poor man lying on the pavement with stumps where his feet should be. You can joke with each other. And you can cry inside yourself at your very core when he or she smiles at you in a way that cannot be fake. You both understand, and you share your understanding.

It is unjust and foul not to give to them. It is unjust not to give a good chunk of our income regularly (and, it must be said, more productively) to the valiant organizations that address Third World misery. But there is a way of feeling sorry for these people when you are with them that is not right.

Here's the first paragraph of Mark Tully's *No Full Stops in India*:

> 'How do you cope with the poverty?' That must be the question I have been asked most frequently by visitors to India. I often reply, 'I don't have to. The poor do.' It's certainly true. I live a very comfortable life in Delhi, while the taxi-drivers who have lived opposite me for fourteen years have to sleep in their cars in the cold winter and on a charpai or light bedstead in the open during the hot weather. I have a three-bedroomed flat. The taxi rank is their home. My foreign guests expect the taxi-drivers to take them back to their hotels whatever hour of the night it may be. Before leaving,

> they will check the fare with me to make sure the taxi-drivers don't get a few more rupees than they are due. That's the way my guests usually 'cope with the poverty'. (p. 1)

I'm glad I read that before I went to India. I found the first part, about how he doesn't have to cope with the poverty, a bit hard, but now I understand it. Either you join Mother Teresa or you don't. Maybe you have a right not to. But you don't have a right not to join her and also to go on about how awful it is for the poor. That is unfair to the poor.

The part I was really glad I read was the criticism of his English friends. Twenty minutes in a Delhi taxi is about £1.00, a buck and a half. Imagine making sure that he doesn't charge £1.20 when it should be £1.00. I always paid a good deal more than they asked. I hope I would have done so anyway. But Tully ensured that I would.

I'm trying to convey a subtle truth here, which I don't see clearly, whether or not you do. Of course we should feel racked, in our Western comfort. But I'm sure it demeans the recipient to feel heartbroken when you give. The beggar is more human than you think. He is just as human as you or I. You owe him more than pity, and he can give you something too. And that is true even though it is also true that his life is subhuman, and that not only his outward life but even his inner life is subhuman.

But now, back to that Bombay morning.

Sunday, January 3

So: Bombay International Airport. A shack, more or less. A scrawny cat, forecasting the hunger of the people, stalking the battered baggage carousel. My bag comes through.

It is 6:10 A.M. Had I arrived at the appointed time, 1:30 P.M. the previous day, Ram would have met me. But I did not expect him to meet me this morning, because this plane, as he must have discovered, was scheduled to come in at 4:00 A.M. So I expected no one to meet me, but I had my money, my phone numbers, my tickets …

A room (forty feet square or so) between the baggage place and the open air. An incredibly shabby counter with a shabby ill-lit office behind it. Indian Airlines. I go to the counter to ask if I can still make the 6:50 A.M. to Goa. That plane is canceled, a teenage girl says, because of the airline pilots' go-slow. There is one at noon and one at 5:30 P.M. I am on the waiting list, number seven for the 5:30, number twenty-one for the noon. Sounds pretty bad to me, but she is encouraging. Those are good numbers, she says. I can hardly see her because the hole through which we speak (she is behind bars and dirty glass) is so small. I figure I'll take a taxi to the domestic airport (Santa Cruz) and ring Ram from there. The girl plays, ineffectively, with her computer. Then she makes a phone call that tells her to make another phone call, which she tries to make. What's going on is obscure, and she's only a kid. So it seems sensible to go to the domestic airport and make further inquiries there, and I say goodbye to her, in a kind way.

Out through the door to find a taxi. A happy surprise. A slight man stands outside with a placard: PROFESSOR COHEN, BRITISH COUNCIL. I had not been told that I would be met in Bombay. I step forward and, inappropriately, as far as he is concerned, I shake his hand vigorously. I hadn't realized that he was a driver, or that it was inappropriate to greet a driver like that. He takes me to Ingrid Almeida, who works for the Council, and who is waiting in the Ambassador car that he drives. The car is a strange blend of posh and dingy. Ingrid shows me a fax, which had not reached me, and which says that I'd be met at Bombay and which juggles around with the rest of my flights. I tell her what I know about my Goa flight. She knows it too, but she has different waiting list numbers, less good ones.

The unreceived British Council fax not only promised a reception at the airport in Bombay and rejigged my flights but also misnamed my Calcutta Indian Institute of Management lecture. The fax said "Quality Market and Private Property." This made me think that my prospective audience would think that I was going to draw curves plotting amounts of expenditure on videos, cars, fur coats (quality market) as against amounts spent on housing (private property), as a function of income level. Wrongly believing, at that point, that the India Institute of Management was a conventional business school, not then realizing that it was or housed a hive of lefties and Marxists, I couldn't see what else they would make of that title. I also couldn't understand how the Council had devised such a title. A few days later it dawned on me that I must at some point have said "Equality, Market and Private Property," and all they'd done is economize on an "E" and a comma.

Ingrid has brought 7,500 rupees (seventy-five one-hundred-rupee notes, fixed together with a stout copper staple) from the Council, to cover the Bombay/Goa part of my visit. About £180. But, she says, I shall be there one night less, because of the delay, so it would be hard for her to explain 7,500 rupees to her superior. Did I think I could manage on 6,000? If not, she'd find a way of explaining, but it would be hard. Since it's easily worth £36 to me to relieve her anxiety, I tell her not to worry. She says if it turns out that 6,000 was not enough, I can apply later for the extra. I am conscious of the difference in living standards.

We drive to the *Kamat Plaza* hotel, which is between the two airports. She explains to the hotel man why I hadn't appeared the previous night. (Ingrid doesn't know that I anyway would have stayed with Ram.) The hotel is cheapjack, but clean and with a certain innocent charm. It has a swimming pool, but I am supposed to avoid ordinary water: that's what all the guidebooks say. Ingrid asks if I want tea or coffee. I recall they are made of water and I decline. We go to the hotel café. We order fresh orange juice: no ice, please. I am worried they might dilute the orange juice with water. We sit, and nothing comes. Fifteen minutes later we ask for the juice. The man says it is being made. Then seemingly safe juice comes, I drink it, and it is very good.

At this point fifteen young African men and women, full of smiles and excitement, enter the lobby of the *Kamat Plaza*, in the charge of an Indian woman. They all wear wreaths of real flowers around their necks, which they were no doubt given at the airport. Ingrid quietly explains that they should not be blamed for not knowing that you are supposed to remove the wreath as soon as it's been put on, in order not to project that you deserve it. It seems to me that the correct procedure is a waste of beautiful flowers.

It is now 7:15, and I ring Ram's flat from the hotel. Madhura, his wife, explains that Ram has gone to the airport, and that he'll be ringing the flat for information. So, on Ingrid's advice, I tell Madhura to tell Ram to come to the *Kamat Plaza*. Ten minutes later he is with us, warm, handsome, jovial, and friendly. I am profuse in my apology that I did not tell him I'd be late. He is covered in shame that he failed to meet my plane. We agree to stop apologizing to each other.

Ram and Ingrid and I go to the domestic airport, to firm up my reservation, a kind of task with which Ingrid seems to be familiar. It is 8:00 A.M. They say come back at noon, the airport manager will be there, get a permit from him to see the duty manager of Indian Airlines, and maybe I can go to Goa on the 1:30 P.M. (there is no longer a twelve o'clock flight). Ram suggests that we go to his flat for breakfast, and I agree. Ingrid says, "I'll tag along, if you don't mind."

So we go to his flat in the V. K. Ramachandran van, Ram and Jerry in front, Ingrid behind. No seat belts in the cars and no lane discipline on the roads. I mean *no* lane discipline, you change lane *whenever* there is or appears to be a gap and everybody toots their horns all the time. Horn tooting is a means of propulsion. Trucks say "HORN, PLEASE" on their rears. Strange three-wheeled scooter-rickshaws, cars, trucks, bikes, pedestrians confidently weaving a domino-course zigzag through the moving cars, and bored-looking cows wandering around, scavenging.

Bombay has eleven million people, with thousands of new people coming in every day from the countryside. Five of the eleven million live on the streets and in "clusters," which are side-by-side makeshift mud-hut slums. It is mostly such slums that were burned down with Muslim families in them when terrorist politicians unleashed fire on Bombay a few days later, six hundred to seven hundred people being killed in a few days. "Communal riots" is the wrong phrase. It's not thousands massing in frenzy. It's dozens, forming hit squads, organized by the Shiv Sena (the army of Shiva) or the Bajrang Dal (the party of Hanuman, the monkey god, Hanuman who helped Ram retrieve Sita from Ravan when the latter had stolen her) or by mere gangsters who burn down hutments and sell something a bit better that they put up on the space to somebody else. And there are counter-Hindu Muslim hit squads too.

Words *can* describe the clusters, but you'd need millions of them. Tremendous variegation. Quite out of the question to take photographs. "Look, here is the leper by the side of the road, here is the bent woman with a jug of water on her head and a skinny baby in her arms …"

What surprises me, because of my stupidity and ignorance, is the intensity of activity. In the West, many of the poor don't do much. They languish between welfare payments, often in decent flats, now and then a little moonlighting, or a little crime, a drink in the pub. Here it is endless bustle. Men hurrying to menial jobs, or shitting at the roadside. Kids playing, yelling, dousing themselves with water. Women cooking. Men gossiping and smoking. All kinds of containers made of tin and plastic in arms and on heads used to carry precious (though bacteria-ridden) water to the shacks, from distant standpipes. An enormous amount of rigorous washing of clothes, and the clothes they wear are certainly clean. In some places dozens of colorful ramshackle shops front the road, with hutments behind. And lush fruit and vegetables on sale that I'm supposed to eat only if I peel it first. Better not try.

It was stupid to have expected the Indian poor to be inactive. Unlike our poor, if they're inactive, they die. Consequently, and also because of its close community setting, their life, hard though it is, has substance and direction, which the life of the poor in the Western welfare state often lacks. These poor people are not unemployed. Still, you are overwhelmed by the difference between their lot and yours, within the sameness that we are all human.

Through slums and more slums, some with television aerials, and some with tall blocks of flats behind them where middling classes of people live, clerks and better-off traders. A mile of sewer stench, then another mile, just as slummy, visually, but no smell. Then a different kind of smell, rotting things, with an ammoniac soupçon of pee. Scavenging docile cows and dogs and the odd goat. A family eating at a fire with a skinny baby lamb or kid in attendance. Terrific sounds of bubbling cooking oil.

More slums, and then up a hill and through a gate with guards to the precincts of the spanking-new Indira Gandhi Institute for Development Research, where Ram and other economists live and work and teach. (In India there are always guards. In that Bombay International Airport room, where Indian Airlines had its grimy office, there was a guard, one guard, with an old rifle. It would have been a piece of cake for me with three or four other Oxford dons or Jews from Montreal to rush him and remove it. He looked anxious, no swagger.)

Ramachandran has a modest flat of two/three rooms with, right now, a dozen people in it, including Ingrid and me; Ram's wife, Madhura; Parvati, his sister, who is a journalist for *Frontline*, a good *Time*-like left-wing magazine from which I learned a lot; Parvati's husband, Sonny, a silk farmer: they are visiting from the South, from Bangalore; two small girls, each a year old or so, one Ram's and Madhura's, one Parvati's and Sonny's, playing in the care of two servant-nannies, one of whom traveled up from Bangalore with her employers; a visiting Finnish academic, expert on the Harappa civilization, and his wife, a psychotherapist; a woman preparing a meal in a (by our standards) underequipped kitchen; another woman sweeping; a child at the table, a boy from the slums, seated with a newspaper beside Madhura, being taught by her how to read, and you have to suppress the rush of emotion inside you when you realize the full meaning of this drop-in-the-ocean-of-injustice scene.

It is thirty-three degrees Celsius and I am overdressed. I retire to a back room to change into light clothes. I shave ("You can have hot water in ten minutes." "No, it's fine.") and I come out still reeling with fatigue but full of happiness, to join the melee. A wonderful breakfast. Soft, baked semolina cake and hot spicy vegetable stew to eat it with, to dip it in. Wheat and rye and oil. Perfect food for me: I love the mixture of the bland farinaceous and the hot stuff. ("I hope the food isn't too spicy for you?" "Oh, no, not at all …")

Time rolls on. It's 11:30 A.M., and we have to go back to the airport. So Ram, Ingrid, and I drive back to the airport. In the divide between the two sides of the broad slum-flanked highway sits a man with no legs (below thigh-level). He hobbles over during the red light and we give him money. He is energetic in his arms-propelled motion. Not pathetic. All in a day's work. A boy comes to my window "No Momma, no Poppa" and I give him five rupees to take back to his parents, or his "beggarmaster," the person who leans on him for a cut, if he has one. Another boy comes selling a shabby balloon with a bit of water in it. He wants one rupee. I give him two: whatever happens to come out of my small-notes pocket, the hundreds safely in the other one. For I've now instituted a vestmental division of labor. One pocket for them, one pocket for me.

Then back to the airport. Only passengers are allowed into it, because of security. It is evident to Ingrid and me that I couldn't conceivably negotiate my waiting list place myself. I wouldn't know what to do. So she asks to be allowed in. The guard tells her to go to the office of the airport manager: there is an entrance outside, on the airport parade. A room with two men lounging at a desk. Another room behind. The two permit Ingrid to go into the back room, where she gets a man to stamp a piece of paper for her, after a curt exchange in (I suppose) Marathi, the language of Maharashtra, of which Bombay is the capital.

We are allowed to enter the checking-in hall. We go to the office of the duty manager of Indian Airlines. 12:15 now. Several uniformed somethings-or-other in his office. He says, come back later, it'll be all right. Ingrid is visibly perturbed, losing her cool, feeling impotent, but pretending otherwise to me. We wander around. A waiting list queue is established for the flight to Goa. I wait. Ingrid goes back to the duty manager. She's away a bit too long for my peace of mind. She comes back. She says the duty manager says it'll be all right. "Big deal, what he *says*," I think.

Then we turn out to be in the wrong queue. Another queue, or, rather, mass of people massing a man. I join the mass. Eventually, I reach the front wave. In the mill of competition to be served by the man, a brown arm suddenly sideways from behind me overtakes my own arm. This arm thrusts forward a signed-by-some-official chit. I protest, exercising (involuntarily, I hope) the legacy of centuries of imperial authority, Mughal and British: "I was here before you" (a funny thing to say, in retrospect). The arm's owner grumble-shouts back. I gently and firmly push back the arm. I look at him and he breaks into a warm and total smile. I smile richly back. Inside, I cry. He asks me where I come from and how many children I have (often the first question from a friendly stranger). Two inner humanities meet, humanities infinitely more precious than Sony Walkmen, chilled champagne, Harley-Davidsons, Mont Blanc pens.

If only we knew how to make an economic system out of our humanities. For what does it profit a man, to gain the world, and lose his soul?

Finally, the plane. A splendid airbus, only one-third full. Why so empty, you wonder, with all that competition for seats? Because that competition was for a smaller plane, now replaced by this one. One hour later we land in Goa. Ingrid said she'd ring Peter de Souza, … but he isn't there. I don't panic: I have my tickets, my phone numbers, my heightened inner humanity and perfect happiness. I decide to ring Peter. There is no phone in Arrivals. There is a phone in Departures, but that means climbing and descending stairs with my luggage and I know I shouldn't carry the big bag because of my liability to hernia. I didn't think of retaining a porter, so I carried. A woman in Departures runs the phone. I reach Peter easily. He will be there in forty minutes.

I wait in the departure hall, with a bottle of Bisleri (still mineral water). It costs 20 rupees, 50 pence. I must be acclimatizing, financially, since I remark to myself that that's an enormous price. Peter comes. He has evidently expected a stiffer, more donnish, type. I think he prefers what I am to what he expected. He is very Western. He is of Catholic descent, as are 35 percent of Goans, because Goa was ruled, from soon after 1500 to 1961 or 1962, by the Portuguese. The local language is Konkani, which is not at all like Hindi.

Goa is big. We drive for thirty miles or so through beautiful villages lined with palm trees, without luxury and without slums. Around 8:00 P.M. we reach Panaji (also called Panjim, its old Portuguese name). We pull up at the *Mandovi Hotel*, overlooking the broad Mandovi River, near where it meets the sea. Goa, a beautiful ungarish resort coast of white-sand beaches, fishermen and fish, beautiful men and women, and, in the hotel, a huge two-and-a-half-room suite for me, £22 a night, overlooking the river.

Having parked my bags at the hotel, we drive to Miramar Beach, where the sea begins, and we walk and discuss political philosophy as the sun sets. And Peter tells me about Goa and about India, and about the current harrowing ethnic *travail*.

Then back to the hotel, and I tell Peter that I must collapse, and he needs to leave anyway.

A short solo walk along the front, where the ferries ferry sightseers. Then a superb buffet dinner in the hotel. Goa is famous for its food, and this hotel is supposed to be the best. Their specialty is fish, and it is not mine, but I manage plenty of vegetables, hot spices, and naan. Peter, later: "I hope the food wasn't too hot for you."

Then, around 10:30 P.M., the weary wandering Jerry, who hasn't slept for thirty-six hours, settles into a huge bed, for a happy, peaceful night.

Actually, the night started peaceful only because of a benign power cut. Let me backtrack.

The reason why Peter had to leave me in the early evening was that he was going to a wedding reception, in the hotel I was staying in, on the floor above me. After the dinner described above, I took another short walk, and, exiting from the hotel around 9:30 P.M., I came upon Peter, now dressed not ordinarily as before but in a Nehruvian tunic. He was the only arriving guest wearing Indian clothes, apart of course from the many saried women. He explained the next day that the tunic was a modest political statement. One mustn't cave in completely to Western culture.

Preparing for bed, I could hear loud jazzy music upstairs, and I wondered if my exhaustion would make me sleep anyway. Just then the lights went out, apart from a little one evidently powered by a hotel generator. That silenced the wedding party and secured my sleep. Apparently, about a half hour later the electricity, and the party, revived. But by then I was safely in the arms of Morpheus. Or Ganesh? Or Hanuman? Or Durga? That would have been exciting.

MONDAY, JANUARY 4

Up at 7:30 A.M. and a local paper (the *Gomantak Times* has been pushed under the door. An item on the front page: "Oxford don to conduct workshop today."[4] (Oh, Morris Winchewsky, could you but see what you have wrought!)[5] I am overcome by the irony of it. I feel humble and inappropriate, silly to be made a fuss of. A morning constitutional through the Panaji melee, in advance of Pe-

[4] Editor's note: The item consisted of the following three paragraphs:

> Dr. Gerry Cohen, the only Marxist to have ever held the Chichele Chair of Science [*sic*] and Political Theory at the prestigious Oxford University will conduct a workshop on the future of Socialism at the T B Cunha Memorial Hall here from 10 am to 4 today.
>
> The workshop comes at a time when there is almost universal disenchantment with Socialism following the disintegration of the erstwhile Soviet Union.
>
> It also ironically coincides with a deep recession in the free market economies with the rate of growth of the most advanced industrial countries expected to be as low as 2 per cent during the year 1992, while surprisingly the Republic of China which continues to be a bastion of Marxism is expected to register a growth rate of 14 per cent.

[5] [Here Cohen invokes the name of his primary school in Montreal. See the opening paragraphs of Chapter 9 of this volume for a sketch of this "pro-Soviet communist private Jewish school."—Ed.]

ter's arrival: we will walk together to the socialism workshop later. Hundreds of charming tiny ramshackle ill-lit poorly furnished shabbily decorated shops, all open to the perfect sunshine air. And booming endless traffic, with few points where a pedestrian can cross without daring, so I imitate the natives and I learn how to dare.

The shops have everything from soup to nuts including the kitchen sink. Auto parts, shoe requisites, a lending library that hires out old magazines and even old newspapers, tangerines, pots and pans, greasy cogs and wheels, smells of spicy breakfast bits, a general air of hum and busy-busy. Not poverty, by Indian standards, just a low but livable standard of living.

I stroll along the front smoking a small cigar. They stare, and I stare back. They smile, I smile. I smile, they smile. They are amused by my cigar or by my baseball hat or by my smile and I enjoy their amusement. No perceptible tourist-phobia. But the ubiquitous taxi drivers do resent the fact that you don't need them.

At 10:00 A.M. Peter arrives. We have a full day ahead. First, Jerry on "Is There Still a Case for Socialism?" Then Dr. P. R. Dubashi, a former high civil servant in Delhi and now vice-chancellor of the University of Goa, will offer his "Reflections." Next, Professor Adi Doctor (I kid you not: that's his name), chair of political science, will speak on "Gandhian Socialism." Finally, Professor R. A. Sinari, chair of philosophy, will explain "The Enigma of Human Rights." In between there will be discussion, and lunch.

It takes four or five minutes to walk to the venue, the T. B. Cunha Memorial Hall. We might have met at the university, but the Indian Science Congress is happening there (Prime Minister Rao made a speech to open it the day I got to Goa). So, happily, we are not in the sticks, where the university is, but in the warm grime of the town.

T. B. Cunha, it turned out, was a leader of the liberation (from Portugal) movement. I gather there wasn't much of a movement. Nehru's takeover of Goa, resisted by the Portuguese, was not in response to intense popular demand, which is not to say that the locals were sorry to see the Portuguese go. Salazar had wanted to burn down part of Panaji as a farewell gesture, but the local Portuguese governor wouldn't play ball with that.

I didn't learn much about Cunha. There was a colored photo of him on the wall sitting at a desk in Western suit and tie, looking more like a middling clerk with his glasses and meek expression than any kind of revolutionary leader. The hall itself was, as Peter had more than once warned me, modestly appointed. When we arrived, there were about thirty people there—it rose eventually to forty. I was introduced on our arrival to about ten of them, including the notables whose contributions-to-be I cataloged a moment ago, and also three trade unionists, including the local trade union supremo, a bearded Marxist in a Fidelista outfit, with a challenging facial appearance and physique.

They offered me tea. I knew it would have milk and sugar in it—I take tea with neither—and I was going to decline and then I realized how ungracious that would be. So we drank tea, the ten of us, at the back of T. B. Cunha Memorial Hall, while the rest waited in their seats. Then Vice-Chancellor Dubashi and I took our places on a small platform with a table and Bisleri (the mineral water), and Peter made his way to the podium, at our left, on floor level. There was a mike, which seemed at first excessive for a room of forty people, but I came to realize that it was necessary to overcome the roar of the raging traffic below.

Peter spoke at some length, twenty minutes or so. He explained who I was, and what the hall was in memory of (it was quite newly opened, this hall). He explained what the program would be, and how we would end around 4:30, when, by fortunate coincidence, a party of activists who were spending a few days walking from one end of Goa to the other would arrive in the square beside the hall to stage a demonstration against the communalism racking India, against the fascist BJP, VHP, RSS, Shiv Sena, and Bajrang Dal, the semifascist politicians fanning the flames against the Muslims.

At the end of his speech Peter presented me with Nehru's *Discovery of India*, inscribed "To Professor Dr. Gerry Cohen, from your friends and admirers at Goa University, 4 January 1993," and signed by Peter and by Sinari. Moved to inner tears, I resolved to read the thing, which will take me ages, since I read slowly and it's huge. I look forward to reading it. Open it anywhere, and you can see that Nehru was brilliant and encyclopedically erudite, and that he had a good style. Had I been Lady Mountbatten, I, too, would have fallen for him.

Then I gave my talk on "Is There Still a Case for Socialism?" with as much verve as I could muster. I spoke for fifty-five minutes. I could not tell how much was understood, but I could tell that they were not bored. I imagined that the unboring thing was not the content of my talk but the person from afar, the style, the occasion, etc.

When I finished there was a trickle of applause. Then Dubashi was introduced by Peter. Almost notelessly, he gave a forty-five minute account of the development of the idea of socialism, from early notions of comprehensive planning through the von Mises/Hayek critique, the Lange/Taylor response, experiments in market socialism in Eastern Europe, the Fabian and social-democratic traditions, etc. Most of it was not new to me, but the organization of the material was superb, a very impressive performance. Dubashi had studied at the LSE in the Laski/Titmuss days and he remembered it all. His attitude to socialism was one of friendly skepticism. There were a few questions and answers, and then we milled around before proceeding to lunch.

We trotted round the corner, twenty of us or so, to a very simple vegetarian restaurant. Glorious food, served thali-style. I occupied a booth with Dubashi. He ate in the Indian manner, with his right hand: you use the chapatis to scoop up the cooked vegetables, rice, and spices. I tried the method, with indifferent success, and often I had to use the cutlery that they also provided. “I hope the food isn't too spicy for you.” “No, it's fine,” I said (it was about 50 percent of the strength of a vindaloo in England). Towards the end of the meal Dubashi had only rice and yoghurt left. How would he manage *that* lot with his right hand with no chapati or roti to stuff it in? He managed. He poured the yoghurt on the rice and messed it all around and pushed it into his mouth. I was delighted by this method of eating. I could not imagine Oxford's Sir Richard Southwood, our vice-chancellor, doing the same.

Peter had been in a distant booth during lunch. As we were leaving the restaurant, he expressed a hope that the food had not been too hot for me. There was a bowl of hard, dry, small, green peppers just beside us, the really fierce ones. “Look,” I said, “I love hot food, even stuff much hotter than what we've just eaten. Would you like to see me eat one of these peppers, neat, right now?” “No,” he said, “because I could not know that you were not enduring it through immense effort of will, to prove your point.” He was, of course, right, and I was glad that he did not accept my challenge.

Between lunch and the afternoon session a young journalist from the *Panjim Herald* walked back with me to the *Mandovi Hotel* to interview me. I've done such interviews before, always with a sense of awkwardness since, because they know I'm a professor of politics, they think I must know about politics, which I largely don't. So I did my best. Asked to comment on whether the BJP was a fascist party, I declined. (Peter later said that I could have said without pretense of expertise that *if* a political party promotes ethnic conflict to gain political advantage, then it is fascist.) The text of the interview is about 80 percent faithful to what I said. The headline—“India still imitates Western ideals: Cohen”—is an embarrassment. I don't think of Thatcherism as an *ideal*, so I didn't mean that when I said that the IMF was imposing it on India. And in a number of other respects I had not “opined” what she said I opined.

The interviewer was a young woman, midtwenties or so, thin and pretty. A Goan recently married and recently relocated from Bombay. I was much more interested in *her* perceptions than in talking about Indian politics. I asked her whether she didn't agree that my hotel rooms were sumptuous. She refused to answer. So I asked her whether she was a journalist or a diplomat. (Gently, I didn't give her a hard time.) So she said every journalist had to be something of a diplomat. We walked back to the T. B. Cunha Hall.

Professor Doctor was the first item on the afternoon's agenda. He gave an admirably clear and, for me, instructive exposition of Gandhi's socialism, emphasizing how it differed both from capitalism and from Western socialism in its aspiration to preserve village ways and values. Then he explained why he “couldn't accept the whole Gandhian package.” It didn't allow sufficiently for innovation. The little modification he proposed seemed to me to explode the whole package, as I later said in the discussion.

After Doctor's talk there was a general discussion, in the course of which I became aware of a stunningly beautiful face at the back of the room. Large brown eyes. Perfect cheekbones, a face satisfyingly symmetrical along every axis. I learned more about her the next day, as you will hear.

Salient contributors to the discussion were, first, in order of speakers, Manjit Singh, a nonbelieving unturbaned Sikh from a Punjab village, where, he later told me, a letter could arrive and be unread for three months because no one knew how to read. He had certainly read a lot, Marx and Parsons and Durkheim, and his theme was that our theorizing didn't connect enough with real life. A kind of *German Ideology* protest. He spoke quickly and with great animation. A beautiful face lined with a medium-sized beard. Then there was another sociologist. "How would you construct the possibility of inequality?" he asked me. He brought out the Oxford don in me, but I restrained my response. I tried to tease him into greater clarity but, *obscurum per obscurius*. Another major contributor was the Fidelista trade union leader, who asked me some very broad questions that were hard to seize, and who directed a lot of fire against Dubashi for his failure to understand socialism, and against Gandhi for being generally out to lunch. Dubashi replied forcefully. "But what do you understand by socialism, how does it work?" he shouted, pounding the table. Fidel: "It does not help when you pound the table." Dubashi: "All right, I'll ask you again, without pounding the table: How does socialism work, what is it?" "Socialism is rule by the working class." *Mazel tov*, I thought. And thank God Dubashi is here to catch the flak: otherwise, for sure, I'd be the target.

Time was getting short, and Professor Sinari offered not to give his talk. The offer was semisincere, but we all thought it out of the question to accept it, and we successfully prevailed upon him to proceed. His talk was about the individual versus society, this terrible conflict. For the second time in my life I experienced the word "opine" used without irony. (The first time was from a Bombay Parsee undergraduate, Jamshed [Jimmy] Maneck Kanga, in the Philosophy Department at University College London, reading an essay for me in a tutorial in 1963. And the next time, after Sinari's use of it, was in the *Panjim Herald* article commented on a few paragraphs back.) After Sinari spoke, I taxed him for presenting too absolute an individual-versus-society antithesis. I asked him whether he wouldn't, if given the choice, continue to be a professor even if he wasn't paid to be one, if he was assured his present salary whether or not he kept his job, and would get no more if he kept it. (This was supposed to show that his self-interest to some extent coincided with his social contribution.) He said he would say "Yes" because he didn't want people to think badly of him. So I added the Oxford-like stipulation that they would admire him no matter what his reply was. I can't remember how he coped with the escalated challenge.

Discussion continued. The last questioner was the woman with the beautiful face. She asked two questions, with a clear line between them. The first went like this: "Professor Cohen. If I am a worker I will vote for a socialist party. If I am a boss I will vote for a capitalist party. So how can we ask whether capitalism or socialism is objectively better?" I don't remember her second question. I found that first one morally crass: the beautiful face seemed not to front a beautiful soul. I denied her premise. Some workers vote for capitalism and some capitalists vote for socialism. Since *they* manifestly address the issue in an objective spirit, so can we. I don't know whether the answer pleased her.

Then we heard the arrival of the march in the square, so we broke up and a number of us trundled down. There was a stage with a proscenium arch on which some of the marchers were singing a tuneful song about India being one nation. I bought a pamphlet called *Cry, the Beloved Country* which strung together newspaper extracts detailing the destruction of the Ayodhya mosque and the subsequent events. I stayed there about fifteen minutes. There was no welcoming crowd, just twenty or thirty people thinly scattered. Then I repaired to the hotel to read the *Cry, the Beloved Country* pamphlet and to rest before going out to dinner with Peter, Doctor, and Sinari.

One reason why I needed to read the pamphlet was so that I could be more forthcoming than I had been with the *Herald* journalist the following morning when a journalist from the *Times of India* was scheduled to interview me. I didn't want to repeat the mistake, pointed out by Peter, of failing to project a little benign anti-BJP propaganda.

Peter came at 8:00 P.M. in his Maruti and we drove to the restaurant. A beautiful place full of palms and coconuts and fishermen's nets and candles. Doctor and Sinari were already there. They had each had a beer. I tanked up on screwdrivers. The food wasn't all that great, but very welcome. "I hope the food isn't too strong for you." "Look, I don't want to be ungracious, but I'm surprised everyone asks me that. Our vindaloos, etc." But "vindaloo" turns out to be a misnomer. In Goa there is *pork* vindaloo, a particular dish (which I didn't sample: mostly on the trip I steered off meat, except for seekh and chicken kebabs), and not a particularly fierce one, and "vindaloo" as a general term is absurd. There is also, apparently, no such thing as "meat Madras." They laughed at the linguistic deformations on English Indian menus.

And then into Peter's Maruti and back to the hotel for a good night's sleep.

TUESDAY, JANUARY 5

At breakfast, confirmation of the thesis that one thing the British Raj left behind was a class of relatively well-off Indians contemptuous of those who are not well-off and sycophantic towards well-placed Anglos. As I have said, Goa U was hosting the Indian Science Congress, and the *Mandovi Hotel* was full of mostly Indian but also foreign delegates to the congress. One of each sat breakfasting at a table adjacent to mine, a mustached Indian and a muscular, tall Australian, sporting a purse on a belt on his waist that I tried and failed not to feel contemptuous about. I eavesdropped. The usual academic chitchat. "Did you go to *X*'s paper on … ?" "No, I had to chair *Y*'s …" Then: "You really must come to Delhi. We would love to …" "Well, it might be difficult …" "I will give you my card. We could make sure that you …" "Well …" "How are you getting to the university? (Laughing with fake embarrassment) I have been given a car. I would be very glad to drive you." "Well, I'm afraid I have to go a bit later. I have to prepare a …" I suppose the words in the interchanges don't reveal the sycophancy. It was the syrupy manner. Then the Australian left, to prepare his … Then the Indian's manner changed. He said to one of the waiters, "Bring me Equal." The waiter was nonplussed. Harsher: "Bring me Equal, the half-sugar, half-saccharin." With imperious disdain, "with wrinkled lip, and sneer of cold command" (Shelley). "We have no, Sir." With contempt: "Yes, you do, go to kitchen." So he did, and, to my surprise and disappointment, they did have it. Which, so the customer thought, justified further disdain. I felt like saying something, but I didn't think it right to do so.

A wander through the jam-packed streets after breakfast. Emaciated women curled up on the pavement offering bananas and tomatoes. Begging men with leg-stumps. Barefoot kids running gaily around in the grime in the sun. Then up to my room to await the arrival (10:00 A.M.) of the correspondent from the *Times of India*.

He seemed a depressive type. No oomph. Asked me questions about socialism on the world scene. I answered unfluently and awkwardly, occasionally pleading ignorance. He never asked me about Indian politics, so my previous evening's study of the political pamphlet didn't get used that morning.

The interview dragged boringly on. Then, around 12:30, it sort of fizzled out, and the *Times* man said a photograph was needed. A man could come from the *Times* to take a picture. I demurred: enough time had been spent. Then I remembered that I had a camera myself. But the reel of film was near the beginning. I hesitated to say that I didn't care if most of the reel was wasted: you don't like to display indifference about wasting £3. Then a discussion about whether the film could be cut in two. Then lots of pictures were taken, some (it turned out) good. Then goodbye to the *Times* man, as Peter and I pile into the Maruti in search of a photography developing studio.

The one we found was very busy: all those Science Congress types flapping their shutters. But they could do it by tomorrow. And they *could* cut the reel. So back into the Maruti and off to stately Old Goa, to look at the sixteenth- and seventeenth-century churches the Portuguese left behind. These were massive affairs, of not bad but not terrific (remembering what was going on in southern Europe at the time) architectural quality, and with third-rate paintings of the Madonna and so forth, some in European style and some tinged with Hindu Krishnas and Radhas milling around the cross. Some *very* good wood carving on pulpits and what looked like small cantorias. All these buildings listed by the relevant Indian ministry, but pitifully decayed decoration. They could be made to look much better.

There was also an interesting museum, with a downstairs containing dozens of devotional Buddhist and Hindu sculptures from many periods and many parts of the country, and, upstairs, a set of rooms displaying paintings (except for the last one, represented only in a photograph) of the Portuguese governors of Goa. Since this governing began around 1500 and lasted for more than 450 years, and no one seemed to have been in post for more than three or four years, there were something like 125 paintings, some quite good, all the governors in ceremonial dress. I wondered whether the short terms meant that the governorship was a plum for which there was a queue or a drag which the Luso-grandees would quit as soon as they could. Peter favored the former theory. I thought that was patriotism, but I did not say so.

Back to town, whirling through the thronged streets in the Maruti, to meet Manjit Singh at a modestly appointed restaurant, and now it's around 2:30. The food was alpha-double-plus, wonderful homemade thali. The bill for the three of us, each of whom fed substantially, for a lunch, was around £1.10, the Bisleri water included. I magnanimously picked up the tab, and Manjit hoped that I hadn't found the spices difficult to cope with.

We go to a public telephone office so I can ring Ram in Bombay to tell him when I'll arrive the next day. Into a booth with such a loud fan that I cannot hear anything. I am permitted to turn off the fan. I reach the Indira Gandhi Institute office, and they say that they will get Ram to come to the phone. I wait and I wait, the rupees pile up. On advice from Peter, I hang up, in order to ring again a few minutes later by which time Ram should have got there. I do that, several times, but these times failing to make a connection. So I settle for a fax, which takes another ten minutes.

To the hotel, to arrange a taxi to take Manjit and me to Baga Beach. Peter asks the taxi driver how much he'd charge to take us to the beach (a half-hour drive), wait there for an hour, and then take us back. 250 rupees. Peter bargains him down to 190. (250 rupees is £6.) So we wend our automotive way through countryside and villages to Baga Beach. The trip is better than the beach. I am enthralled by the palm-tree villages, the picture-postcard tropical lushness, the busy gaiety and the old churches, the narrow unobtrusive road, overhung with foliage. And then we get to Baga Beach.

Baga Beach is a beach. A rolling sea into which I wade. I do not swim because I do not want to have to park my glasses. No great desire to swim anyway: I'm not a beach man. Then we regain the taxi, drive back through the country and the villages to the *Mandovi*, and embrace goodbye.

It's six o'clock, and Peter will fetch me at eight to take me to have dinner at his house twenty minutes away to meet his wife Lijia (an economist), and his widowed mother. We reach Peter's place which, as he had apologized, is beautifully situated, a huge coconut tree in the garden, and beautiful in its architecture and its appointments. Nothing overdone. Lijia is also beautiful. We have pleasant conversation over good, stiff, booze, something local I forget from what plant, and I get very merry inside. Peter's mother arrives and joins us, an elegant woman of sixty-seven.

Usual dinner party chat enlivened by the topics of Goa and creeping fascism in India. Then excellent food, buffet-style, which we take out with us to the verandah, where we'd been drinking. Somebody hopes that the food is not too strong for me. (It wasn't.) Then Peter drives me back. We are stopped by the police. They take our license number. They say, in friendly fashion, that they have to do random stops and report license numbers, to show that they are invigilating, ensuring security. Peter says it could be that they stopped us because he was wearing a kurta. We discuss kurtas. He says they are cool in this hot climate. I find that ridiculous, since they go down to the shins. He rebuts. He struggles to defend the best in Indian civilization.

WEDNESDAY, JANUARY 6

Another perfect morning. Armed with my Cadogan Guide to India (which I recommend, except that it exaggerates the health dangers), I do a Cadogan-guided tour of Panaji. First the splendid Church of the Immaculate Conception, which is just opening for business (it's 10:15), the shammes busying himself with sweeping and polishing up. A very fine church, smaller than but as good as what you get in Old Goa. I ask the shammes how to get to the mosque and the Hindu temple, and he points me in the right direction.

It's a bit difficult rendering his instructions, the map, and the streets congruent, so I seek further help from an eager passerby. It turns out he is eager because I am a potential customer at his garment shop. "You only have to look, not buy." "I'm not shopping this morning, give me your card and I'll come by later." (I have learned how to be mendacious.) "Ah, but, but …" He tries a bit more, and then sees there's no point. Then I come upon the masjid or mosque, which is a shop-front affair, with a rude sign on the front. An anteroom and an inner room, in which one man is kneeling and another is prostrate. I remove my sandals and socks at the entrance and I slowly proceed inwards, charmed by the small scale and the magicness of the sanctum. But the kneeling man swings his upper body and head to the left and stares at me rigidly. I look at him, not knowing what to do. He goes on staring, not quite menacingly. I feel intrusive, naturally, so I retreat to my socks and shoes, not knowing how much fear and how much respect there is in the mix of motives moving me.

Back on the street, I progress towards the Hindu temple. There is a dusty unkempt courtyard and, near a tree, old women sit offering garlands of flowers and other paraphernalia. I say, meaning it, that I'll buy when I come out. So it's off, once more, with the socks and sandals. The temple is pretty new, and concrete-ugly. Ugly idols here and there, and an altar at the far end. Worshippers come and go, singly, and here there is no projection of hostility or suspicion. ("If the goy wants to pay his respects to Vishnu, let him pay his respects to Vishnu.") At the altar I see some of those garlands and bits of food on plates. So now I realize they are sacrifices to whatever idol—my eyesight fails me—is behind the glass behind the altar. So, having meandered round the temple a bit, I go outside, slip my sandals on again, and buy a garland to pay my respects to Vishnu, or whoever is in the glass case. Once again, stray worshippers come and go. Some bow, some kneel, it all seems such a potpourri, a microcosm of the run-down supermarket shelf of god-choices that is popular Hinduism.

After the temple, says the Guide, walk up the hill to the Archbishop's Palace. Neither the Guide nor the map shows where that is, but, I figure, up is up, so I proceed to the back of the temple courtyard, where several lounging laborers—there's some kind of inscrutable building work going on in the courtyard—flank some stairs, and look at me with unfriendly curiosity. Up through stairs and lanes and the back gardens of attractive dwellings and guarded public buildings to the palace, which is lousy-classical in style. A small child approaches, asking for I cannot tell what: he isn't begging. In front of the palace entrance there is a trench with three or four diggers in it, sweating in the thirty-degrees-Celsius-plus sun. As I leave, one of them stares at me with what looks like intense resentment. If it is resentment, then it's justified. How did I earn the right to stroll in the sun he sweats in?

Later that day, I take a flight to Bombay, where Ram meets me at the airport. We put my bags on a trolley and roll it to the car park where his van is. Packed, we drive off through the slums and the stench to the Indira Gandhi Institute. Arriving, we open up the back of the van to take out the bags. WHERE IS MY BLACK BRIEFCASE? Not in the back. Not in the front. Not under the seat. Zapped. Rumbled. We must have left the briefcase on the trolley.

It had my tickets, my money, a few hundred pounds in cash (I hate traveler's checks), and, worst of all to lose, my lectures. I did not feel *as* bad as you will imagine, because, on the advice of my Cadogan Guide, I had written down the numbers of all my things, my tickets, my passport, etc., but I did feel *awfully* bad. Bye, bye, briefcase, what will I do?

Ram says we can get a temporary passport. But it is Saturday night and I am due to fly from Bombay to Calcutta the next morning. We call in at Ram's flat and decide to return to the airport. I remember, vividly, Hume's *Enquiry Concerning Human Understanding*, how struck I was when I first read this passage, thirty-three years ago: "A man who at noon leaves his purse full of gold on the pavement at Charing Cross, may as well expect that it will fly away like a feather, as that he will find it untouched an hour after,"[6] and it is now nearly an hour after, and Bombay airport is full of desperate characters, on the make.

We drive back to the airport, through the slums. I am conscious that the

[6] [Section VIII ("Of Liberty and Necessity"), part I—Ed.]

people in the clusters have no reason to sympathize with me (cf. "Incentives, Inequality, and Community," p. 274, example (c)).[7] Ram says, "If it's there, it's a freak." I'm glad my friend is honest. Ram says: "We have to figure out what we're going to do if it isn't there." I say: "I can't cope with that yet, emotionally. When we know it isn't there, we'll figure out what to do."

How was this possible? Could someone have snatched it from the trolley as we rolled it to the car? I suppose I thought I was in Ram's care and he thought I knew how many bags I had. I realize I can ask Michèle to fax my lectures, and I feel better: but the faxing would take hours.

The trip to the airport is swift, since now it's too late for plane departures. We are there, at the car park, in less than twenty-five minutes. The trolley is where we left it, with no bag on it. We get out of the van. Two kids, around seven and eleven, stand nearby, smiling. Seeing them, Ram says: "I think this story is going to have a happy ending." He is right. They explain that when they saw the bag they thought it might be a bomb so the airport police were called, and they now have it. I am over the moon, and I am grateful that India has terrorists.

The kids lead us to the nearby police station. The bag is produced by Captain Khan, who is friendly but *very* mildly sardonic. He says: "Check the bag." The outer zip-pocket, which contained the passport, money, and tickets is empty. "Yes, this is my bag, but the papers aren't here." "Check inside," says Captain Khan. And there they are. "Check the rest." So I shuffle through the jumble: "Well, it's all here, except I can't find the malaria tablets." I say that not out of anxiety, but because Captain Khan has told me to check thoroughly. Ram: "I don't think anyone would take your malaria tablets." We don't bother about them. I make to go, but another policeman gets me to sign a statement saying it's all there. (Which it was: the tablets turned up later.)

Bag safely in hand and back to the van, the boys in train. I give them each one hundred rupees: you can eat decently for two weeks with that. A thirty-year-old man appears, claiming a role in the affair. So he, too, is remunerated. Then back for the third time that evening through the slums and stench and—now—fog.

At Ram's they have already dined—it is 10:45, and they could not know how long we'd be. I present, from my suitcase, a bottle of Bushmills Single Malt, originally intended for Rajeev and Tani in Delhi, but the retrieval of the bag is a reason to be festive, so it seems right to release the bottle now. Ram and I drink well before and with an excellent meal.

Next morning, at 6:15, Ram will drive his sister Parvati with husband Sonny, little daughter, and servant to Bombay's Victoria Terminal (VT), where they

[7] [The example, from Cohen's Tanner Lectures, is as follows: "I might persuade my fellow middle class friend that, because my car is being repaired, and I consequently have to spend hours on the buses these days, I have a right to be grumpy. The same conclusion, on the same basis, sounds feeble when the audience is not my friend but a carless fellow bus passenger who is forced to endure these slow journeys every day."—Ed.]

will take the train back to Bangalore. I am offered the opportunity to come with them, which I accept with enthusiasm, since it will be my only chance to see Bombay proper (I've now seen the slums of Bombay improper five times).

Ram takes me to the guesthouse, whose name is more attractive than its rooms are. Fine on the outside, but the chamber is grim, large with hardly anything in it. A *very* loud air conditioner, which would ensure, for me, a sleepless night. "Can't I open a window?" "No, the mosquitoes will come in." Then he turns on some device which exudes a scent meant to frighten the mosquitoes away, and which therefore frightens me. And he takes his leave.

I cannot have that air conditioner on: I'd rather die of suffocation, in my sleep. So I turn it off. But I notice that the windows are screened, and I manage to open them. I am nervous about all this antimosquito preparation, and I haven't yet bought any Odomos, for my skin. I falsely believed that the mosquito fuss was to do only with malaria. It wasn't. It was also to ward off merely unpleasant nonmalarial mosquitoes. But there were few mosquitoes here, and they were puny by comparison with our Laurentian heavies. Had I known that a large part of the point was to protect from mere annoyance, I would not have been anxious. Also, and less rationally, had I known that malaria was a disease *carried* by certain mosquitoes, as rats carry the plague, as opposed to *inherent* in the sting of some mosquito types, then that, too, would have reduced my anxiety. I see that, given everything else that I knew and did not know, such information would not have reduced the probability of a malariagenic sting, but somehow its not being of the essence of some mosquitoes to malariafy me if they stung me would have been reassuring.

So there is the mosquito anxiety, and the Bushmills Single Malt, and also a mildly raucous party outside or a few doors away, and these assaults conspire to produce poor sleep, maybe two or three hours before my alarm goes at 5:50 A.M., and I rise exhausted but excited, the second condition defeating the first, to prepare for my tour of Bombay.

Why am I writing all this? I hope you find it (intermittently) entertaining, but it's not my purpose to entertain. India gripped me, and I don't want it to let go. As long as I write, it stays with me, I don't have to say goodbye. So this morning (January 27 [when, having been back in England for several days, Cohen wrote this part of his account—Ed.]), I think: today I am going to see Bombay, and then I shall fly to Calcutta. And I'm excited. I can predict, perfectly, what's going to happen, because I can remember it happening. "Something began me and it had no beginning: / something will end me and it has no end" (Carl Sandburg, *The People, Yes*). "And nothing happens but the wheel turns, and remains forever still" (T. S. Eliot, *Murder in the Cathedral*).[8] *À la recherche du temps* not yet *perdu*.

[8] [This line in quotation marks does not occur in *Murder in the Cathedral* and is probably a concatenation from memory of the following lines from Eliot's verse drama: "That nothing lasts, but

THURSDAY, JANUARY 7

So I rose, feeling very weary, tried unsuccessfully to make the shower work in my guesthouse room, and settled for an invigorating hot shave and a face- rub with a tissue impregnated with alcohol and scent from a pack bought at Heathrow. I decided not to have coffee or anything because I wanted a tranquil stomach to accompany me down the long length of Bombay from Gorgaon (where Ram's institute is) in the North to VT (the Victoria Terminal) in the South.

Ram's van (which could be called the Ramachandranvan) pulled up at the guesthouse at 6:10. It wasn't because the Bangalore train left very early that we were setting out so early, but because Ram wanted to avoid the morning rush hour traffic, both ways. Sonny suffers from asthma, and he had had a bad night. I offered to forgo the front seat, but this would not be heard of. So Parvati, Sonny, baby, and Nanny sat in the back and I settled next to Ram in front.

First some slums, then left, instead of right (which was to the airport), and new territory to explore. I don't remember it well, but a fascinating long drive through varieties of accommodation including charming tree-lined middle-class streets already filled with briefcased walkers at 6:45 A.M. Some of these quite near more hovelish areas, in one of which we see burned-out taxis that had been torched the night before, which turned out to be the eve of the second and larger wave of Bombay killing. I was lucky to be leaving Bombay that day. For that day the killing started in earnest, curfews were imposed, the airport was closed, Goregaon itself was hit, and tens of thousands of people fled Bombay in packed trains.

Then through the center of Bombay, which could be a Western city. Very few people sleeping on the streets: this could be part of central London, in that respect. Handsome office buildings. Billboard ads for cigarettes smoked by "gracious people" and New Year's greetings from Air India, promising to keep the nation united. Benign mix of politics and commerce. And then the "Princess's Necklace," the curve of lights along the arc of the lovely bay, the Necklace not at its best because there is too much daylight competing with it.

A little way into town from the shore, we reach a Gothic extravaganza, with Hindu bits here and there, and ridiculously overextended horizontal gargoyles on its tower: the Victoria Terminal. Tremendous Indian hubbub and we drive into a small space and it is time to say goodbye to the Bangalore-bound. It is hard to find a porter (which is bizarre, a counterexample to the overemployment everywhere in such places in India), so I take a heavy bag from the van to the pavement fifteen feet away. Sonny (whose asthma forbids him to be a porter) is mildly shocked: "*You* shouldn't have carried that" (his emphasis). I would have loved to go inside the terminal, but parking was impossible. So back up through Bombay to the institute for breakfast with Ram and Madhura.

---

the wheel turns" (p. 38) and "That the pattern may subsist, that the wheel may turn / and still / Be forever still" (p. 41).—Ed.]

Ram wants to talk to me about self-realization in Marx. His idea is that it supplies an interpersonal metric of advantage less bedeviled than utility with problems. I shift into academic gear, and we talk through breakfast and then when I gather my things, black briefcase included, in the guesthouse. I grind ruthlessly against Ram's claims, which he hopes to turn into an article. He is entirely responsive, sees my points. It is five minutes before the driver is to take me to Bombay airport for the Calcutta flight. Ram regrets that our conversation will be aborted: I am in good form, and he is learning. So I say, "Well, you could come with me to the airport," my motives a mix of wanting to continue to discuss and not wanting to lose his excellent company.

He accompanies, and we are so engrossed that the beggars get short shrift. Ram begins to see that his idea doesn't work. I feel guilty as we reach the airport, and Ram says, "I'll stick to economics." Should I have been gentler, less ruthlessly Socratic? No, one mustn't patronize. We say goodbye.

It is nearly two hours before flight time. I have arrived early, against Ram's advice, because of recent difficulties in securing flights. But all goes smoothly. I check in, and I settle down in the waiting area to read more about Ayodhya and its aftermath, in *Frontline* and in *India Today*. Taxonomy of fascism: Advani, Joshi, Vajpayee. How the BJP evolved out of the Jan Sangh that I remember from the fifties. (And there is nothing new under the sun: nothing happens, but the wheel turns, and remains forever still.) Tired of reading, I wander around. I take myself to an empty area to smoke a small cigar. A friendly middle-class Indian notices me and stares, so I stare back smiling. He smiles: "Mr. Caine?" Either he thinks I look like Michael Caine (that flattering comparison has occurred many times: I prefer it to another one that is sometimes suggested, with the late Marty Feldman), or he thinks I *am* Michael Caine. Not knowing whether I am correcting him, I indicate that I am not Michael Caine. He is keen to extend our acquaintance (does he hope it will pay off some day, as Mr. Mukherjee—see below, January 9—certainly did?). He has just come from the famous (cf. Ingrid's efforts, January 3 above) duty manager of Indian Airlines, and he is headed for the Calcutta waiting list queue. He hopes to see me later. He looks a lot like the January 5 breakfast sycophantic contemptuous-of-waiters Delhi-ite: could it be the same man? He goes off to his queue, and I wonder.

In due course, we board. I sit at a window. The format is two-four-two, and, in the seat beside me, a young Indian woman, pretty but a bit overweight, settles in. I read the page proofs of Bernard Williams's *Shame and Necessity*, which, so far, is very good, Bernard at his current best, saying persuasive and antiphilosophical things about moral responsibility. After twenty minutes or so my companion opens a conversation. "You are a teacher?" "Yes, how did you know?" "From what I see you are reading." All done with gentle grace, not a milligram of intrusive force. She is in market research. But she trained as a psychotherapist, and she'd rather be doing something else. She tells me about her past work in the Bombay slums, among other things finding out why the dwellers would not use rudimentary toilets that were provided, why they preferred the open ground. Then: "How many children do you have?" As usual, this precedes any inquiry as to whether one is married: often, that question never comes. I am delighted by her unflirtatious openness. No Western woman could strike up a conversation like that without a hint of flirtation: it isn't in our culture. In that and other ways, this is a more human culture: why not exploit the natural tendency of people to like people? (True, I have met many Englishmen who don't like people, even at All Souls. But I'm not yet convinced that such dislike is natural.) She is going to Calcutta on business for a few days, and she will stay with her grandmother.

Ten minutes before landing in Calcutta I walk to the rear of the plane, to refresh myself. I pass by the Mr. Caine man. "Where were you?" he asks, "I looked for you in the waiting room." "Well, I was there." The tone of his question reinforces my suspicion that his desire to interact with me was Mukherjeean—for possible future benefit.

We reach Dum Dum airport (the dumdum bullet, a smart weapon, is so called because it was devised in these Calcutta outskirts). The young woman and I wait together for our bags. She complains that they hadn't allowed her to put her bag in the cabin. When it arrives, I agree with them: it's certainly too big, but I don't say so. My bag takes more time, so I bid her goodbye. She says, "I'll wait with you." For a minute or two I am under the illusion that she waits because she wants more of my company. Then I hypothesize that she waits not for that reason but for the hospitable one that she doesn't think it right to abandon an ignorant stranger before he has his bag. The plane was a bit late, and her grandmother must be waiting, so I say: "I'll be all right, you must go." "Are you sure?" "Yes, and thank you so much." We shake hands.

My own bag comes, and I heave it over and onto the trolley. Forgoing various importuners who offer taxis, I progress to the outside gate, where a Thomas Cook driver should be waiting, laid on by the British Council, Calcutta branch, through the work of Ms. Usha Lumba. There he is, with a placard: "Professor Cohen and Ms. S. Cohen." (So the message hadn't sunk in that Sarah, who was originally coming with me to India, wasn't, in the end, to be with me, and I feel a powerful regret that she is not.)[9] The driver sets himself to push my trolley, but two airport entrepreneurs descend on it at the same time. I protest that I am attended to, thank you very much, I even with amusement try to shoo them off, but nothing doing. And my Thomas Cook man, who is a frail fellow, while they are robust, hardly tries to dissuade them. So, with me not knowing why they are in our party, the four of us proceed towards the car park, the three Indians pushing the trolley and me carrying my black briefcase. The bags are put in the

[9] [Sarah is Cohen's daughter.—Ed.]

back of the Ambassador, as many as possible of the three each doing as much as possible to assist in the heaving, and then one of the uninvited two, the other having taken possession of the trolley (Could it be that it was to get the trolley that they accompanied us? Unlikely, but not impossible), approaches me as I enter the front of the car and says something in Bengali. I don't know what he's saying, but I reply with a few rupees. And we are off, just the driver and I.

I expect Bombay-ish slums, as we rumble towards town. But there are no slums, just open fields with, sometimes, better-than-slum huts lining the avenues, and lots of cycle-rickshaws. And the traffic is an exhilarating chaos, far more adventurous even than Bombay. On undivided roads there are no painted lines and the number of lanes in each direction varies, a function of the volume of traffic in that direction and (maybe) the daringness of the drivers. Routinized games of chicken. The tooting horn is king. Taxis terrorize motor-rickshaws (also called three-wheelers) and motor-rickshaws terrorize cycle-rickshaws. Here there are no ordinary person-pulled rickshaws: they're restricted to the center, and they really are a heartbreaking sight.

(Someone told me that the life expectancy of a man once he becomes a rickshaw-puller is five to ten years. I couldn't imagine sitting on a person-rickshaw, yet he would want me to retain him, wouldn't he? Still, I couldn't do it … I suppose that, if I lived in India, I would have servants. It wouldn't be fair not to employ some unemployed people. Karl Marx: "In the social production of their life, men enter into relations that are indispensable and independent of their will. The sum total of these relations constitutes the economic structure of society, the real foundation, upon which rises a legal and political superstructure, and to which correspond definite forms of social consciousness. … Then begins an epoch of social revolution."[10] Then? When?)

I am energized by the rapid pulse of life on the Calcutta streets. People cooking, running, carrying, selling, yelling, sobbing, begging. Millions of people on the streets all the time. Very few tourists visible. A fine billboard near the *New Kenilworth Hotel*, showing a man with a bandaged face: DO YOU SEE A HINDU, A MUSLIM, OR A MAN IN PAIN? Cry, the beloved country.

And then the *New Kenilworth Hotel* which is on Little Russell Street, in between Shakespeare Sarani and Ho Chi Minh Sarani. Did Ho Chi Minh read Shakespeare, or only Molière, when he was a student in Paris? (Ho Chi Minh Sarani is so called, was so named by the communist government, because the UK and US consulates are on it.) I have a British Council letter on which it says that my room was confirmed that morning by the hotel manager. The man at the desk doubts that. His computer reassures him, and I get to my room, 517, which is not a suite, as in Goa, but perfectly adequate. The air conditioning is

[10] [This is a quotation from Marx's preface to his *Contribution to the Critique of Political Economy*. See Cohen's *Karl Marx's Theory of History*, pp. vii–viii and x.—Ed.]

silent. But there is a hammer tapping upstairs, which, they say when I ring, will stop at 6:00 P.M., and it does.

I go for a stroll through the nearby streets, including Chowringhee Road (also known as Jawaharlal Nehru: all Calcutta streets have two names, old and new, for the sake of confusion, and few people seem to know both names of any given street, I learn, later, when taking taxis). It is very hard to cross these streets, since there are no lights, but I try to learn. I buy Odomos, the antimosquito skin cream. I look through the books on a Paris-like street stall. I need to buy a short-sleeved shirt, for this evening, since I have no clean ones. One establishment only makes them to measure. Another obliges. It is *so* alive, *so* much activity, like being in the middle of a multicast Hollywood movie.

Then back to the hotel and there is a message for me at the desk. MESSAGE: Love from Michèle. She had rung. I am overwhelmed by the love through the distance and I cry with happiness as I go up the lift to my room to ring Amiya Bagchi.

Amiya Bagchi is a Marxist, director of the Centre for Studies in Social Science in Calcutta, where I was supposed to speak today, but couldn't because of the Indian Airlines strike, which delayed my arrival by twenty-four hours. He is most cordial on the phone, invites me to come down to his home for a drink that evening, anytime. I say I'll be there by eight. He tells me what to tell the taxi, and I write it down: Number 428 Jodhpur Park, a house with a red gate, not in the park itself, but near the Bata shoe shop on the road to Jadavpur. (I am surprised that Bagchi has a whole house, in crowded Calcutta.) I show this written message to the hotel man in charge of taxis and he explains in Bengali to the nice young man who will taxi me there.

So off we go through the melee. A marvelous ride through undisciplined traffic, at one point a red light simply ignored through the whole of its phase by the throng of cars and other vehicles: the only "stop" that's obeyed is the *mudra* of a traffic policeman. The driver says in bad English that he has studied English, and we pidgin-chat. He can't find the house, he wanders around, but eventually he succeeds, after getting some instructions from a street seller. I ask him to wait while I check. Amiya comes to the door, preceded by a servant. Actually it is not a door, but a folding, locked gate, the kind that is a pattern of diamonds when it's extended. We go to the taxi, but I have nothing smaller than a hundred-rupee note. Amiya vets the price I've been asked to pay, which is forty rupees (= £1). It should have been thirty, he says, so it's not too bad. (The price was preagreed, not metered.) The taxi driver tries various shops for change, and then we find him at a nearby shop, where he gets ten tens for the hundred. Risking Amiya's disapproval, I give him fifty. The taxi driver would like to wait, but Amiya says it will be easy to get another one to take me back to the hotel, so we dismiss him.

We enter Amiya's house and I realize I have left a plastic carrier bag in the taxi. So we rush out to see if it's still there, but it isn't. I don't normally lose and leave things. Evidently, I am out of sorts these days, too excited to pay proper care. We both expect that the driver will drop the bag at the hotel for me, and it does reappear, the following day.

Amiya's house seems large, on two stories. I have to say *seems* large because I am shown through only part of it, another mysterious section, where the kitchen and (presumably) bedrooms and servants are, being apparently (from something that happened the following evening, I infer this) off-bounds for me. We go up the stairs through a study to a sitting room. One can see at a glance that this is a massively erudite man, wonderful books from all over the world, books about Western painting, all the big collections of Plato and Aristotle and Homer, journals and so forth (and later he says this isn't his library, which is at the Centre). To my disappointment, I notice there is just juice and mineral water on the table. I am interested in something stronger. I don't say so, but presently he says: what would you like, beer, vodka? I am partial to straight vodka and that's what I choose. He apologizes that it is Indian, but I find it good: not as good as Russian, better than ordinary Smirnoff's.

Our talk ranges widely, much of it about people we both know or know of. Two sophisticated Marxists, or anyway it seems politic for me to maintain that persona. We discuss Amartya Sen, and Maurice Dobb.

Amiya is between fifty-five and sixty, un-Westernized in appearance. A Bengali way of speaking that requires from me a little extra attention to get the phonemes right. I am talking about his accent only: his sentences are entirely elegant. And he wears hanging garments that I cannot remember exactly or even describe to the extent that I can remember, but they are not what any Westerner would wear. He is very friendly, but also a little correct. I feel that we belong to different generations. He says he will come tomorrow afternoon to hear my talk at the Indian Institute of Management. I am grateful. Amiya's wife, Ratna, arrives. She teaches English at Jadavpur University. She is jolly and warm. We both know Ketaki Keshari, who, like Ratna, read English at Somerville. Ratna will be in Oxford in June, and I urge her to look me up, and I hope that she realizes that I mean it.

It is 10:00 P.M., and it is clear that there will be no food beyond nuts and crisps. (Not that Amiya ever suggested there would be food.) So I say that I must go back to the hotel, and he says yes, I must not keep you from your dinner. We trundle out and he quickly finds a cab, the driver showing confidence that he knows how to find the *New Kenilworth Hotel.*

The driver is a strong, tough-looking type. Next to him sits a friend (taxi drivers in India are often accompanied by a friend), and I relax in the back. The streets are less crowded now. I realize we are moving in the right direction, northwards and a bit east, but when we get to what must be the right general area, he pulls up at the wrong hotel. He more or less believes me when I say that it is the wrong hotel, and I also say "Shakespeare Sarani, Shakespeare Sarani." So he zooms off, somewhere. He stops at a shop and gets instructions. Zooms off again and gets nowhere. Stops again for more instructions. Zooms off and finds the hotel. Stops in the forecourt of the hotel. The meter says thirty. Expecting him to expect me to haggle it down because of his incompetent extra driving, I give him fifty, a whole £1.25. Then, bravely (for he really is a tough-looking young man), I lean forward and grab his head and shake it back and forth, in merry admonition, and, as I had hoped, the two of them find this very funny, and we say goodbye. (Apparently, had I said "Theatre Road," its old name, instead of "Shakespeare Sarani," the driver would have understood.)

The weary traveler deserves a little self-indulgence. I take myself to the Indian restaurant in the *New Kenilworth Hotel.* Fawning maître d', and very nice decor. Good beer, and I order a slap-up vegetarian meal, overriding the waiter's warning about spiciness. I eat with gusto, and I read *Frontline* as I eat. There is a picture of L. K. Advani (parliamentary leader of the opposition, leader of the BJP). One of the waiters takes an interest, looks at the picture. "Bad man, very bad man," he says. Another comes over and agrees. In contradiction to his stance of fawning correctness, the maître d' smiles benignly, does not reproach the waiters for interfering with the customer, and I am glad. And I am also glad that, as I hastily infer, the common people of Calcutta are not fodder for fascism (and, in fact, Calcutta was not among the worst-hit spots in the post-Ayodhya storms).

Nicely pickled on vodka, beer, and Indian pickles, I ascend. I ring Michèle and tell her what her message meant to me. Then I retire. No mosquito worries in this air-conditioned room. There had been lots of mosquitoes at Bagchi's, and he said he could turn on the air conditioner, but that there would then be noise. I preferred not to have noise, and the mosquitoes surrounded me even though there was Odomos on my arms (the only time I applied that redoubtable stuff). He offered me a blanket, but it was a very warm evening, and I declined. I was no longer worried about malaria, for some reason (maybe Amiya himself had enlightened me) and these mosquitoes were impotent fleas compared to our Laurentian ones. "I hope the mosquitoes weren't too fierce for you." "No, not at all, as a matter of fact …"

Good night.

FRIDAY, JANUARY 8

Calcutta morning. After breakfast, I spend an hour or two working in my *New Kenilworth Hotel* room, to the sound of the tapping hammer, which they had assured me would not tap today. I ring to ask how long it will last: "We are renovating the hotel, and we beg your indulgence." I grant it. I am conscious, working on my papers, that I am sacrificing experience of Calcutta magic. But life isn't all beer and skittles.

I leave the hotel around 11:00 A.M. to take in the scene. I am struck, as in Bombay, by the volume and intensity of human activity. The father of a family which evidently spent the night under a piece of cloth on poles in the Jawaharlal Nehru Road is vigorously cooking a wonderful breakfast. A man sits on a box while another (squatting) man shaves him, with a cut-throat razor. The traffic is terrific, the battle of the motors and the rickshaws. I obtain fifty two-rupee notes from a bank protected by a man with a rifle, to give to beggars, who do not throng but who appear now and then. Madonna-and-child beggars have to be favored several times, because they follow you. I try to cross the Jawaharlal Nehru Road, in order to reach the precincts of St. Paul's Cathedral, a stone's throw away. I am defeated by the host of vehicles. "For heaven's sakes, Jerry, *they* cross the road, surely you're not going to not see the cathedral because you don't have the guts or recklessness to cross?" I try again, and once again I am defeated. Then, a providential gap, and I scurry across, and into the grounds of the cathedral.

These lack the good order of an All Souls quadrangle, but they are serene and soothing. The cathedral itself is second-rate. Indians on bamboo scaffolding are repairing exterior moldings at a pace which suggests that the pile will look as good as new in AD 3000. I enter through the unimposing west front. The interior is full of memorial tablets and statuary, commemorating various British contributors to and takers from India. I inspect for about fifteen minutes.

Then back across the grounds to the edge of the road, and this time I *have* to cross it, otherwise no hotel and no lift to the Indian Institute of Management, scheduled for 12:30 P.M. A bespectacled schoolgirl, slight and frail, unfilled little briefcase, surveys the traffic. If she can cross, surely I can too. I will watch how she does it, or, better still, I will cross by her side. We weave through gaplets in the traffic, and she is unaware that she is helping this cautious Western Jew, and there is some pathos in that.

At the hotel the plastic bag has been returned, with the cashew nuts, the sweater, and the map in it. As always, the Thomas Cook driver laid on by the British Council is on time. I sit in front and his friend therefore has to sit in the back. His friend has a bit of English and we discuss how long it will take to get to the institute. The going is slow, lots of traffic, dark buses chock-a-block with passengers, rickshaws, trolley cars less dense with people than the buses are. Had we set out a half an hour later it would have taken hours to get there, instead of the forty-five minutes it actually took, because there were disturbances in the city, with overturned buses halting the traffic. I *think* this was to do with Mamata Banerjee's (she, a Congress politician from Delhi) thespian protest against Mr. Basu's (he, the Communist Party [Marxist] chief minister in the Bengal government) administrative treatment of a deaf-mute girl whom she had dragged with her to Basu's office, out of which Mamata herself was dragged by guards when Basu refused to see her. The newspaper headline that morning had said that she was beaten, and the journalists were now boycotting the state government, but the story didn't confirm the headline: she was dragged, not beaten. My sympathies are with Mr. Basu and against the transparently dramatizing Mamata (that was certainly her forename: I might be misremembering her surname), who is exploiting this deaf-mute girl, whatever the rights and wrongs might have been of what Basu did about her case.

An ugly billboard inscribed "Indian Institute of Management," with "Dunlop Tyres," and the Dunlop logo, underneath, means that we have arrived. Left turn through the guarded gates into the grounds of the institute, which are lush, with nice buildings. A huge campus, with only several hundred students, all postgraduate. I am received by Dr. Anup Sinha, who is relaxed and genial. I explain that I will give my talk on "Is There Still a Case for Socialism?" and not, as intended, on "Incentives, Inequality, and Community," or, as advertised, on "Quality Market and Private Property." That is fine. (The reason why I gave "Is There Still a Case?" is that I had intended to give it the previous day at the Social Sciences Centre. That occasion having been canceled because of travel delay, "Is There?" is what I wanted to give in Calcutta now that I could give only one paper here.)

We talk a bit, and then a young sociologist called Munshi bursts in, eagerly, very pleased to meet me. He has criticized my criticisms of the labor theory of value. He has two papers he would like me to read. He says he realizes that on trips like the one I'm on one accumulates too much paper, so he will send the papers to England, but postage costs a lot, and he will send them only if I undertake to comment. I promise to comment. He says he is not coming to my talk because he has another engagement and he is not so interested in "Quality Market and Private Property," but he wants to hear what I would have said in "Is There Still a Case for Socialism?", which is why he has come to join us for lunch. I explain that, since transport problems prevented me from presenting "Is There Still a Case … ?" the previous day, as scheduled, at the Social Science Centre, I would present it here, today, at the institute. It is now 1:40, and the talk is at 2:45. Dr. Munshi says that in the new circumstance he must and will come to my talk, he will alter his arrangement, but now he will not have to stay for lunch, because he needn't find out about "Is There Still a Case … ?" over lunch, and he is very busy. He leaves.

Anup introduces me to a number of his colleagues, and we proceed to the lunchroom. There is a superb buffet, about nine dishes, and, after the first seven, a border-sign in front of the last two: NON-VEG. I appropriate an assembly of delicious vegetable substances, and a lot of us, eight or nine, sit down at a long table, Nirmal Chandra opposite me. A few of the lunchers show knowledge of and interest in my work, and that gives me satisfaction. Nirmal Chandra studied economics at University College London, so there are landmarks and people for us to talk about. He is friendly, but with a certain English-type reserve, while the others are more fully available. A number of them hope that the food is not too strong for me. In fact, it's about 75 percent as hot as an average (what we call) Madras. They all have glasses of tap water before them, which they don't drink, but somebody obligingly gets the waiter to bring me (only) Bisleri. They drink the tap water when they've finished the food (it is no doubt India Institute–processed tap water), while a waiter brings (only) me a superb rasmalai, which I visibly enjoy so much that he then brings me another one, and I am not sorry.

People enter in respectable numbers, fifty or sixty, and I write some things on the board. I read my paper, and the discussion afterwards reveals that Marxism is not yet dead in India. Tough questioning, some of the "What about China?" variety. Two long interventions from Amiya Bagchi, manifesting erudition and intelligence, but quasi-Continental-obscure. Nirmal Chandra, too, asks lots of sophisticated paleo-Marxist questions. He is evidently profoundly skeptical about me, though possibly also respectful. The discussion goes on for an hour and more, and it had the energy in it to go on much longer, but it is stopped by Anup at around 5:00 P.M. A gentle patter of applause, as in Goa, most hands clapping mildly, for thirty seconds.

I am pleased by the result. Evidently, they were not bored, and for me that's the main thing. And it is nice that the India Institute of Management, which I thought would be some sort of business-conformist organization, so that I was surprised that Rajeev had put it on my itinerary, turns out to be a red nest, or at least to have a red nest.

Bagchi's driver—paid by the Social Science Centre, but he *is* Bagchi's driver—is in attendance, and Amiya, Nirmal, and I take our leave of the rest and pile into the Ambassador. We drive a short distance across the campus in the twilight and pull up near a path which, I learn, leads to a café. "You can leave your bag in the car, the driver will wait for us." I say to Nirmal: "One man's poverty is another man's amenity." "Well, of course" he replies, almost, but not quite, contemptuously. The café is like several I went to, in and around campuses. Incredibly basic in decor, you could think you're in a Victorian slum. After our refreshment, Bagchi says that we will go to his house, and later his driver will take me back to my hotel.

The drive from the IIM, Calcutta southwest (though still on the eastern side of the Hooghly, which I never got to see) to Bagchi's house, Calcutta southeast, not far from Tollygunge, is along a single miles-long, one-and-a-half-lane-wide huge arc of a road created, it seems, by settlers who are two or three cuts above slum-dwellers, and every hut facing the road on both sides for all those miles is a tiny shop selling food, carpets, tools, whatever. It's six or seven o'clock now, quite dark, and the road teems with relaxed people all a-bustle, and I am a goggle-eyed child.

We reach Bagchi's house. Nirmal greets somebody, whether a relative or a servant I do not know, and he and Amiya pass through a curtain to a room downstairs left, and I make to follow them—I thought we were a trio—but I am gestured away by Nirmal: my place is, once again, as last night, up the stairs to the right, and Amiya will join me presently. He does, and soon Nirmal does too, and various servants relay messages and take instructions in Bengali, in matter-of-fact unservile ways.

Tonight I choose beer rather than vodka, good Kingfisher beer, and after two bottles I am—for me, by my standards—pretty drunk. Mostly we gossip-talk about the English, and I go on about how like Jews Bengalis are: clever-clever, fractious, disdainful. I illustrate what I mean by disdainfulness by telling a joke about two conversing Jews. "So how are you, I haven't seen you for a long time?" "I'm not very well, I have cancer." "Cancer? What kind of cancer?" "Of the skin." "Of the skin?! That I don't call cancer. Now my Uncle Morris, *that* was cancer …"

More on the English. I point out that despite thirty-one years of living in England I have virtually no friends there who are not Jewish or not women or not North American. Purebred male goy Brits I find hard to get close to. Or not Brits, but Englanders proper: the Scots, if not the Welsh, are more human, and the Irish are practically Bengali. Bagchi recalls a conversation in Cambridge with Piero Sraffa who had gone on in a similar vein. Sraffa said: "The only Englishman I know is Dobb … Actually, do I *know* Dobb?" And we all laugh.

Ratna comes in, and she is flattered, she says, that I remember her name. Which says something about (1) Bengali sexism, and/or (2) her unawareness that, to a *langue-maternelle* Anglophone, "Ratna" is not an easy name to forget. Nirmal's wife, a doctor, also arrives.

Emboldened by the Bacchic atmosphere, I offer to give—no, I *announce* that I will give my impersonation (a certain routine I've invented) of an American philosopher visiting Britain and meeting his English colleague, Nigel. They are taken aback at my transformation without permission of the living room into a stage, but the performance is successful, and I get the loudest applause I've had in India so far.

It is 10:00 P.M., and for some time Nirmal's wife has been ineffectually nagging that they should go, that he should stop drinking, saying these things in an Indian way, because they are the right things to say, and not clearly meaning them, despite the fact that she is pretty worn out with a hard day's doctoring. So now we rise to go, and Amiya says, to me, but you haven't eaten, would you like something, there is something, before you go? No, thanks, really, I'd really rather eat after the drive than eat first and then go back to the hotel (which is true). So we say goodbye and come away.

And now the maelstrom streets are empty, which is a damn good thing, because the shape of Nirmal's course as he drives is a sideways back-and-forth weave, I kid you not. A good sixteen-foot width of road he uses as, back and forth, he drives ahead, and I am amused. It is not dangerous, because the road is empty. Nirmal says that he only drives at night, and one can see various reasons why. Daytime he takes the claustrobus.

In the hotel it is too late to go to the excellent Indian restaurant, but there is an all-night café, where I order yet another Kingfisher and some sort of vegetariana. A noisy, flush-faced, words-slurring, cigarette-smoking Indian from Long Island happens in, brags his way 'round various waiters and tables and settles at my table, with my leave, because I think I'll find his company amusing. He describes his wealth and high status, promises that if I have any difficulty with flights he'll fix things for me, drops names such as Peter O'Toole, and I can't now remember the other ones. "Oh, Peter is very fond of living in Hampstead ..." He orders a beer, but it is 10:50 and the bar closed at 10:30. I pour half my Kingfisher into his glass. He says I must come to his room, he will show me pictures of his house on Long Island. I tell him (what is true) that I am not a night person. He accepts that. He says, you should have been in my room last night, I had two of the most beautiful young Bengali women there. He is about fifty-five, and I find that report quite disgusting. But I didn't do anything, he adds, I can't do sex any more, not very often, I find it difficult. I boast that I can still do sex. Then you should have been in my room last night ... I don't utter the rebuke that is in my mind. He sails off, reminding me that if I have any problems with flights tomorrow, he can fix them, he knows this politician and that businessman.

Up the lift and into bed for a peaceful, beery night.

SATURDAY, JANUARY 9

My last day in Calcutta, how sad.

At breakfast, I notice a Gujarati man from Cardiff with whom I had chatted amiably on the transcontinental trip, in some or other queue. He also notices me, and we talk. Ahmedabad, his hometown, was, the previous couple of days, engulfed in carnage on a scale surpassed only in Bombay, and I ask him if he has managed to go to Ahmedabad, since I know that he had intended to. No, he is waiting for things to calm down. I tell him that I am less innocent, India-wise, than I was a week ago. He understands, and he indulges me. We part again, no doubt forever, without exchanging names.

Usha Lamba of the Council has laid on a driver to take me to the airport, leaving the hotel at 4:30 P.M., the plane scheduled to take off at 7:30. So I have a whole day to myself: what should I do? I know I haven't seen the worst of Calcutta, which I *think* is near the Howrah Bridge. It would be easy to get there, but I decide that it is impossible to go Leontius-like (see Plato, *Republic*, 439) to Howrah, to see human misery. If other engagements had taken me through Howrah, it would have been OK to stop. But to go there precisely in order to see extremes of suffering is not on. I decide that the more moderate deprivations visible here and there in Chowringhee will have to suffice.

It was another warm and sunny day, but I took my retrieved sweater with me, in a carrier bag, because one of my destinations was the India Museum, and

I thought that it might be air-conditioned (which it was not) and I had experienced fierce air conditioning in the hotel restaurant and elsewhere. I proceeded through charming streets displaying a plenitude of life. A boy of ten or so busy at a pavement water pump, filling a large bucket with water, pouring it over his sparsely clothed body, pumping, filling, pouring, pumping, filling, pouring, several times. Men running a Heath Robinsonian juice-squeezing machine to get juice to drip out of a vegetable I could not name, something like bamboo stalks. Quite a few unhealthy-looking apparently unowned dogs, snoozing in the gutter. These dogs are sadly cut off from humanity: they show neither friendliness nor aggressiveness to people, no people-induced excitement of any kind. If a person approaches such a dog, it limps away, not, it seems, in fear, but to relocate itself in a fresh nonhuman space. These feral dogs seem not to be dangerous.

There was a lot of begging that morning, on the way to the India Museum, and one beautiful woman clutching a baby was extremely persistent. My initial five rupees seemed to prove nothing except that I was generous enough to be worth further nagging. "No Poppa, baby, baby," with her right hand gesturing at her own mouth, over and over again. One curious thing was that all that could be true, yet it wasn't being said because it was true, and it was said with poorly acted pretend hysteria that she could well have been aware I was aware of. Just a language of begging. So I gave her another five, but she continued to walk by my side, half a step behind mine, gently tugging at my shirt. So I devised a plan. I would give no more until I reached the museum: in fact, I had nothing small enough to give (small enough to make me willing to give); and then I would get change and give and say goodbye. So I reached the courtyard of the museum, passed through the gate while signaling to her—she could not pass through that gate—to wait, paid my one-and-a-half-rupee or so entrance fee, got ten ten-rupee notes for a hundred-rupee note, gave her a ten-rupee note, and accepted her pleasure and surprise. Then she arranged her hands flat, upright and together, in that Hindu gesture, and said goodbye.

Before that lady began to accost me, I stopped at a stall, just a box at the pavement's edge, where a kid was selling books and things, and I looked through a great wad of postcards, none showing the sights, but mostly with pictures of Ganesh, Shiva, Hanuman, and other gods and godlets. I selected a few for purchase. The kid then called a superior, who had been lounging against the building, in the shade, to fix the price. It was two or three rupees, so I gave five. The kid smiled, and I felt ashamed.

The museum was in bad shape, decor-wise, truly decayed and dingy, in a condition opposite to that of the National Museum in Delhi, on which more later. The India Museum is a sort of British Museum, Natural History Museum, Science Museum, all in one, a Victorian pile with a large courtyard. I focused on the sculpture, which was pretty good, particularly the items in the Gupta so-called wet style, so called because the drapery hangs tight on the body, as though wet. Beautiful pieces, from all over the subcontinent, from many periods and kingdoms. But I could not find the magnificent portions of the Bharhut Stupa that were pictured in my book on *Indian Art*, by Craven, and said to be in this museum. Who to ask? “Excuse me, Guv, can you direct me to the Bharhut Stupa pieces?” I tried the counter where they sold a disordered miscellany of art pamphlets, but the woman didn't understand. A well-dressed man overheard my inquiry. “It is there,” he said, “in that gallery,” pointing to the one I had combed from end to end. “Well, I looked for it there, I didn't find it.” “Go back and look again, there are many alcoves.” So I did, and there were many alcoves (though not more than the first time), but I didn't find any parts of the Bharhut Stupa. So I gave up.

I hadn't intended to look at the stuffed animal displays, but a trip to the toilet was indicated, and, since that was on the upper floor, and so were the animals, I toured them too. Once resplendent but now shabby displays, but lots of interested local people, taking it all in. I wished I could fund a renovation.

So back out into the sunshine, and I was pleased, but also a little disappointed, that my beggar lady had not waited outside the hour and more that I'd been in there. I proceeded further north up Chowringhee, where there were lots of shops, and I bought a brown belt from a sidewalk merchant. The type I wanted was, in the token he had of it, a bit too long, so we had to go up the street to a shoeshine man and cobbler whom he got to cut it and redo the buckle, but I was to return with my vendor to his patch while the cobbler did that: I was not to stay and watch. Did he think I might learn his tricks, his trading links, and set up as a rival? He wanted ninety rupees, so I gave him a hundred. I don't know how much the cobbler got.

By now it was twelve-ish, and I was hungry. Down a medieval lane a street caterer had just made samosas and puris. So that was my (superb) lunch, taken with soda water from another nearby stall. This is the life for a Montreal Park Avenue street boy. More food stalls, more bookstalls, more dogs, more kids douching themselves with pump water, a poor woman dead to the world on the pavement with her baby, and a little lamb, stock-still, nothing tethering it, standing by. More beggar-ladies, requiring multiple givings of alms. More wagons on which that strange vegetable was having its juice pressed out with a strange machine, cogs and chains and levers. Then a coconut seller, with a pile of green coconuts before him, and a superb machete. He cuts a large hole with the machete, you take a straw and suck, and you get a superb and (so they say) very healthful drink. Then your otherwise unused coconut joins the large pile of empties at his side. Very nice way to wash down the last bits of samosa and puri. (The man selling those had forgotten to express a hope that they were not too strong for me.)

Having dealt with several enbabied women, none of whom were as relentless as my first such customer, I decided that I should buy some stamps for my postcards. So I entered what was called a “Post Office” in Little Russell Street. On the customer side of the counter there was no one. On the personnel side there were nine or ten people, at least seven of whom were pretty clearly doing nothing, and, not for the first time on this trip, I had to repress Thatcherite reflections. Behind what seemed a likely wicket I asked a woman if I could buy stamps. She gestured towards another woman, several persons along, indicating that the latter was the one to whom I should apply. This woman was, however, asleep, her head on her arm on her desk. I hesitated, but I did want to buy some stamps. So I made some kind of noise which roused her. She looked at me with terrible exhaustion on her face, and I felt a rush of sympathy for what was evidently, at least psychologically and at least right now, a miserable life. I said I wanted six airmail stamps, for postcards. She said they were eleven rupees each (I later discovered that they should have been six and a half rupees each). I gave her a hundred-rupee note, which she took to a man at a desk at the back. He recorded something in a Dickensian ledger, and gave her the thirty-four-rupees change. She then fussed through a dog-eared book, supplied the stamps, passed me the change, and went back to sleep.

It was now one o'clock, and I was near my hotel, with three or four hours of meandering, so I thought, ahead of me, and the bag with the sweater was a nuisance. I decided to park it at the hotel and then proceed south. Entering the hotel, I was called to reception by a woman behind the desk who was on the phone. "He's just come in," she said to a caller, who turned out to be from the British Council.

"This is Mr. Ojha, from the British Council. I must tell you that your Indian Airlines flight to Delhi is canceled, because of the Russian airplane crash at Delhi. I was not supposed to be at work today [it was a Saturday] but I popped in for a moment and Thomas Cook rang to say that if we had anybody who needed a flight to Delhi there was a private plane run by Minnie Pan travel agency that could take them. If you will be ready by two o'clock a driver will come to take you and the plane will leave at 3.30. It is Jagson Airlines." I could not process this properly. "I don't quite understand." "If you wait there I will come." "Can you come soon?" "Yes, I am just around the corner, in Shakespeare Sarani."

It was incredibly good luck that I had happened to enter the hotel at just that time: failing this as yet imperfectly explained rearrangement, I would have had to wait two or three days before I could get to Delhi, and Delhi engagements would have gone by the board.

So Mr. Ojha appeared, and I didn't really understand the arrangement, but I contented myself with the practical truth, or hypothesis, that, if I was ready by two, I could fly to Delhi. I agreed with the plan, and we went up to my room where I began to pack, with such calmness as I could muster, and he began to make and cause phone calls: to Thomas Cook, to Minnie Pan, to the British Council. Then he said he would have to go back to the Council for a document, and that I must wait in my room because Thomas Cook will ring to confirm from Minnie Pan. So I said, but you *will* come back soon, I'm relying on you. He assured me that he would.

Presently, Dr. Munshi rang, of the India Institute of Management, to talk about socialism. Fearful that a theoretical exchange would prevent Thomas Cook from giving me the message from Minnie Pan (if that's what I was waiting for), I apologized that it was simply impossible to talk about socialism now, because I was expecting an important phone call and I was leaving Calcutta in twenty minutes. "Write to me and I'll reply." (I think he mistakenly thought I was trying to brush him off. Anyway, I haven't heard from him.)

Mr. Ojha came back, as promised, with a document, and he explained what I had to do, except that the phone rang and he squared it all up with Thomas Cook. "When you get to the airport you must go to the flower shop and there you will find Mr. Edgar Allan Peacock, of Minnie Pan." "Edgar Allan Peacock? Is he English?" "No, he is a Christian from South India … Just go to the florist and Mr. Edgar Allan Peacock will give you your ticket. But now you must write me a letter saying that you will reimburse the British Council for the fare." So, somewhat slyly, I wrote a letter saying that I would reimburse the British Council for the fare with whatever money I recovered from Indian Airlines for the canceled flight. He didn't demur, because there was no time, and the phone rang again. It was Mr. Mukherjee, Mr. Peacock's assistant, to say that he was going to the airport and he would make sure everything was all right. He was leaving in ten minutes. It occurred to me that, if such a thing was possible, I would be better off traveling to the airport with Mr. Mukherjee, since he was, after all, Mr. Peacock's Minnie Pan colleague, than trying to find Mr. Peacock on my own. I suggested this to Mr. Ojha. He saw the wisdom of it, and, after two more phone calls, it was settled that I would travel with Mr. Mukherjee, that he would collect me, with a driver, at ten to two. I was very glad that I would be in Mr. Mukherjee's hands.

So I checked out of the hotel, and Mr. Mukherjee appeared at two o'clock with a Thomas Cook driver. "I am Mr. Mukherjee. I am Mr. Peacock's assistant. They told me to come and collect you because you are VIP." That's pronounced *Vee*EyePee, by the way, not VeeEye*Pee*, in Bengali. This seemed not to fit the actual causal genesis of our traveling together, in which, so it seemed to me, I had played a more active role, but I let the matter ride. "Also I am going to the airport because I live right near the airport."

So I said goodbye to Mr. Ojha, and I thanked him profusely for having saved my bacon, and off we went to the airport. Mr. Mukherjee was an affable young man in his late twenties, not yet married, because "here we do not marry until we are twenty-eight" (which is false, I gather), but possessed of a fiancée, and looking forward to a "nonarranged marriage," which, others told me, only 10 percent of marriages in India are, though the percentage is much higher among the better-off, and there are a large number of what are called "arranged nonarranged marriages," whose character I could imagine, but the criteria for which were never precisely specified for me. Mr. Mukherjee was very educated, and manifestly intelligent. He had degrees both in chemistry and in Japanese, and his English was nearly perfect. He hoped to get a translator's job in Japan, after he was married (his wife would come with him).

He told me that he liked working for Minnie Pan, because he met many VeeEyePees. He took their addresses, and one day he would travel abroad, and he would have many people to look up. So I duly volunteered my address. I remarked that the road to the airport was uncommonly free of traffic. "That is because it is only used by VeeEyePees." I doubted that premise, and also, the other, implied, one, that there weren't many VeeEyePees, since they seemed to be the medium in which some locals lived and moved and had their being. I questioned the first premise only: "You mean, only VIPs are allowed to use this road? How could that be, since nobody checked?" "No, it is not a question of permission, but mostly VeeEyePees go to the airport at this time." That seemed to imply that there were lots of VIPs, since there were, surely, lots of planes: I could see plenty in the sky. I gave up the interrogation.

We reached Dum Dum Airport, ahead of time. Edgar Allan was not at the florist. We sat in the waiting area. Mr. Mukherjee had to show a pass to enter it, but I didn't, since it was assumed that all whites were *bona fide* travelers. We waited. Then Mahesh appeared, another Minnie Pan traveler, agent for a finance company in Delhi, glad, as I was, that we were (so we then thought) getting to Delhi early. We waited. "Don't worry," said Mahesh. "Mr. Peacock will come."

In something approximating due course Mr. Peacock arrives, with one woman and one man. The man is our third traveler, an Indian who works for another branch of Peerless Incorporated, which has recently absorbed Minnie Pan. I don't know why the rather attractive woman is there: only later did I learn that she was another one of Mr. Peacock's assistants. She bombards me with questions. "Where do you come from? Where were you born? How many children do you have? What is your profession? Do you like Oxford? How far is Oxford from London? Do you drive?" Her intense interest flatters me. Mr. Peacock himself is portly, mustached, with an air of being in the know that is reassuring. "We will leave soon, don't worry." (Is he coming with us? I don't know and it doesn't matter.) We wait. Mahesh wonders whether there will be a meal on the plane. If not, he hopes it leaves soon, because he doesn't want to have to wake up his wife (who goes to bed early, because their young kids are exhausting) when he gets to Delhi so that she can make his supper.

We wait. Now it is four o'clock. The pilot appears. He says all is set fair for the flight, which will take four hours, the winds being adverse. The pilot is self-possessed and handsome, so I experience further reassurance. We wait.

At 4:15 Mr. Peacock says, "Come, we are going to board you now. We have to go through the VeeEyePee lounge."

So we leave the waiting area, and we exit from the building, two porters pushing a trolley bearing the bags of Mahesh, the other Peerless man, and me. Also in our assortment are Messrs. Peacock and Mukherjee, the woman assistant still asking me questions ("Where will you fly from Delhi? What are you lecturing about? Where did you study? Do you like London? Have you been to New York?"), and the three travelers.

The building housing the VIP lounge is one hundred yards away. When our party is within twenty-five yards of it, a man in overalls emerges from it, waving his arms back and forth across one another in the air, like a tarmac groundsman directing a taxiing plane. "No, not VeeEyePee lounge, not VeeEyePee lounge," he shouts. How he knew who we were, if he did, and why Mr. Peacock immediately submitted to his authority: these matters were unclear. We complied.

Back, then, to the waiting area in the original building, and it is approaching 4:30. We are to go through Jumna Airlines (not quite the right name, but I don't remember the right one, so I'll use it). That is, our carrier is Jagson Airlines, but Jumna will help with security and ticketing. Mr. Peacock waits at the Jumna counter. We wait in the waiting area. Mahesh is now certain we will leave too late to get to Delhi before his wife retires, and he is more concerned than before about eating. We are told that there will be a hostess, and a snack.

Finally, at 5:20, Mr. Peacock equips the three of us with very homemade tickets. Now you can go, he says. He, Mr. Mukherjee, and the woman point us towards Security, and then say goodbye. At Security there are no passengers and about fourteen soldiers, many with rifles. The porters put our bags on the X-ray conveyor belt. "Where are your boarding cards?" a soldier asks. We show our tickets. "Those are not boarding cards, we cannot let you through without boarding cards." Mahesh: "We don't have boarding cards, this is a charter flight." The soldier trots over to the office of his superior who confirms the absoluteness of the boarding card condition.

We're uncertain what to do. The Peerless man has the good idea of going back to the main part of the terminal to see if he can retrieve Mr. Peacock. This he is allowed to do, and he returns with Mr. Peacock, who says to the soldiers: "They don't need boarding cards, it's a charter flight." This utterance reassures and activates the soldiers, and the X-ray machine. We reach the far side of security. We are on the threshold of the tarmac.

A conversation now occurs, not in English, between the superior of the two porters and Mahesh and the Peerless man. Mahesh rotates his head halfway, back and forth, in the gesture that those unfamiliar with it might classify as a form of negation, but I know, by now, that it means: "What you say is interesting, I am considering it." So I ask him what the porter has said. Mahesh: "He will not take the trolley on the tarmac unless we give him money, because trolleys are not allowed on the tarmac. It is blackmail." He is curiously calm, as if this refusal doesn't matter, as if going to Delhi doesn't matter. For the first time on the trip the ugly American within me stirs. "Ask him how much he wants, Mahesh." He asks (he hadn't yet been told!). "One hundred rupees. It is blackmail." I figure an extra £2.50 is worth it to get the show on the road, but I don't want to appear high-handed. I say: "Look, unless you think we shouldn't pay, on principle, I'll gladly pay the hundred rupees." Mahesh does the head rotation, and he and the Peerless man accept my suggestion.

So I promise one hundred rupees, and that brings us to the edge of the tarmac, but we have no instructions about where to go. There are seven planes on the tarmac. On six you can see the colors and the names, and none say "Jagson Airlines." The seventh is in the distant dark: you can't see any writing on it. Mahesh infers with perfect confidence that that seventh plane is ours: it's small, which ours is supposed to be. I am skeptical about the reasoning, but there is no alternative.

So the five of us, three passengers and two porters, proceed towards the little plane, while menacing big ones are revving up nearby. Thirty yards from the plane I voice a suspicion, "Look, the plane is dark. There is no one on the plane." Mahesh: "No, don't worry, the pilot will be there."

But the pilot isn't there, no one is there, and the door is locked. It is, however, the right plane: Jagson Airlines, an eighteen-seat "Dornier," two propeller engines. It looks like a fun plane. To fly in, not to just look at.

Mahesh: "We will wait. The pilot will come." Nobody comes. The head porter (of the two) says that they must take the trolley back to the airport, it is not allowed on the tarmac. Here I protest, because I know that my bag is much too heavy for me to carry by hand back to the air terminal without threatening myself with a hernia. (Strangulated hernia January 1988 nearly killed me, and there was also a plain hernia operation in March 1989.) My protest is calm and firm, and the porters respect it. It is six o'clock, and we wait. Then the superior porter says that he will go back to the terminal and try to find the pilot. We are grateful. But he proceeds to take the bags off the trolley, so that the trolley can be returned as a by-product of this assistance. This (a) casts doubt on the true purpose of his projected visit to the terminal, and (b) reactivates my hernia anxiety. So I forbid the removal of the trolley. He begins to gather a resistance to my prohibition. An *impasse* seems to be imminent. But then we see four figures approaching in the distance, side by side: something like the last scene of *Casablanca* is about to be played out.

The four turn out to be the pilot, a copilot, a hostess, and a freshly discovered passenger (the ferreting out of whom from who knows where might have been the cause of the further delay—he keeps remarking on his luck, anyway). *Now* the bags are safely removed from the trolley, the hundred rupees are transferred, the big bags are put in the back, we take the little ones into the cabin, the hostess boards too, and pilot and copilot settle into the cockpit.

There are nine seats behind one another down each side of the small plane. Mahesh sits in the third seat down the left, I on the fourth seat down the right, since I do not want to presume too much on his friendliness. He quietly says, pointing to the three seats ahead of me: "These seats are also available," which I rightly take to be a friendly invitation to sit beside him, and I do. We chat, and then he reads the *Times of India* while I read Malcolm Muggeridge's morally repugnant book of homage to Mother Teresa (understand: he, not she, is morally repugnant).

The right-wing engine revs up. But then we hear an exchange between the pilot and the man in the control tower, who says, firmly, "We don't have the receipt for your airport fees." "But I paid, I paid." "But we don't have your receipt."

So now our pilot leaves the plane to trudge across to the terminal to present his receipt. He is gone twenty or twenty-five minutes. While he is gone, the passenger door of the plane has to be kept open, because, with the engine now turned off, there is no other way to put air into the cabin. The open door means that hundreds of mosquitoes fly in, attracted by the lights. The usual (in my Indian experience) pathetic mosquitoes, without much sting, but this time their numbers compensate for their individual inadequacy.

The pilot returns, and the right-wing engine revs up again. It revs up for five minutes while the left-wing engine stays silent. Now it is my turn to reassure Mahesh: "Don't worry, we will leave soon." It is 6:30 P.M. At 6:35 P.M. the left-wing engine gets into the act. At 6:38 P.M. we are airborne. It is fun to be in such a small plane. Delhi, here we come.

It is cold in the cabin, and I am wearing sandals (with socks). The back of the seat in front of me folds forward to horizontal, so I use it as a leg rest. But my feet are still cold, and I feel the incipience of a sore throat (that's all I need, now). So I make my way to the back of the plane and I ask the hostess whether there is a blanket. "No, would you like me to tell the pilot to turn on the heat?" "Well, yes, that would be very nice." So she does, and he does, but too late to prevent the gathering sore throat from establishing itself. I am a weensy bit pissed off that the heat hadn't been turned on right away, instead of what was forty minutes into the flight. Then Mahesh imitates my use of the seat in front as a footrest. Then the hostess distributes the meal: one of those curious Indian cheese sandwiches of a fairly but not completely insipid kind, with no crust on the soft, square white bread, that cautious people like Peter de Souza prefer to the who-knows-what-they-were-fried-in samosas that I choose in preference to these mega-goyish sandwiches at snack bars. Mahesh is unimpressed by the meal, but it is enough to ensure that he will not have to wake up his wife. I am content with it: at least there aren't too many calories here, even though there is also a dry cake to go with the sandwich.

The flight is smooth, all four hours of it. At Delhi Airport we see that the place is virtually shut down, the wreck of the Russian airliner (miraculously, no one was killed or hospitalized, despite the fact that the plane somersaulted) still strewn on the main runway, and I am once again grateful to Mr. Ojha. It is 10:30 P.M. and it is quite cold, maybe three degrees Celsius. A bus takes us from the little plane to the terminal, and in the bus I hurriedly withdraw my solid shoes from my heavy bag (which Mahesh has kindly carried onto the bus for me) and change out of my sandals, not wanting to make my sore throat worse. (I should say that I'm not one of those people who very much minds sore throats, and I didn't much mind this one: I just didn't want it to get worse. In the event, it lingered through the Delhi stay, mainly when I got up in the morning, but it didn't get worse.)

In the terminal the guards look astonished: where did these passengers materialize from? We then proceed to the desk where you can prepay for a taxi, thus (a) avoiding rip-off, and, more importantly, (b) removing any incentive a driver might have to take a circuitous route. I am in Mahesh's unobtrusive, kind care, and it is 118 rupees. Mahesh says goodbye, and that he will get in touch with me at the *Imperial Hotel.* (He didn't, but he might have tried. The hotel confused me with a certain Mr. Coons when others tried to get me.)

We drive into town along clear, broad, well-paved avenues in the fresh cold evening. There is nothing higgledy-piggledy, no tumbledown this and that, no people by the roadside. I am in mourning. I have lost my India. This is not my Technicolor India. This is a modern city. (Later, I discover old Delhi, which is thoroughly, variegatedly, human.) After twenty or twenty-five minutes we pull up on Janpath, at the *Imperial Hotel*, whose exterior neon sign is so crude that I wonder whether it's the right place. But it is, and a turbaned and floridly attired doorman helps me out, and I give the taximan a princely twenty-rupee tip.

The hotel is sort of Edwardian (not *Edwardian*, Edwardian), or, perhaps, nineteen-twenties-ish, the flapper era. Full of obsequious attendants and unobsequious desk clerks. Incipient sag in beams and some uprights, but retaining a great deal of between-the-wars-like splendor that I like a lot. *Certainly* more agreeable than the rather more fifties-ish decor of the *New Kenilworth* lobby in Calcutta, and cuts above the modest *Mandovi* initial self-presentation. Later, having gagged at the garishness of two expensive *Taj* hotels that I saw in Delhi, I was very grateful, quite apart from the matter of cost, that Rajeev had booked me into the *Imperial.*

The clerk at reception asked me to confirm my identity more than once. (I learned later that Rajeev had rung to cancel that night's reservation, because he was rightly sure—though wrong in the point of fact—that I could not make it to Delhi that day. Hence the clerk's puzzlement, but he did not explain it to me.) Then he sorted the matter out, and I was given the key to room 126. Real skeleton key, none of the punched-card *Kenilworth* nonsense. (Fine if you're staying in Seattle or Leicester or Lyon, but inappropriate in Calcutta.) One or two—who can remember?—liveried bellpersons escorted me up by lift to the floor above, round a couple of corridor turnings, and here was the room. Capacious and serene, everything I need, desk, loo, separate alcove for clothes and fridge, two good beds to choose from, telly.

It was 11:20 P.M. I hate ringing people at that hour, because I hate being rung at that hour myself, and I figure I can't tell who else also hates it. But I thought I had better ring Rajeev, since we were due to go to Agra (Taj Mahal and other goodies there) the next day, and I had decided in the course of the Jagson Airlines saga that I had had enough of travel for a while, that spending from Saturday night to Friday morning in Delhi without leaving it would be paradise, a relief from all the jerks and palaver and heteronomy of being moved and not moving in the traveling I'd done. I must ring Rajeev to tell him to cancel the Agra trip. I would have to see it next time (I had resolved that there must soon be a next time).

So I rang Rajeev, who wasn't there and Tani answered. Tani, who had evidently been awake, expressed surprise that I was in Delhi and said that she was sorry, but Rajeev, not expecting me to arrive, had canceled the Agra trip. I explained that I was very happy about that. It was settled that Rajeev would ring me the next morning.

Then it was 11:27 P.M. or so, and, two days earlier, during our Calcutta phone call, I had asked Michèle to ring me at 11:30 P.M. at this hotel on the Saturday night. She punctually did, and I was so full of the bizarre Jagson Airlines trip that I spent most of our ten minutes expounding it, step by step, on the phone. Then I washed my face, which I had been wanting to do ever since entry into the room, but the phone calls had had priority. Then I went down to the twenty-four-hour café.

When I was registering in the lobby there was a young (thirty or so) Canadian man with a backpack, negotiating for a room. Now he was still in the lobby, wondering about a bite to eat. So I suggested that he join me and we went to the hotel café. There he explained that he'd been working in India for several years, in the countryside, for a Canadian engineering firm, working on schemes to regenerate land that has suffered from too much irrigation, something like that. He affected a laid-back nonchalance that was nearly irritating, and he'd just returned from a trip home to Winnipeg or some other faceless western Canadian town. He said how bad the North American Free Trade Agreement was for Canadian jobs. But the solution, apparently, was to remove all that excessive welfare state structure. The solution was to let capitalism rip. I found that depressing, but I was in no mood for polemics.

The menu promised lots of succulent spicy veggie delicacies, but they were all "off," and I had to settle for one of those preposterous cheese sandwiches, with a side order of Uncle Chippies (which are crisps). I longed for a beer, and so did Grant, or Brad, or whatever he was blandly called. We checked out the beer price. It was 170 rupees (£4, \$6–7) for a bottle of Kingfisher (which is big, and delicious). Brant (or was it Grad?) thought that was too much, he'd forgo it, so Diamond Jim GA offered to pick up the tab, and Bland accepted. We ate, we chatted, we parted. Drunk as a lord (one Kingfisher is quite enough to make me drunk, when there's not much food in me), I rolled myself up the stairs and I washed and went to bed, very happy, and, uncharacteristically, content to postpone unpacking until the morning.

SUNDAY, JANUARY 10

A wonderful Delhi morning, sun shining in a clear blue sky, the sixty-degrees-Fahrenheit crispness every bit as good as eighty-degrees-Calcutta torpidness, and I don't mind my slight sore throat. An excellent Indian veggie breakfast, but I can't remember exactly of what. (The earlier parts of this trip are easier to remember than the later, partly because they were intrinsically more dramatic, and partly because their earliness meant that they hit me with more force.)

Then some pleasant pottering in my room, unpacking my things, basking in the thought that I wouldn't have to repack for another 120 hours. It was forbidden to open the windows. PLEASE DO NOT OPEN WINDOWS BECAUSE OF INSECTS. There seemed not to be any insects, but at this stage I obeyed the rule. A couple of days later, I began to break it, harmlessly. It was more agreeable to look at the green parakeet in the tree outside my room without a piece of glass between us.

Rajeev rang, and we agreed that he would come to the hotel at 1:00 P.M., and we would do sightseeing. That settled, I left the hotel to take a walk.

My destination was Connaught Place, the hub of New Delhi, which meant turning left at the end of the hotel driveway. That is a place at which are perched petty entrepreneurs, black-market money changers, hopeful auto-rickshaw drivers, and so forth. Seeing me about to proceed left, one of these apprehended me and advised that, since it was Sunday, everything up towards Connaught Place was closed. The things for tourists were somewhere else, and he would take me there. I disbelieved (and I was right) that *everything* would be closed, and I anyway thought that if a person with no interest in my welfare advises me not to go left, then that is a good reason to go left.

So left I went, and I did not regret it. There was a great deal of life, but, unlike Calcutta's, and old Delhi's, this life was tourist-oriented. So, what the hell, I *am* a tourist, what right have I to disdain it? A series of feeble temptations designed to part you from your money. One man after another offering a miniature wooden chess set, quite attractive too. And when you say, "No, I'm not interested," they take that to mean, "Yes, but please reduce your price." So they go down to 30 percent of the original, and then leave you alone. At the corners of streets snake charmers sit. I'd always been intrigued by the idea of snake charming, so I stopped at the first charmer I saw. He began to play his wooden flute, and he removed the lid from one of his six wicker baskets. A sleepy cobra emerged, erecting its head as best it could on its weary neck. Immediately realizing that (1) it must be defanged and (2) it must be drugged, I lost my interest in snake charming. The show didn't improve when the charmer removed other lids and eventually there was a chorus line of spaced-out snakes. My soul's reaction was in Yiddish (*"Oich mir a shlang!"* Which is, word-by-word "Also to me a snake!", which means "That they call a snake?"). So I gave him five rupees and I came away.

Along this stretch of the Janpath Road, from the *Imperial Hotel* to Connaught Place, there are also shoe-shine men, hawkers and traders of all kinds, stalls where samosas, puris, and other delicacies can be had, and three types of beggar: children, women each with a single baby clutched to her breast, and diseased or infirm people. Here the begging seems to be more of a regular business than in Calcutta, because here it is a street for tourists and businesses, more than a street which people make into a home. Local people are not importuned by peddlers and beggars. This was confirmed by the interesting case of Narinder Singh, the Sikh from Norway that I met (see January 15 below) on the plane back to England. A not-very-observant Sikh, he doesn't always wear a turban, and his hair is not uncut, though it is longer than is conventional, with a kind of little ponytail when the turban is off. He reported that when he walked along Janpath and Connaught Place with his turban on, he was not approached by anyone, but that, when he did not have his turban on, he was regarded as fair game.

I walked along that street, Janpath, buying and eating and giving alms for several of the mornings and early evenings of my six-day Delhi stay. I don't remember which incidents happened on which days, so I'll just describe a clutch of undated incidents here.

There was an episode with a shoe-shine man, who, looking at my shoes, said, correctly, "These have not been shined in India." He proceeded to rectify that, and one thing he did was drop a great dollop of white cream on the front part of my brown Ducker and Son left shoe. I was apprehensive about a stain, but he reassured me. "It's only cream." And, indeed, it was fully absorbed within twenty minutes, to the benefit of that shoe. When, on the following day, he again offered to shine, I pointed out that it would not compliment him for me to accept his offer, since his shines were surely worth more than a day's wear. He took this in good part, and I promised (unfulfilled) to come back in a day or two.

The begging women were moderately persistent, but content with a little less than their Calcutta counterparts, further evidence that here in Delhi anyway it is a tourist business, with, no doubt, menacing organizers in the background. And there were many child beggars, of great charm. Some spoke quite good English. One boy, very attractive and around ten years old, asked me, after I had given him a few rupees, whether I would take him back to my hotel. This was a puzzling question, since he must have known that the huffy hotel would not allow a ragged waif through its doors, unless, perhaps, a guest absolutely insisted, as only one guest in a million would. So why did he ask that question? I hoped it was not some sort of prostitution proposition.

One evening a particularly heartrending thing happened. It was dark, and, needing aspirins, I was out in search of a pharmacy. Daringly, I walked right (not left) down Janpath, where it's dark and where there are not many shops, just to make a change. There was a stall selling all kinds of good-looking nuts. I stared long enough at the display to feel obliged to buy when the stallholders made some kind of inquiry. So I pointed to the peanuts, and I said I'd have five rupees worth of them. A pair of scales were then used in a simulation of precision weighing, but I'm sure that I was given lots less nuts than five rupees should command, and I didn't care. I really didn't want to eat the nuts, because of my regard for my figure, but I couldn't buy nothing. Then a sad-looking darling little boy of six or so approached and asked for money. Darling though he was, I was not prepared to give a hundred rupees, and I had no smaller note. So I gave him the nuts, expecting that to be a mere first move, expecting him to demand money instead or in addition, and then I would go to a shop and get change if I could, the nuts having served as an earnest of good intention. But the boy didn't complain, he just quietly took the nuts, and peacefully ate them. I progressed back left up Janpath, and he walked sort-of-behind sort-of-beside me, very quietly, and carefully, not ravenously, eating the nuts, in a trancelike state. Then I got to the shops and there was a woman there who was his mother or his boss, clutching a baby, and she began to approach me, but he intervened, to show her the nuts, with pride and satisfaction, saying something which probably meant "Look what the man gave me." She looked at him as though he did not know the value of things, but in an excusing attitude, and I felt gutted.

The most resourceful urchin was a kid of ten or twelve whom I met at the far end (from Janpath) of the Connaught Place circle. He was carrying a bag which contained requisites for shoe shining. He proposed a shoe shine and I said that I did not want one but that I would give him money. He spoke very good English. He said that he did not want my money. What he wanted was that I should buy him a shoe-shine box, because the police hounded him and prevented him from plying his trade because he did not have a proper box. If you give me a box, I will not have to beg any more. Just give me 150 rupees, and I can buy a box, and I will not have to be a beggar any more. All said chirpily and with charm, no wailing or nagging or anything like that. So I said, "Here is fifty, now you've got fifty, so you only need two other people as kind as I am and then you can buy your box." "But, no, Sir, there is nobody else as kind as you are, Sir, so if you do not give me more I cannot get my box." This was so amusing that it did not occur to me to counterargue that he could make up the missing hundred from, say, fifty niggardly handouts. We walked a long way together discussing I forget what—not just the box—and I gave him no more. I learned later that Narinder Singh, in his turbanless mode, was approached by the same boy with the same story. I can't remember what Narinder gave him, but it was also considerable.

Another thing that happens along Janpath if you are a tourist in the morning is that you are bugged by Kashmiri (so, anyway, they style themselves) merchants whose display rooms are in the hinterstreets and who plead with you to come and see their wares because (1) you will get the chance to buy beautiful stuff, cheap, and (2) they are oppressed, displaced people who need your custom. It's hard to integrate these two appeals, to your cupidity and to your generosity at one and the same time, but one young man is sufficiently unyielding that I finally yield, and I follow him through streets off Janpath to an upstairs showroom which has in it six or seven men, no customers, and lots of well-presented dry goods. I am interested in scarves, as possible gifts for folks back in England, and they show me nice ones. I buy two. Then, the carpet selling starts. To deal at once with all my reasons for not wanting to buy one, they say that I needn't give them any money, that they can ship a carpet to Britain and I can pay somebody there. But I buy no carpet, although they are very beautiful.

I'm not much of a shopper, and in Janpath there's a great place to go if you're not much of a shopper and you have to buy gifts for a dozen people. It's called the "Central Cottage Industries Emporium." It's run by the government, it's like a department store, with many separate bits, fur, leather, wooden handicraft, children's toys, clothes, bolts of cloth, etc. The stuff comes from all over India, and there's no question of bargaining, which is a relief. The salespeople, I discovered, are salaried: it isn't franchised out. Nor do they get a commission. "So you are on a salary?" "Yes, Sir," the salesman replies, "very handsome salary, Sir." (I don't ask how much.)

You say what you want at a particular counter, they give you a slip of paper, you pay at a central cashier, and then you collect all your wares at a central point. Satisfyingly orderly. Credit cards are accepted, but, when I queue and finally reach the cashier, he says that my credit card is acceptable only on display of a passport. So I have to go back (ten minutes' walk, maybe fifteen, if beggars are not ignored) to the hotel to get it. I go back, I return, and once again I'm in the queue with my bills, and, this time, my passport. He tots up my bills. "It is more than 2,600 rupees. We cannot take credit card for more than 2,600 rupees." It does not occur to me to split the bills into two sets and pay for one set with Access and the other with Visa (the total is only 3,700 rupees). So, for the first time on this trip, I do what the guidebooks say there's no point doing: I protest. "Why didn't you tell me about the maximum when you sent me off to get my passport?" "It is not possible to do credit card for more than 2,600 rupees, but if you see the general manager he will give you a permission and then you can pay." This sounds to me like a half-hour job, with only a possibility of success, but he reassures me. "It is easy, he is downstairs where the goods are collected." But I noticed a long queue there. "You do not have to queue. You can go behind the counter to his office." I find this general manager, who is young and obliging. He tries and fails to make a phone call. So, since the phone call doesn't work, he signs a permission anyway, and from there on it is plain sailing.

And while one wanders shopping and seeing snake charmers and so forth along this Delhi tourist drag, from time to time an elephant appears ("Curiouser and curiouser," cried Alice!) and that adds to the variety.

Back to chronology, but by now (date of writing February 17) it's getting difficult to remember at the previously sustained degree of detail: Oxford professors should be given a couple of weeks off to record what happened when they return from places like India. I'll press on as best I can.

It's 1:15 P.M., January 10, Sunday. Rajeev rings from the lobby of the *Imperial Hotel*. "Come up." So, in a minute, there he is, impresario of this trip, my former student and present benefactor, to whom I express warm, sincere gratitude, as I open the door. We will do some sightseeing, but first we will have lunch in the hotel.

By 1:40 or so, we are eating outside on the terrace in perfect, sunny weather, under a parasol. Rajeev asks me to tell him *everything* that's happened so far. "You really want me to tell you everything? Because I can do that, but you must tell me when you're getting bored." "Don't worry, I'll tell you." So I go through much of the experience that you've now read about here, and he is evidently amused by how strongly it all impacted on me. We have chicken tikka, of excellent flavor but not tip-top texture. Rajeev hopes that it is not too strong for me. It isn't.

Then into Rajeev's van to go to his beautiful three-layered flat in Aurangzeb Road, to which he has recently moved with Tani, their two girls, Aranyani and Vanya, and Pratap and his wife, their helpers. Nice representation of Ganesh on a living room table. (I am now feeling a bit inhibited about going on like this, since Rajeev and Tani will be given a copy of this. I beg their pardon and I rely on their generosity.) Tani is to join us on our sightseeing. But she takes too long to get ready, or is busy with something she cannot leave, and we go off alone, to the Old Fort.

In the outer precincts of the Old Fort there is a large Sunday crowd of individuals and families buying food and drink at stalls, and milling around in holiday fashion: an exhilarating scene. The Old Fort itself is a huge space enclosed by an impressive wall, largely intact, and with interior structures, the best of which, and the most impressive building I saw in India—but I did not visit many buildings—being the "Mosque in the Old Fort," exquisite stone and marble, very heavily decorated with no feeling of overdecoration. I was very taken with this building.

We go back to Aurangzeb Road to see if Tani is now ready, to come with us to see Humayun's Tomb: the color photograph of it in Craven's *Indian Art* book had impressed me tremendously. Tani is now ready, so off we go to the tomb, and it is a splendid thing, except that the Jamuna River is not as close to it as it was when the Craven photo was taken, so you do not get from any point this marvelous photo view of a serene river with an elegant classical (that is, Mughal-classical) structure just above.

On an outside wall of the tomb (it's not really a tomb: it's a vast, blue, single-story building, with a sepulcher in the middle of a set of passages) a youth is chalking something on the wall, while his friend watches. Tani admonishes him, and, amazingly, he respects her command, stops, apologizes, and looks a bit ashamed. Try that one on, *mutatis mutandis*, in London or New York, and see how well you do in the juvenile correction department. I spit on a tissue and try to rub the chalk off the stone, but it stays. Since, however, the stone is otherwise free of graffiti, they must have a way of cleaning such things off. This miscreant can't have been the first to try to leave his mark on the stone.

That is enough sightseeing for one day, so Rajeev and Tani drop me at the *Imperial*. Rajeev had told me that it was somebody's birthday party that evening, and I could come, but he appreciated that I might be too tired. I want to come, and it is arranged that I will take a taxi to the Bhargava residence, to get there at 8, and then we'll go to the party.

So I engage in some restful solo pottering in my room, reading, drinking mineral water, playing patience and some invented (by me) card games, which simulate baseball. Then a taxi to Rajeev and Tani's driven by a Sikh accompanied by a friend. I am a *little* anxious when he does the wrong turn at Aurangzeb Road and can't find the block, but all is well in the end.

At Rajeev and Tani's there is a visiting friend from Bombay, Roshan Shahani: she is a leading writer on music, and she is seated on the floor of the living room with a woman singer called Shubha Mudgal, and a man. Shubha is singing, beautifully, certain wail-like Indian songs (I am totally ignorant about Indian music) to Roshan, and commenting on them. I am invited to sit down and listen, and I do, while Rajeev and Tani deal with their girls. Roshan introduces me to Shubha, but not to the man accompanying her, whoever he may be. (A lover? A servant? Rajeev also couldn't say, when I asked him afterwards.) I'm a bit unsure about how to comport myself, internally and outwardly, so I'm not entirely comfortable, socially, sitting on the floor listening to the songs. In due course I slope off to an adjacent room, and I hear Roshan and Shubha discuss which songs are Ganpati and which are not. I am more intrigued by this edible word, "Ganpati," than by the music itself, which is also intriguing, but too alien for me to really enjoy. "Ganpati" becomes one of those phoneme-strings that I say over and over to myself, aloud, when I'm alone,[11] other such strings on this trip being "VeeKayyyRamachandran," "Vajpayee" (a BJP leader), and "Hanooomaan" (the monkey god). Later, reading in Britain, I learn that "Ganpati" is just another

[11] [After his return from India, Cohen started calling Michèle "Ganpati," which soon became a mutual term of affection. This was shortened to "Ganpat," then to "Ganni," the latter of which stuck, and they never called each other by any other name until his death.—Ed.]

(more affectionate?) name for "Ganesh," the multilimbed god with an elephant's head. Here's how he came to have an elephant's head, if I correctly remember Rajeev's explanation. He was a son of Shiva and Parvati, and he was lurking outside his mother's bedroom, because he wanted to see her. Coming upon him during his lurking, his father Shiva, not knowing who he was, chopped off his head. Then Parvati explained to Shiva that this was their son, Ganesh (either Shiva was an unobservant god, or he had many sons), so Shiva willed that Ganesh would get a new head, of the same kind as the head of the first creature he would thereafter meet. The first creature Ganesh encountered was an elephant, which is why he now looks as he does. You can see representations of Ganesh in any museum that has a decent range of Hindu sculpture.

Rajeev joins me in the room to which I've retreated, and we do some preparty drinking, me whisky and he rum. We talk quietly so as not to interfere with the Ganpati or non-Ganpati songs Shubha is singing. Soon the vocal display stops, things loosen up, and the Bhargava kids, Aranyani and Vanya, tumble into the company, in their pajamas. Aranyani has recently recovered from a bout of typhoid. She looks well. In the original plan surrounding my visit, the Bhargavas were to have had a holiday in Goa, the last part of which was to have overlapped with my own Goa period. But they were prevented from doing that by the pilots' strike. Rajeev says that was good fortune because it would have been awful for Aranyani to have had her typhoid while they were in Goa.

Writing about Rajeev and Tani, and knowing that they will read this, and knowing that they will know that others will read this, I am forced to reflect on the morality of producing and distributing this thing. I have despised novelists I know who sling in identifiable people and incidents from their own lives, where the descriptions invade privacy and must be excruciating for the people concerned, and I am not going to tempt you to read them by telling you which novels I have in mind. You could say: if I am worried about how Rajeev and Tani *will* feel, I should also worry about how Peter and Amiya and all the rest *would* feel to know that their thoughts and actions are being publicized like this. Well, I am worried, and I am confused. We don't think it wrong to talk to people about other people. We think it's wrong to *gossip*, which is telling people things about other people that are titillating, or in a prurient or judging way. I am certainly not going on in *that* fashion. So what is the difference between a sequence of morally permissible one-to-one narratives and this one-to-many performance, albeit a longer performance than is usual? How can the method of delivery make a moral difference?

I try to entertain Aranyani and Vanya, and I have delayed till now saying that they are utterly beautiful little girls, for fear that Rajeev or Tani might think I'm trying to flatter. Well, this narrative is becoming too second-order, too self-reflective. So, from now on—I'm sure *they'd* prefer this—I shall write it as though their relationship to it is as third-personal as everyone else's that I mention. Early in our Delhi experience together, after I'd thanked him for something or other, Rajeev proposed a pact: no more thank-yous either way. It seems to me in the spirit of that to engage in no further apologizing and moral self-scrutiny.

We drink a bit more, and then we're off in Rajeev's van to the party. It is one floor up in a block of flats, except that it is not exactly a block of flats, because there is no independent door to the flat above, it's just a set of rooms, a good set of large rooms, radiating off a large staircase landing. There are quite a few dozen people there, and plenty of drink. The average age is thirty-five to forty (Rajeev's kind of age). The tenor of the talk and the demeanor of the people (all middle-class intellectuals of one kind or another) derive from the radical culture of the sixties in Britain, but the safe end of that culture, not the wild Hippie Angry Brigade end or anything like that, and also, now, twenty-five years later, somewhat faded, and there is something mimetic, not autochthonous, about the expressions and attitudes. In other words, and not to put too fine a point on it, there is a certain coloniality here, exported mild radical slightly subchic. I try not to feel superior about that, and I succeed (it's easy for a Jew from Quebec not to feel superior about that), and, anyway, Rajeev agrees with my depiction. One woman is talking about how inferior so-called Indian food is in Britain. She doesn't go to restaurants when she's in London, but sometimes, when she's dying for a thali, she goes to Drummond Street, but it's not the same. (Well, the best of Drummond Street is just as good or better than most of what *I* had in India, though not as good, nothing is, as the *very* best I had. But anyway, maybe food is a matter of taste, maybe I'm wrong that it's an objective matter. Then again, how can anyone think that a Montreal bagel isn't objectively better than a New York bagel, if you'll pardon my misuse [in its second occurrence] of that term?)

One person at the party is Pankaj Butalia, a film director, and friend of Rajeev's, who urges us to come and see a preview of a film he's made for Channel 4 (UK) on Thursday evening, at 6:00 P.M., at the French Cultural Centre. He is earthy in appearance, and I look forward to the film.

At this party no food is cooked in the kitchen of the flat we are in. But there are lots of bowls and plates on a large kitchen table, and rich smells emanating from the flat below, where, I think, the parents of the woman whose birthday it is live, and all that is reassuring. The food comes and everybody tucks in avidly. It is excellent, but not as good as Drummond Street.

A further floor up there lives, among others, an academic who is at the party and who makes some hugely funny jokes. I am sorry to say that I forget these jokes now. It is February 18, and the memories are decaying.

Rajeev and I are tired, it is nearing midnight, and we want to go home. But Tani is in the middle of what seems to be a Tani-admiring clutch of people (there is much to admire in Tani) and she is unresponsive to Rajeev's repeated suggestions that we leave. And Jerry is becoming (unjustifiably) impatient, because I am not a night person, and Tani is, I see, having a very good time. Rajeev and I are watching and waiting on the central landing, Tani is in a bedroom with these apparent admirers. Rajeev explains, or explained the following day, that he does not think it fair to curtail Tani's fun, since she gets less of it than he does. Still, after twenty to thirty minutes of us waiting she smilingly joins us, and they drive me back to the hotel.

MONDAY, JANUARY 11

Such a beautiful morning that I disobey the instructions against doing so and open the windows of the hotel room. I breakfast (by chance) with two gents in their midseventies, Americans who (still) teach philosophy at Wake Forest University, Winston-Salem, North Carolina, and who have just got back from Katmandu. They'd been in Delhi for a conference on Indian philosophy, they'd made side trips to Agra and Jaipur, and, now, Katmandu, but they hadn't yet seen anything of Delhi itself, and this was their day to do that, since they were flying back to the States that night at midnight. We talk about political philosophy and it turns out that the livelier of the two, Bob, was raised as a socialist, and that, in 1932, when he was fifteen, he introduced Norman Thomas to a North Carolina audience. Thomas got nearly 900,000 votes for president that year, on the Socialist ticket, and Bob claims that Roosevelt took a lot of his program. I recall Thomas being vilified in the fifties in the Montreal communist movement for being financed by the CIA (which, it later emerged, he truly was), and we talk amiably about all that. They are very kind and intelligent gentlemen, Americans of the most attractive sort, and they invite me to give a talk at Wake Forest the next time I am in the States. It is impossible to say no, but we shall see whether this happens.

I spend the morning carrying out some selection of the touristic activities on Janpath described in the generalized depiction of Janpath mornings given at pp. 71–74 above. At twelve o'clock Rajeev comes, to squire me around more of Delhi. I show him scarves I bought at the Kashmiri shop. "They are nice, but they are not real Kashmir." Idiotically failing to connect "Kashmir" and "cashmere," I wondered how he knew where they came from. I hadn't thought they were supposed to be "cashmere," just "Kashmiri." Did Rajeev conclude that I was naive, no *mayvin* (Yiddish for streetwise expert) when it comes to scarves?

We will go to Old Delhi, to the Muslim area where the Jama Masjid (mosque) is. We go by taxi, to avoid parking trouble. We travel a good while and reach the appointed quarter, which is the opposite of the grand empty avenues of New Delhi. It is alive with the multifarious activity that I love—that almost everyone would love—being surrounded by. Our first stop is a restaurant, in the immediate interior of a maze of lanes, called Karim's, quite famous, I understand, or so I was later told, on the homeward plane, by Narinder Singh. In this maze of lanes, Rajeev explains, a person could be killed, his dead body lying there for two or three days without anyone doing anything about it.

Karim's is a simple place in appearance with plain booths, full of non-middle-class locals. In our booth two friendly Muslims sit across the table from us. They do not speak the same language as Rajeev, but a certain kind of lively food-centered conversation goes on. We eat (I think) a dhal soup, and then (I know) the most perfect seekh kebab I have ever known or will ever know, the taste ambrosial and the texture seductive beyond belief, a somewhat resistant exterior with a differently textured inside, soft to just the right extent. It is so good, this kebab, that I succumb to Rajeev's suggestion that we order another round, and we do it all again. I suppose this meal, though limited in size, was the most orgasmic one I had in India.

We pass out of the lanes to the broad busy road where the entrance to the Jama Masjid is. Desperately debilitated men in a collapsed state flank each side of the entrance walkway, too depleted to flourish their mendicancy. Up the steps to the portico, where we check our bags and shoes. Too bad about having to shed shoes, because it is a nippy day, and I have a lingering condition of now-you-feel-it-now-you-don't sore throat courtesy of the Jagson Airlines Calcutta-Delhi trip forty hours ago. The praying area of the Jama Masjid is topologically similar to the Mosque in the Old Fort, but much larger, and with less impressive stonework. In each of its four or five large bays there are one or two worshippers (there were none in the Old Fort Mosque, which is now probably just a monument) who seem unirritated by tourist wanderings, and there are hardly any tourists anyway. We walk across the vast raised piazza, which has cloisters on the side opposite to the praying area. But we, or, anyway, I, get cold feet, so we go back to the portico, regain our shoes and bags, and get back to the road.

Now we will visit the vast Red Fort, which is not too far away. Rajeev suggests a cycle-rickshaw, and I agree: this being my first (and only) trip in such a conveyance. It's excellent passing slowly through the milling life in that sort of carriage, and, so far as I can see, on this sort of flat terrain it's no worse to be a cycle-rickshaw driver than a taxi driver, as far as exertion and nuisance are concerned, except that you don't make as many rupees. We reach the precincts of the Red Fort. The rickshaw man tells Rajeev to give however many rupees he chooses, and he gives, I think, five, and asks me with a trace of anxiety whether I think that was all right.

So we pay our half-rupee or so each, and we enter the Red Fort. There's a forecourt, and then a corridor in which there are dozens of tourist jewelry and trinket shops, and Rajeev warns that the jewelry here is overpriced, not the real thing. Then an immense open space, with structures around the sides. In one of these there is a huge high throne, where Mughal emperors sat giving audiences to mortals assembled below. The wall decoration of this place, which is called Diwan-I-Am, is less good in real life than in photographs I'd seen, because it's shabbier in real life. A Muslim man begins to shadow us, stopping when we stop, moving when we move. He continues behind us as we pass to a structure of a more devotional sort. I remark on this to Rajeev, how curious it is. Eventually, we shake him off.

We leave the Red Fort, and then an episode occurs with a climax, to be described, that is the only harrowing thing that happened to me in India. Outside the fort, there is a Muslim woman with a baby, maybe a year old. She begs, we give. She follows us, she begs again, we give again. Maybe three times, and then we both feel that enough is enough. She is not of the same mind, so she follows us, as we look for a taxi, relentlessly begging as we keep on saying "No." It is my intention to supply a terminal ten-rupee note once we're in the taxi. We get into the taxi, I in front, Rajeev behind, and my front door is still open. I give her the ten, which appears, finally, to satisfy her, whereupon together, she and I together, close the front door, and you'll presently learn why I emphasize that we do it together.

I emphasize that because, as the door shuts, it catches the finger or hand of the poor little baby boy, at the forward end of the door. He cries, and I open the door. I look at the hand, which seems not to be severely injured. The baby is moving it freely, and his crying is a normal child-with-a-substantial-but-not-unbearable-pain crying, not a howling shriek. Mother keeps gesturing at the hand, with renewed begging. So I give her a hundred rupees and I close the door, ashamed that I have not invited them into the taxi, the shame tempered by my confidence that the injury is not really serious, which is confirmed by the lack of change in the way she begs: she is not beside herself with anger and despair.

The taxi has to traverse a congested intersection before it can take the main road back to New Delhi. It proceeds at a walking pace, and the mother walks beside it, knocking on my window. I am silently crying but I don't know what to do. It seems awful to do nothing and crass to give more money. I am crying and I know that it will take several hours to recover from this. It is one thing to not help the poor as much as you can, it is quite another thing to be a cause of additional pain to them. Is this how *I* cope with the poverty (see the quote from Tully at pp. 29–30 above), by riding away from it in a taxi?

"Should we have offered to take her to a hospital?" "She would not have come to a hospital," says Rajeev, who is also shaken up. "We would have had to force her into the taxi, she would have been afraid, such people do not go to hospitals for a thing like that, you have to understand, she is subhuman." And you have to understand that he says that with compassion, and what he meant was that she had been dehumanized by her conditions. "Where does such a person live?" "It could be she has a husband who works on a building site. If so, that's probably where the three of them spend the night, under a blanket on the site." And the taxi takes *me* to the plush *Imperial Hotel*, where Rajeev and I part, until tomorrow.

I spend a couple of hours at the hotel slowly recovering from this terrible episode. After some time I am sufficiently recomposed to look forward to the visit of Daniel Nelson, a friend of my London friend Tia, a dedicated journalist of wide Third World experience who has just arrived to spend a year working for a campaigning (on the Third World environmentalist front) magazine called *Down to Earth*. I tell Daniel the horrible story, we drink at the *Imperial* bar, I notice my Wake Forest professor friends having supper in the adjacent café, and they say they'll write to me. I wish them a good journey, and I'm glad that, unlike theirs, *my* plane won't take off at midnight. Then Daniel and I go to a restaurant in some hotel, recommended by Rajeev. The lighting there makes the place gloomy, the food is good but not great, and I know that I am not my usual vivacious self for Daniel, because I am not fully recovered from the afternoon.

We part quite early, tenish. And so to bed, to forget about the day.

TUESDAY, JANUARY 12

I woke, as I did most mornings in Delhi, after a good sleep with the slight sore throat imposed by Jagson Airlines and a stubborn infected spot in the area of the palate where it meets the insides of the top two front teeth, a soreness not relieved by various mouthwashes that I tried nor by the salt and boiling water that I occasionally obtained from room service. I was well rested, despite the fact that sleep was interrupted around 2:00 A.M. by a phone call from Maggie, Miriam, and Sarah in London.[12] I had tried and failed to reach them several times, once putting a message on the answering machine, and this was their response. It was not that they didn't know they were ringing me at an unholy hour but that they thought getting in touch was so important and exciting that, having failed earlier, they thought it right to persist in trying, and they happened to succeed on this particular occasion. One thing that had thwarted them was the hotel's mixing me up with a certain Mr. Coons, which will also explain an episode on the evening of this day and which I hope explains the fact that Mahesh never got in touch with me. Anyway, it was marvelous speaking to them and it was excellent how generous they all were in their attitude to the good time I was having, how readily they shared my excitement.

So I went to breakfast and had porridge or pancakes served by one of the *Imperial*'s variously dressed waiters. Some of them wear functional clothes, but others wear ceremonial garb of different kinds, plumes and sashes and so forth, maybe going back to fashions for servants laid down by Mughal emperors and preserved by the Raj. I thought it was demeaning for them that they should wear such costumes.

On this day at 3:30 P.M. I was to lecture at the British Council: a car would come at 3:00 P.M. I had no prior engagement, so I spent some hours in the

[12] [Cohen's first wife and two daughters—Ed.]

flaneur-type activity on Janpath that I had come to like so much, bought the scarves I mentioned at pp. 73 and 78 above, gave alms to a charming girl of ten or so who seemed intrigued by something about me other than my power to exude money and who accompanied me a long time chatting with me and then with all the charm she could muster (which was an enormous amount) pleaded with me to give her my topi, which is to say my Montreal Expos baseball team peaked cap which I always wore against the sun (I get a headache otherwise) and which I did not give because I had not seen any good substitutes that I could buy and I judged that my necessity would in this case take priority over her delectation. But it pleased me that she wanted the hat, because she wanted it with the passionate yearning of a child, not in the canny style of a little beggarmaid, and I thought: at least this couldn't be shared with a beggarmaster.

I wondered a lot about beggarmasters. I wondered about how pervasive they were, about whether they initiate operations or prey, more Mafia-like, on preexisting operations that they regulate and control. I also wondered about something which is rather important from the point of view of whether one should give alms or not. That is, how are they, the beggarmasters, paid? If (1) they are paid a fixed rent, then every penny you give the beggar benefits the beggar, helping either to pay that rent or forming part of his surplus above it. If, on the other hand, (2) the beggar is just given a wage out of what he brings in, a fixed wage, then, beyond a certain point (and even before that point if the wage is guaranteed regardless of what's brought in: a likely story) you're only feeding the beggarmaster. And it could also be (3) sharecropping, each getting a proportion, in which case you benefit both with every rupee you give. I suppose the first or third system is used: the second presents too little incentive to the beggar. And maybe it is the first system in particular that is used, since the third system has monitoring problems: can't they fake how much they've collected, misrepresenting it in a downward direction, or do they simply have nowhere to hide it, or are they cowed by there being such a massive penalty if they lie that they are terrified into probity? But, as long as the second and unlikely system isn't used, Western sophisticates who say: "You're only benefiting the beggarmaster," are taking an easy way out. They could still say: "You're only supporting the begging system," and I don't want to go into that argument here. But I would like to know what's known about the lot of these people, and these kids. There is a surface gaiety in the kids, on a sunny day, but God knows what's really going on there, what the basic structure of their lives is.

I didn't want much of a lunch in advance of the British Council lecture, so I bought samosas from a stall and munched as I walked, sustaining superb stings and thrusts of hot spice. And I spent time pottering and reading and lecture preparing in my room.

The driver came and we traversed the short distance from the *Imperial* to the brand-new British Council building on Kasturba Gandhi Marg. Strange building, quite attractive structural design, the inner part of its facade (if I remember rightly) nicely recessed, but with ridiculously enormous jagged black stripes painted all over it, like some tiger posing as a zebra. Jazzy, anyway, not dull.

Into the building, which is already (it's 3:10) milling with people bound for my lecture, and I am greeted by the diminutive Mrs. Chandrika Grover, who is not the Westernized sophisticate I had expected her to be from correspondence—she is the Council worker in charge of my arrangements and my grant—but a truly shy but very attractive personality. I was also greeted by the first secretary at the Council, who introduced himself by surname, which, benignly, I have forgotten, both barrels of it. He seemed agitated when I arrived. He fretfully scanned the people coming in. "I'm just wondering about how many people there'll be. We're planning to hold it in the lecture room, over there, but if too many people come we'll have to have it in the auditorium, and the trouble is that later on there's a concert in the auditorium by Margaret Fingerhut ..." "Well, it's fine with me either way." "Well, yes, let's hope we won't have to move to the auditorium." "You mean you're actually *hoping* that not very many people will come?" (I say, smiling: I mean, what kind of impresario is this?) "Well, yes, I mean no, it's not that, it's just that the auditorium ..."

Vay iz mir! Is it incurable, this English non-life-affirmingness? Does it survive (maybe it's reinforced by) the grand tour around the world's embassies, the trip on an elephant through the bush which—I later learned—the first secretary did in Rajasthan with his family? And why do I have *any* sort of feeling of apologetic awkwardness when I'm with a cold public school posho like this?

Rajeev and Tani arrive, and Vidhu Verma, who was supervised by me for the M.Phil. at Oxford, and Daniel Nelson. A thin turbaned man comes up to introduce himself. He recites his spiritual credentials, which I don't quite catch. I make to shake his hand but then I see that his hands are bizarre, some webbed fingers, some twisted ones. So I do not shake his hand in the conventional way but sort of gently squeeze it, because his approach is so warm and friendly.

The people have been filing into the small room, which holds about sixty. There are about ten or fifteen who can't get in, but apparently that's not enough to order a shift of room. I am introduced to the head of the Council, one Robert Arbuthnot who speaks English upper class but seems entirely human, and Vice-Chancellor Baxi, who is also human, and who will be introducing me. People keep trying to press in, so the first secretary relents and declares that, alas, we have to move to the auditorium.

We file out and cross the lobby. A good auditorium, with a piano on the stage, which has some relation to the anxiety about using the auditorium that the first secretary expressed: maybe one should not ask, "Is There Still a Case for Socialism?" in the presence of a piano. Now there are, I don't know, about 120 people, which is not that huge an audience, but I am glad that it is bigger than anticipated, and also glad that we weren't originally supposed to be in the auditorium, for then this crowd would look small, a failure. And there I am waiting to be introduced with my pretty left-wing text on my lap, feeling a *bit* sheepish about voicing these left-wing formulations in the presence of the first secretary and Robert Arbuthnot, who do not look like they subscribe to *Militant*.

Vice-Chancellor Baxi, an amiable and un-self-important man, rises to introduce me. I must say, it's a full introduction, none of that "needs no introduction" guff. He introduces me as one of the founders of analytical Marxism. The other major figure is Jon Elster, but my work is better. Elster adopts a schoolmasterly tone towards Marx in *Making Sense of Marx*, the very title of the book manifesting that inappropriate posture (in fact, I myself advised Jon against that title, for that reason). Cohen's *Karl Marx's Theory of History*, on the other hand … Then, the most unexpected thing: "I was particularly pleased, as a lawyer, that he had used Hohfeld's analysis of rights in his reconstruction of the base/superstructure distinction." (So he actually looked at my book, recently, or years ago. And what is this very miscellaneous audience going to make of *that* erudite remark?)

So, well-introduced, I approach the mike, and this is a portentous moment for me, and I say, voice breaking against my will to conceal emotion, "It's a very great pleasure and a privilege to be here and I am grateful to the British Council and to my Indian friends for making this possible." And then I deliver my lecture, conscious of a certain incongruency between its red content and this blue venue, or venue with blue hosts, anyway, but I just press forward because there's no business like show business, and I try not to notice, too often, the first secretary's unapproving (not disapproving) facial expression.

A trickle of applause, and plenty of questions afterwards, one long and not very penetrable one from the turbaned man with the misshapen fingers probably to the effect that the spiritual is more important than the material; another from a young academic woman, a sociologist or political scientist who spews forth unstoppably, the apparent purpose of her performance being to display her familiarity with a number of academic words, some, I fear, of European origin, such as "postmodern," "anomie," "structuralism," "false consciousness," and so forth, these words occurring in random concatenation, with copulas and prepositions stuck in now and then for the sake of grammar. It was total bullshit, of one familiar variety.

After forty-five minutes or so the event is declared complete, and, as we file out, Arbuthnot says he liked my point that it's false that the only way to get people to do good work is to pay them a lot: he's glad, he says, that I emphasized that people can work from a sense of service. (Did he give my left-wing point a "white man's burden" spin in his mind?)

Into the lobby and I am captured by Achin Vanaik, a kind of Marxist with a recent Verso book on contemporary India and an article on communalism in a recent *New Left Review*. I didn't know, in the course of this conversation, that he had those credentials. He came on as a courteous but firm Marxistically informed interrogator who had noticed quite a lot of Marxism being shed by me in the course of the lecture and who wanted to know what, if anything, was left. "So you don't any longer believe in the leading role of the working class?" "No, I really think that's obsolete. Of course, it would be very nice to believe ..." "And state planning is completely out?" And so on, until I begged off. I found answering him hard, because, when I give a lecture and there's questions afterwards, in the hall itself I'm all alert and keyed up, and then, when we leave the hall, I relax mentally, and I find it very hard to field further questions creatively, especially relentless and highly motivated ones of the sort Achin was throwing at me.

Anyway, I beg off, I say goodbye to Rajeev and Tani (whom I will see that evening at a reception at the first secretary's private residence) and to Vidhu, and I fall into the just-the-two-of-us company of Daniel Nelson and me, and we walk through the raging traffic to the *Imperial Hotel*. We amusedly co-observe various rum street scenes, and we part at the hotel, with a loose arrangement to meet the next morning, or the one after that, at the National Museum.

It is 5:30 or 6:00 P.M., and in two hours' time I am to be driven to the reception for me and for Margaret Fingerhut the pianist at the private residence. I spend an hour or two flaneuring on Janpath and pottering in my room, and settle down to wait for the driver. He doesn't come at 8, which is peculiar, because these drivers are normally punctual to a fault, and at 8:20 I decide that at 8:40 I will take the water buffalo by the horns and ring the first secretary. This is preempted when, at 8:39 precisely, he rings to inform me that the driver came by twice, and they said I wasn't in my room. He supposes it was the hotel desk's fault, and I confirm that. (This was the second or third time that they confused me with Mr. Coons, one other time being when Sarah was ringing me, and a possible third if Mahesh indeed tried to reach me.) He tells me to take a taxi to his place. A man will be waiting for me outside his house.

The floridly turbaned man at the hotel entrance commands a taxi through his microphone—taxis wait in a queue in a crescent off the main hotel driveway—and we are off, to Vasant Marg, Vasant Vihar. There is the usual taximan's confusion once we are near our target, but he is correctly instructed by some folks on a nearby street. At the first secretary's house it is his own driver who is there to escort me in. He explains, kindly, that he did try hard to pick me up, and I equally kindly acknowledge his efforts.

Inside, there is a landing by the door, and then we descend a few steps into a large and pleasantly appointed room, about thirty people in groups of four and five engaging in lively talk. I am disappointed that Mrs. Chandrika Grover isn't there: I guess she is too junior to merit an invitation. I join a group containing both Rajeev and the first secretary, and I ask the first secretary lots of questions: does he own this house? does he rent it? does the embassy lay it on? where did he study? what did he study? He did graduate work on stories used by Shakespeare for some of his plays: this fact makes me like him a bit more.

I also meet the first secretary's English wife, who, as is usual with English people, or maybe one could say as is usual with people, is warmer, more friendly, more human-being-enjoying, than her male mate. Then the first secretary splutter-stutters a suggestion that I should meet a man (whose name I forget) who is the head of something like a council for race relations. The splutter-stutter occurs because what he really wants to say is that the man is a lefty, like me, but what he actually says is something like, "He's, well he's, rather your sort of person, your, so to speak, line of country." I find the first secretary's shilly-shally discomfort ridiculous, but I am happy to meet the man, who is wrapped in a pure white dhoti, ravishingly handsome with a large black beard. We talk about his time when he was posted in London, and then we are interrupted by the arrival of food, a superb buffet on a long table.

While making my way into this food, I chat with the wife of the race relations man, who is beautiful, in the manner of Radha in certain traditional paintings. I don't know how we reach this topic, but we talk, as we eat, about the problem of not getting fat. She says that when they lived in London it was no problem, she would walk to work and do a lot of other walking, but, here in Delhi, it is too dangerous for a woman to walk on the streets alone. (Several people said that was true of Delhi, by contrast with other Indian cities. Maybe it's because New Delhi is underpopulated and what people there are get ferried in cars and taxis, so there aren't enough people on the streets for walking women to be safe.)

I had reached the party at 9:00 P.M. Now it is 10:25, and the first secretary's wife comes up to me and says: "I know you unfortunately got here late, but would it be too awful for you if you left now? The thing is, Margaret Fingerhut is exhausted, so she needs the driver to take her back now, and he could drop you too." I am surprised by that, since I surely could stay a bit longer—I'm enjoying the food, beer, and company—and then take a taxi, but I don't point that out. Instead, I excuse myself for a moment and ask Rajeev, who has not (yet) been asked to leave, whether he'd be able to take me back to the hotel. He says, yes, though first he and Tani have to drop by somewhere else. So I say, fine, and this turns out to be a good turn of events, because the drop by somewhere else, as you'll learn, is quite interesting.

So I tell the first secretary's wife that it's all fine, I'll stay a bit and my friend will drive me back. Then Margaret Fingerhut and others gather themselves up to leave, and, as they move towards the landing at the door, somehow the rest of us get swept up in this tide, and we are all making to go. But then the first secretary splutters, to five of us, including Rajeev, Tani, and me: "Well, *you* don't *have* to go," in the tone of someone making a logical point, rather than of someone inviting us to stay. So we say, well, yes, we'll stay a bit, and his wife seems genuinely pleased that we will, and we settle, the seven of us, around a coffee table, and drinks are poured. It looks as though the wife is looking forward to a good long drinkful jaw-jaw, but her husband seems not so relaxed. So, after ten or fifteen minutes, I disremember on what pretext, someone, I disremember who, says that we really should leave, and we do.

We drive away, to the large, expensive, mega-garishly decorated *Taj Palace Hotel*. Up the lift and along a corridor to a suite of rooms currently occupied by Shabana Azmi, a Bombay film star and political activist of Muslim descent. (She starred, they tell me, in *City of Joy*, the recent film about Calcutta, which I have not yet seen.) There are four or five friends of Shabana in the room, men and women, some in the film industry and some not, and there is a waiter at a bar table in the background, preparing drinks and snacks. Shabana is glamorous in a warm, unthreatening, way, in a flowing garment. Everyone is exercised by the horrible events shaking Bombay, and they are discussing a meeting some of them are to have tomorrow with Prime Minister Rao. Today some of them have met President Sharma, an old man who told them, so they say, that he did not really know what was going on: they should instruct him. One plump lavishly dressed woman on the sofa says: "The situation is unimaginable. My servants are terrified," and I gulp, silently. The terror is because in this phase of Bombay disturbance the Shiv Sena is targeting Muslims not just in slums and chawls but in posh flats, taking the terror to the middle classes. Shabana is on the phone to Bombay, learning about the most recent incidents. She is animated and distressed in the course of bringing Rajeev and Tani up to date on what is happening. We leave after about an hour, Rajeev and Tani driving me back to my hotel, after which, so I learned the next day, they returned to the *Taj Palace* because Rajeev and Tani had sensed that Shabana needed to talk more with them.

WEDNESDAY, JANUARY 13

This is the morning when I do my shopping at Central Cottage Industries Emporium in Janpath, the course of that having been described at pp. 73–74 above. At 3:00 P.M. I am to lecture at the Jawaharlal Nehru University, on the edge of town. Rajeev picks me up, and, at JNU, we are greeted by the Marxist economist Prabhat Patnaik, who will chair.

It is a long room with a long table, some fifty people already there, among whom I am pleased to see Achin Vanaik, my relentless post–British Council lecture interrogator. I read my paper on "Incentives, Inequality, and Community." They listen attentively, but then there is a silence, which I decide to take in my stride. Finally, it is broken, by a woman who raises questions, not really directed at anything in my text, about caste and inequality. After a couple of disavowals about how I don't really know much about the caste system, I venture my idea, originally devised against certain incautious formulations of Michael Walzer, that the justification of caste in terms of stories about reincarnation shows the hold of the idea of equality on human normative consciousness as such. If you get reincarnated, willy-nilly, through all the caste levels, then each soul enjoys equality of condition, over the long run. If you get reincarnated according to how you behaved in your previous incarnation, then that is a trans-lives form of equality of opportunity. Someone objects that the caste system is accepted by many who do not believe all that. I counter that, nevertheless, if anyone tries to justify it, those egalitarian notions figure in the justification. Then a woman makes the very shrewd point, to which I have no reply, that, even if what I say is true, there is still an endorsement of inequality in that, however climbable the ladder of inequality may be, it is still thought that there should be such a ladder, that inequality is the right way of ordering human relations. Then another woman says that it is highly debatable, anyway, what is inequality and what is not, and many protested against the law reserving 27 percent of certain government positions for untouchables and OBC's (other backward castes). Achin Vanaik then runs through, with great lucidity and economy, five distinct arguments (which he just reports, without affirming) against the reservation policy. I remark that they are precisely the arguments that are made against reverse discrimination in the United States, and I pick off each one of them with a well-placed shot.

We deconvene, and Rajeev and Prabhat Patnaik and I retire to a campus café of the characteristic low-grade sort and drink tea and coffee. I am engaged by the phoneme-string prapatpatnayeek of my host's name, and I repeat it to myself perhaps a thousand times from that day to this.

Rajeev drops me at the *Imperial*, for rest and restoration ahead of a large dinner party that will take place that evening at his home. I taxi there and arrive at 7:30 P.M. There are some familiar faces, Achin Vanaik, Roshan Shahani of Bombay, the music critic, and Shabana Azmi, the Bombay actress. We drink and we eat excellent food courtesy of Pratap, whom Rajeev calls "our man Friday." He is more major domo than servant in his deportment. Roshan had wanted to be back in Bombay by now, but it was impossible to secure transport. Shabana reports on that day's meeting with Prime Minister Rao. She lifts her lower lip and makes it protrude, in imitation of Rao, and mimics some of his statements. "What do you expect me to do? I can't violate the constitution." But, despite the apparent ineffectuality of Rao's meeting with the film industry people, it was part of the pressure to which he was subject in the course of the Bombay and Ahmedabad disturbances, part of the pressure that moved the government to forthright action against the BJP demonstration which was to have occurred in Delhi on February 25 and which government troops frustrated, without excessive force, a victory for reason and humanity.

I enjoyed the party, but I can't remember very much more of it. It took place on January 13, and it is now March 1. Memories are decaying. It is good that this narration is approaching its end.

Thursday, January 14

My last full day in India. In the morning, at 10:30 A.M., I meet Daniel Nelson, the environmental journalist, at the National Museum. My Sikh taxi driver is disappointed by the shortness of the trip. He asks whether I would like him to wait until I am done, so that he can take me to my next venue. I decline, since Rajeev will be collecting me at 12:30, to take me to lunch and then to the Delhi School of Economics. I compensate by giving him twice the requested fare.

The National Museum is beautifully kept, in thorough contrast with the Calcutta India Museum: presumable the money goes where most VIP visitors are likely to come, to impress them. A tremendously stimulating collection of Hindu and Buddhist sculpture, and a huge room of *objets d'art* and tools and so forth from the ancient sites of Harappa and Mohenjo-Daro, the most affecting piece being the Mohenjo-Daro dancing girl, a tiny (five and a half inches high) metal figurine, with bangles all the way up her left arm, bespeaking the pleasures of a civilization about which we presumably know next to nothing. Daniel and I have an excellent time in the museum, and then we wait outside in the sun for a while, because Rajeev is a bit late.

We drive to a complex of flats and offices, where we meet Rajendra Prasad, a Communist Party (Marxist) functionary who coedits a journal called *Social Scientist*. He is serious, bordering on the forbidding, a true functionary, reminding me of counterparts that I knew by the dozen in my Canadian communist childhood and teenhood. The three of us sit at a table in a pleasant café. I eat chapatis and vegetables, and Rajeev eats nothing, because today there is a protest fast by a group to which he belongs, against government inaction against the communal agitations. (The center of the fast was a place in Delhi which had been Mahatma Gandhi's Delhi headquarters. Later that day Tani criticizes Rajeev for having made me lunch with Prasad, when it would have been far more interesting for me, a unique opportunity, to visit the fasting people at the Gandhi place.) Rajendra would like to print "Is There Still a Case for Socialism?" in his magazine. I am glad to oblige, though I silently worry whether the text will be thought not tough enough by the magazine's heavy Marxist readers.

After lunch we drive to the Delhi School of Economics, for my last public appearance. There we meet Bhaskar, now on its staff, and whom I knew a bit when he was studying at Oxford, since we had both participated in an antiapartheid group. We have coffee with Bhaskar and one other person in a lively campus café. I am happy to discover that my faithful Oxford student, Vidhu Verma, who was at the British Council lecture, has come to hear me again. The campus itself is extremely pleasant, full of trees and lawns. The lecture, on "The Pareto Argument for Inequality," takes place in a seminar room, about twenty-five people there. This is my most technical lecture, because I'd been told that the Delhi School of Economics is intellectually advanced, which it proves to be. As I read my lecture, I recognize the recurrently smiling face of a tall thin man sitting opposite me. For a while, I cannot place this face, but then I realize that it belongs to Jean Drèze, the young Belgian economist whom I met in Helsinki in 1988 when I also met V. K. Ramachandran. Drèze is a highly committed egalitarian economist, who writes books about poverty with Amartya Sen, and, I am told, he gives all his money (surplus to the needs of his own reproduction from day to day) away, and doesn't live in any particular place of his own either. It is unsettling facing so severely committed an egalitarian as I read my egalitarian paper.

Afterwards there are good questions from Jean Drèze, Bhaskar, a prof called Basu, and Rajeev. But they're all handleable: the argument survives. Then we drive off, giving a lift to an agreeable young sociologist, and I reach the *Imperial Hotel* for rest and recreation before meeting Rajeev and Tani in the evening to see Pankaj Butalia's film and for a goodbye dinner at a restaurant. In my room I read an interesting article by Rajeev, which distinguishes five meanings of the word "secularism," in its contemporary Indian acceptation.

In the hotel corridor I meet a man who asks me how much longer I am staying. I tell him that I am leaving the next morning. "Then I will not see you again, Sir, I am the man who cleaned your room every day, Sir." This I know is false, because two or three times I was there when the cleaner came, and it wasn't him. But I give him what he expects anyway. (Falsifying his prediction, I do see him the following morning, in a conflict about whether or not to approach me again.)

I taxi to Rajeev's, and he and Tani and I walk to the nearby French Cultural Centre (one minute away) where, at 6:00 P.M., there is a preview showing of Pankaj Butalia's film for Channel 4 UK (it will go out in June) about Calcutta widows who have nobody able or nobody willing to support them and who spend the rest of their lives in exile in a town called Vrindavan where they sing songs and do other devotional things in a temple. The temple authorities give them a few handfuls of rice every day, and each one lives in a tiny space somewhere on a street or in a lane. The film is mostly a collection of autobiographies spoken by these forlorn individuals, why they came to Vrindavan, how they spend their time, what they feel about themselves. It is first-class cinema, a compelling presentation of miserable human bodies and extraordinary shots of how their bodies relate, in a close textural sense, to their crude clothing. And the stories they tell are utterly credible and heartrending.

We watch the film in the French Centre's comfortable small theater, between one and two hundred people filling all the seats. I cannot believe that the audience is not, anyway for the most part, as impressed as I am, but at the end there is only modest applause, and this retroactively reassures me with respect to the mini-clapping that my own various Indian performances induced. Wild applause seems to fall outside the range of Indian conventions. As we leave, it is a great pleasure to join the line of well-wishers congratulating Pankaj on his achievement.

Sobered by the film, we tread back to the Bhargava residence. The atmosphere is downbeat, and I am sorry that it is our last evening. Rajeev is tired, having been up till 3:00 A.M. two nights earlier, at Shabana's rooms, and last night also going to bed late, after the dinner party. Tani is as lively as ever. She brings forth two boxes, each containing a brilliantly painted model of Hanuman, the monkey god, in Superman-like flight. I am surprised to see what look very like wings jutting out behind Hanuman's armpits. "I didn't know that Hanuman had wings." Tani corrects me: "They're not wings. They're part of his dhoti," with massive emphasis on the first syllable of "dhoti." (I have imitated the way she said that a hundred times since, and I have also nagged a number of other people to imitate it too.) I am invited to choose one of these Hanumans as a goodbye present, and I gratefully do.

Rajeev says that beer is absurdly expensive in restaurants (cf. the Canadian's response to its price in the final paragraph of January 9 above), so we drink before we leave for the restaurant, which is in the repellently opulent *Taj Mahal Hotel*. The food is good, but only one dish is supreme, a minced chicken kebab, of a sort English Indian restaurants don't provide, in the shape of the seekh kebab (lamb) which they do provide. This chicken kebab has a truly memorable texture.

Our last supper is friendly, but not buoyant. They are no doubt heavy with thoughts about the awful crisis the country is in, a crisis on which they have both been spending—and will continue to spend—a great deal of their time and energy. They drop me at the hotel. Rajeev says "Jerry, it was great," and I am sad.

FRIDAY, JANUARY 15

Departure day. A British Council Thomas Cook driver turns up at 8:30 A.M. He is a Delhi native, six children, about fifty-five or sixty years old, not a powerfully built man, so that I am very sorry to have to ask him (for antihernia reasons) to carry my heavy bag to the lobby. He is pleasant without being obsequious, and his English is excellent. As we leave room 126, the corridors are filled, as usual, with surplus personnel, and I give my key to one of them. Downstairs, I pay the bill. They ask me for the key. I say that I gave it to a man upstairs. They say, then you will have to wait, we check upstairs. It's end-of-tether time, I am in no mood for needlessly accommodating pointless requirements. So I don't comply, and we pass through the door to the driver's Ambassador.

The road to the airport is heavily guarded, one soldier every ten yards, on both sides. I ask the driver why they're there. He says that a VIP must be coming in. Then I recall that this morning Prime Minister Rao is, at last, flying to Bombay, to see the situation for himself, and the driver agrees that this explains the soldiers.

Not much happens at the airport, except that, after checking in, I have to pay an airport tax at the airport bank that I should have paid before queuing to check in, but this hiccup is nothing compared to the travel hurdling that you've read about earlier.

I board the plane, in subdued mood. Next to me there are two London-born Indian girls, sisters, maybe twelve and fifteen years old, who had been stranded for five days in a hotel near Bombay Airport. They had wanted to visit the city, but the disturbances and the curfews kept them out.

Lunch comes soon after takeoff. The hostess assumes, when I order vegetarian, that I mean European vegetarian, and I settle for what I get because I assume that that's all there is: a rather boring vegetarian meal. Then I see another

European traveler, a woman, tucking into what look like the kind of spicy veggie goodies that so beguiled me when this trip began (see p. 27 above). It emerges that she, too, was given the European vegetarian, but that she knew about the alternative, and protested, successfully. I hadn't realized that there was an alternative, and it is now too late to rectify matters since I've already consumed part of the lousy meal. So I sit there cross, pissed off that I'm denied a final consumption of India because of the false presumption of the hostess. I tell myself not to be so childish, not to make such a big deal of it, and I simmer down.

Then the pilot makes a magic announcement: "If you will look through the windows on the right, you will see Mount Himavant, which is sacred to the Zoroastrians."

Himavant! One of my favorite poems is Eliot's *Waste Land*, much of which I know by heart, and many words in which are an enigma to me, because I haven't read any guide (other than Eliot's own footnotes) to the poem. One of those words, which I have always thought beautiful, is this word, "Himavant," which I knew must be a place-name, but I never knew what place it named. Himavant is introduced near the end of the poem. Right after the glorious lines, "Then a damp gust / Bringing rain," which mean that the parched dead land is finally receiving life-making water, the poem goes like this, "Ganga" being the river Ganges:

> Ganga was sunken, and the limp leaves
> Waited for rain, while the black clouds
> Gathered far distant, over Himavant

I had never been curious enough to find out about Himavant. I had not even pronounced its name correctly, always saying "Hímavant" when I read the poem, instead of "Himávant," which is the correct, and better-sounding, pronunciation. I was excited by the pilot's announcement. It extinguished my morose reflections about the meal that had been denied me, and I swiftly made my way to the back of the plane to look through a window where there were no seats. Here I met Narinder Singh, the Sikh described in January 10 above, who had been visiting his grandparents in Delhi, and who was now on his way back to Trondheim (Norway) where he was studying engineering, having spent most of his life in Bergen, to which his parents had emigrated when he was eight. Narinder and I looked through the window at the marvelous sight, Teheran to our right, behind us, and Himavant in the middle distance ahead, shaped like Fujiyama and rising amid surrounding lower peaks. And, beyond Himavant, the shore of the Caspian Sea.

The day remained clear, and I hung around for hours at the back of the plane with Narinder Singh, chatting and enjoying the great views together, Iran, Iraq, the Kurdish hills, the Black Sea, Romania, me feeling heartbroken with the banal thought that here is this beautiful planet that we have abused so much and on which there is so much misery. For a time we were joined by a friendly American, Jack Zibell, of Holland, Michigan, who had spent two weeks with his wife in Indian villages. Jack and his wife work in their spare time for their local Methodist Church, and Jack had been doing computer-type things, *gratis*, under the aegis of the church, for these villages. He wasn't goody-goody religious or anything like that, just a regular American guy, and he and Narinder and I enjoyed the aerial views together. Jack told me that he had had the Indian vegetarian meal on this flight, and that it was mediocre, nothing like the zinger on my flight to Bombay, which, so he said, he was also on.

Narinder and I held the fort while Jack disappeared for a while. He returned with his wife Karen. Karen was astonished that I had enjoyed my visit to India. "You mean, you actually *liked* being there?" When I recounted something of what I'd done, and how much, indeed, I had enjoyed myself, she said, "Well, you stayed in hotels, we didn't. We stayed in villages, and there weren't proper toilets. I didn't mind that so much but what I minded was people not using toilets at all, just doing it in public. There was a constant assault on the senses. I just can't take this sort of cultural difference." The last sentence activated Narinder Singh: "It's not a cultural matter, it's a social matter. You can't say there's anything wrong with Indian culture. Think of the religions, the ancient books, the painting ..." Karen: "Of course it's cultural, it's a way of life." Narinder: "No, no, no, that's not culture, that's a social thing." I reflect, arrogantly, that I could give a lecturette, right now, on concepts of the social and the cultural, which would dissolve this pointless dispute, but I restrain myself, and I just say: "Look, you're not really disagreeing about the important thing. You both agree that it's off-putting when people shit in public, whatever 'social' and 'cultural' might mean." This satisfies neither of them, but the issue is, as it were, dropped.

I agree with Karen that I wouldn't like to live the way the Zibells did, but I say that I would like to live in India for a while, chiefly because it is so *interesting*. Karen: "Don't you think the interestingness would wear off after a while?" This had never occurred to me, even as a possibility. My bet is that it would not, and I hope I get the chance to test that someday.

I know that this narration has been more about me than about India. But I've never done a piece of writing like this before, and I hope I'll never have to do one like it again. India impressed itself so deeply on me that I have had to recall what you have read, for the sake of preserving it.[13] India taught me lessons, and there are many more to come. For

> The welcome offered to you is your *guru*, the agony inflicted on you is your *guru*,
> Every wrench at your heartstrings that makes the tears to flow is your *guru*.
>
> —Bāul poem, from K. M. Sen, *Hinduism*, p. 106.

[13] [Thanks to Michèle Cohen and Rajeev Bhargava for their assistance in preparing this manuscript for publication.—Ed.]

Chapter Five

COMPLETE BULLSHIT

I. DEEPER INTO BULLSHIT

> **bullshit** n. & v. *coarse sl.—n.* **1** (often as *int.*) nonsense, rubbish. **2** trivial or insincere talk or writing.—*v. intr.* (**-shitted**, **-shitting**) talk nonsense; bluff. **bullshitter** *n.*
>
> —*Oxford English Dictionary*

> It is just this lack of connection to a concern with truth—this indifference to how things really are—that I regard as the essence of bullshit.
>
> —Harry Frankfurt

1. Harry Frankfurt's essay "On Bullshit"[1] is a pioneering and brilliant discussion of a widespread but largely unexamined cultural phenomenon. On being honored by an invitation to contribute to the present volume, I decided to focus on Frankfurt's work on bullshit, partly because it is so original and so interesting, and partly because bullshit, and the struggle against it, have played a large role in my own intellectual life. They have played that role because of my interest in Marxism, which caused me to read, when I was in my twenties, a great deal of the French Marxism of the 1960s, deriving principally from the Althusserian school.

I found that material hard to understand, and, because I was naive enough to believe that writings that were attracting a great deal of respectful, and even

[1] [All page references in this chapter are to this essay unless otherwise indicated.—Ed.]

reverent, attention could not be loaded with bullshit, I was inclined to put the blame for finding the Althusserians hard entirely on myself. And when I managed to extract what seemed like a reasonable idea from one of their texts, I attributed to it more interest and/or importance (so I later came to see) than it had, partly, no doubt, because I did not want to think that I had been wasting my time. (That psychological mechanism, a blend, perhaps, of "cognitive dissonance reduction" and "adaptive preference formation," is, I believe, at work quite widely. Someone struggles for ages with some rebarbative text, manages to find some sense in it, and then reports that sense with enthusiasm, even though it is a banality that could have been expressed in a couple of sentences instead of across the course of the dozens of paragraphs to which the said someone has subjected herself.)[2]

Yet, although I was for a time attracted to Althusserianism, I did not end by succumbing to its intoxication, because I came to see that its reiterated affirmation of the value of conceptual rigor was not matched by conceptual rigor in its intellectual practices. The ideas that the Althusserians generated, for example, of the interpellation of the individual as a subject, or of contradiction and overdetermination, possessed a surface allure, but it often seemed impossible to determine whether or not the theses in which those ideas figured were true, and, at other times, those theses seemed capable of just two interpretations: on one of them they were true but uninteresting, and, on the other, they were interesting, but quite obviously false. (Failure to distinguish those opposed interpretations produces an illusory impression of interesting truth.)

No doubt at least partly because of my misguided Althusserian dalliance, I became, as far as bullshit is concerned, among the least tolerant people I knew. And when a set of Marxists or semi-Marxists, who, like me, had come to abhor what we considered to be the obscurity that had come to infest Marxism—when we formed, at the end of the 1970s, a Marxist discussion group that meets annually, and to which I am pleased to belong, I was glad that my colleagues were willing to call it the Non-Bullshit Marxism Group. Hence the emblem at the head of this article, which says, in Latin, "Marxism without the shit of the bull." (The group is also called, less polemically, and as you can see, the September Group, since we meet each September, for three days.)

2. I should like to explain how this essay reached its present state. I read Frankfurt's article in 1986, when it first appeared. I loved it, but I didn't think critically about it.

[2] As Diego Gambetta has pointed out to me, a mechanism merits mention that is different from the "sunk cost" one that figures above. You can be so happy that you've got *something* (after whatever amount of labor, or lack of it, you've expended) from someone who is reputed to be terrific that you overvalue it. In both mechanisms you misattribute the pleasure of getting *something* to the quality of the text you got it from.

Having been asked to contribute to the present volume, I reread the article, in order to write about it. I came to realize that its proposal about the "essence" of bullshit worked quite badly for the bullshit (see Section 1) that has occupied me. So I wrote a first draft that trained counterexamples drawn from the domain of the bullshit that interests me against Frankfurt's account. But I then realized that it was inappropriate to train those examples against Frankfurt, that he and I are, in fact, interested in different bullshits, and, therefore, in different *explicanda*. Frankfurt is interested in a bullshit of ordinary life,[3] whereas I am interested in a bullshit that appears in academic works, and, so I have discovered, the word "bullshit" characteristically denotes *structurally* different things that correspond to those different interests. Finally, and, belatedly, I considered, with some care, the *OED* account of "bullshit," and, to my surprise, I discovered (and this was, of course, reassuring) that something like the distinct *explicanda* that I had come to distinguish are listed there under two distinct entries.[4]

So, instead of citing cases of the bullshit that interests me in disconfirmation of Frankfurt's account, I now regard it as bullshit of a different kind[5]—which is not to say that I have no criticism of Frankfurt's treatment of the kind of bullshit that interests him.

Frankfurt is partly responsible for my original, misdirected, approach. For he speaks, after all—see the second epigraph at the beginning of this article—of the "essence" of bullshit, and he does not acknowledge that the *explicandum* that attracted his interest is just one flower in the lush garden of bullshit.[6] He begins by saying that the term "bullshit" is very hard to handle, analytically, but, as we shall see, he rather abandons caution when he comes to offer his own account of it.

Consider, then, the *OED* reading of "bullshit":

> **bullshit** n. & v. *coarse sl.—n.* **1** (often as *int.*) nonsense, rubbish. **2** trivial or insincere talk or writing.[7]*—v. intr.* (**-shitted**, **-shitting**) talk nonsense; bluff. **bullshitter** *n.*

[3] His essay begins as follows: "One of the most salient features of our culture is that there is so much bullshit. Everyone knows this. Each of us contributes his share."

[4] Frankfurt himself cites the *OED*, but mainly with respect to meanings and uses of the word "bull": he touches on its definition of "bullshit" only in its use as a verb, I disagree with his discussion of the entries he cites, but it would be an imposition on the reader's capacity to endure tedium to explain why.

[5] Four differences between the kinds of bullshit that exercise Frankfurt and me are listed in n. 27 below. The import of those differences will emerge in due course, but the reader will probably follow me better if he or she glances ahead now to n. 27.

[6] [In his festschrift "Reply to G. A. Cohen," Frankfurt writes: "If I am reluctant to endorse Cohen's claim that the sort of bullshit on which my attention was focused 'is just one flower in the lush garden of bullshit,' it is not because I doubt that his claim is true. It is only because I cannot help recalling that bullshit is an animal product and not a plant" (p. 340)—Ed.]

[7] "Trivial" is very different from "insincere," partly because it has weaker implications for the state of mind of the speaker/writer. I shall take 2 with the accent on "insincere."

The bullshit that interests me falls under definition 1 of the noun, but the bullshit that interests Frankfurt is closer to what falls under definition 2 of the noun. And that is because of the appearance of the word "insincere" in that second definition of "bullshit." In definition 2 of the noun "bullshit," bullshit is constituted as such through being the product of discourse governed by a certain state of mind. In this activity-centered definition of bullshit, the bull, conceptually speaking, wears the trousers: bullshit is bullshit because it was produced by a bullshitter, or, at any rate, by someone who was bullshitting at the time. Bullshit is, by nature, the product of bullshitting, and bullshitting, by nature, produces bullshit, and that biconditional, so understood that "bullshitting" enjoys semantic primacy, is true of Frankfurt's view of the matter.[8]

Definition 1, by contrast, defines "bullshit" without reference to the bullshit-producer's state of mind. The defect of this bullshit does not derive from its provenance: almost any state of mind can emit nonsense or rubbish, with any old mix of sincerity and its lack. Here the shit wears the trousers, and *if* there are indeed "bullshitters," and "bullshittings," that correspond to the bullshit of definition 1, then they are defined by reference to bullshit. But it may be the case, as I meant to imply by that "*if*," that the words "bullshitting" and "bullshitter" don't have a stable place on this side of the *explicandum* divide.[9] However that may be, definition 1 supplies an output-centered definition of the noun: the character of the process that produces bullshit is immaterial here.

Note, moreover, how the alternatives in the brief entry on the verb "to bullshit" match alternatives 1 and 2 in the definition of the noun (even though that entry isn't, as it perhaps should have been, subnumbered "1" and "2"). One can "talk nonsense" with any intentions whatsoever, but one cannot unknowingly or inadvertently "bluff": bluffing is a way of intending to deceive. (I'm not sure, by the way, that the dictionary is right in its implication that it suffices for bullshitting, in the nonbluff sense, that you produce bullshit, in sense 1: innocent producers of bullshit might be said not to be bullshitting when they produce it.)[10]

It is a limitation of Frankfurt's article that, as we shall see, he took for granted that the bull wears the semantic trousers: he therefore focused on one kind of bullshit only, and he did not address another, equally interesting, and academically more significant, kind. Bullshit as insincere talk or writing is indeed what

[8] Frankfurt certainly believes that a person bullshits if he produces bullshit, since he thinks it a necessary condition of bullshit that it was produced with a bullshitting intention. He (in effect) raises the question whether that intention is also sufficient for bullshit at p. 119. But, although he doesn't expressly pursue that question, his definition of "bullshit" (p. 125), and its elaboration (p. 130), show that he holds the sufficiency view as well. It is because Frankfurt asserts sufficiency that he can say (p. 129) that a piece of bullshit can be true.

[9] See, further, the last two paragraphs of Section 4 below.

[10] See, once again, the last two paragraphs of Section 4 below.

it is because it is the product of something like bluffing, but talking nonsense is what it is because of the character of its output, and nonsense is not nonsense because of features of the nonsense-talker's mental state.

3. At the beginning of his article, Frankfurt describes a complexity that afflicts the study of bullshit:

> Any suggestion about what conditions are logically both necessary and sufficient for the constitution of bullshit is bound to be somewhat arbitrary. For one thing, the expression *bullshit* is often employed quite loosely—simply as a generic term of abuse, with no very specific literal meaning. For another, the phenomenon itself is so vast and amorphous that no crisp and perspicuous analysis of its concept can avoid being procrustean. Nonetheless it should be possible to say something helpful, even though it is not likely to be decisive. Even the most basic and preliminary questions about bullshit remain, after all, not only unanswered but unasked. (p. 117)

I have no problem with Frankfurt's first remark, to wit, that "bullshit" has a wide use in which it covers almost any kind of intellectual fault. To circumvent this problem, to identify a worthwhile *explicandum*, we could ask what "bullshit" denotes where the term does carry (as Frankfurt implies that it sometimes does) a (more or less) "specific literal meaning," one that differs, in particular, from the meanings carried by words that are close to "bullshit," but instructively different in meaning from it, such as the word "horseshit," which, at least in the United States, denotes, I believe, something characteristically produced with less deviousness than characterizes the production of (*OED*-2) bullshit. And I think that, for one such meaning, Frankfurt has provided an impressively discriminating (though not, as we shall see, fault-free) treatment: much of what he says about one kind of bullshit is true of it but false, for example, of horseshit.

Frankfurt's second remark, about the difficulty caused by the fact that "the phenomenon itself is so vast and amorphous," is more problematic. Notice that this remark is meant to be independent of the first one (hence the words "For another ..."), as indeed it must be, since no *phenomenon* could be thought to correspond to "bullshit" where it is an undifferentiated term of abuse. In making this remark, Frankfurt must suppose, if, that is, he supposes, as he appears to do, that he will command the reader's agreement, that the reader has some "specific, literal meaning" of "bullshit" implicitly in mind. But that is extremely doubtful, partly because it is a gratuitous assumption (and, indeed, as the *OED* reveals, a false one) that "bullshit" has some *single* "specific, literal meaning." In a word: how can we be expected to agree, *already*, that bullshit is "vast" and "amorphous," when no specification of "bullshit" has yet been provided?

However that may be, Frankfurt leaves these preliminary problems behind, and plunges right into his subject, by reviewing, refining, and developing a definition that Max Black once gave of "humbug" (which is close to bullshit of the *OED*-

2 kind), and then by commenting on an example of real or feigned rage expressed by Ludwig Wittgenstein against (putative) bullshit uttered by Fania Pascal.

Emerging from the Black and Wittgenstein discussions, Frankfurt very surprisingly says that "the essence of bullshit ... is ... lack of connection to a concern with truth— ... indifference to how things really are ..." (p. 125), where that indifference (see the Frankfurt passage quoted in the paragraph that follows here) is concealed by the speaker. It's the word "essence" that surprises me here: it seemed to be implied by Frankfurt's preliminary remarks that the term "bullshit," considered comprehensively, denotes no one thing whose essence one might try to specify,[11] and Frankfurt had not in the interim indicated a particular *region* of bullshit, whose bullshit might, perhaps, be identified by an essence.

Frankfurt later elaborates his definition as follows:

> This is the crux of the distinction between him [the bullshitter] and the liar. Both he [the bullshitter] and the liar represent themselves falsely as endeavoring to communicate the truth. The success of each depends upon deceiving us about that. But the fact about himself that the liar hides is that he is attempting to lead us away from a correct apprehension of reality; we are not to know that he wants us to believe something he supposes to be false. The fact about himself that the bullshitter hides, on the other hand, is that the truth-values of his statements are of no central interest to him; what we are not to understand is that his intention is neither to report the truth nor to conceal it. This does not mean that his speech is anarchically impulsive, but that the motive guiding and controlling it is unconcerned with how the things about which he speaks truly are. (p. 130)

Notice that, when Frankfurt elaborates what is supposed to be a proposal about bullshit, he speaks not of "bullshit" but of the "bullshitter." This confirms that, in Frankfurt's account, it is the bull that wears the trousers. But he wrongly takes for granted that that is the only important or interesting bullshit that there is.

Now, in the light of the semantic promiscuity of "bullshit" that was discussed at the outset of this section, it was, so I have suggested, unwise of Frankfurt to cast his claim as one about the "essence" of bullshit, as he does in the p. 125 passage. He should have submitted his indifference-to-truth thesis as an attempt to characterize (at least) one interesting kind of bullshit, whether or not there are other interesting kinds of it. Let us assess his thesis as such, that is, not with the ambitiously generalizing status that Frankfurt assigns to it, but as an attempt to characterize one kind of bullshit, and, in particular, an activity-centered kind of bullshit. I return to the distinct bullshit-*explicandum*, which corresponds to *OED* definition 1, in Section 4 below.

[11] Does Frankfurt think that the phenomenon of "indifference to how things really are" is "vast and amorphous"? Surely not. Then *what*, again, is he asserting to be "vast and amorphous," in his second preliminary remark, which I criticized two paragraphs back?

Consider Frankfurt's statement, with which we may readily agree, that "[t]he realms of advertising and of public relations, and the nowadays closely related realm of politics, are replete with instances of bullshit so unmitigated that they can serve among the most indisputable and classic paradigms of the concept" (p. 122). I find it hard to align this remark with Frankfurt's proposal about the essence of bullshit: advertisers and politicians are often very concerned indeed "to lead us away from a correct apprehension of reality" (p. 130) and to design what we might well call "bullshit" to serve that end (yet the quoted p. 130 words are used by Frankfurt to characterize the purpose of liars *as opposed* to bullshitters). Is it not a problem for Frankfurt's proposal about the essence of bullshit that those whom he designates as paradigm bullshitters engage in a great deal of what is not, for Frankfurt, bullshitting?

Frankfurt might say (as he must, to sustain his proposal) that, when advertisers and politicians seek to cover up the truth, they are doing something *other* than bullshitting. But when we are inclined to agree with Frankfurt that advertising and politics supply paradigms of bullshit, it is not the subset of their doings to which his proposal points that induces our inclination to agree. I think we are induced to agree partly because we recognize at least some lying to be also bullshitting.[12] Frankfurt's contrast between lying and bullshitting is malconstructed, and he erred, I believe, because he failed to distinguish two dimensions of lying, which we must separate if we are to determine the relationship between lying and Frankfurt's bullshitting.

Standardly, a liar says what he believes to be false: let us call that his standard *tactic* (or, for short, his tactic). Liars also standardly seek to deceive their listeners about some fact (other than the fact that they disbelieve what they say): we can call that the liar's (standard) *goal*. And normally a liar pursues the stated *goal* by executing the stated *tactic*: he says something that he believes to be false *in order to* induce his listener to believe something false. (Usually, of course, what I have called the liar's "standard goal" is not also his ultimate or final goal, which may be to protect his reputation, to sell a bill of goods, to exploit his listener, or whatever.[13] But the liar standardly pursues such further goals by pursuing the goal which liars standardly seek. None of these further goals *distinguish* the liar from nonliars.)

Now, what I have called the "standard tactic" and the "standard goal" of lying can come apart. Consider what was one of Sigmund Freud's favorite jokes:

[12] I suppose all lying is insincere talk, and I do not think all lying is bullshitting: at least to that extent, the *OED*-2 definition is too wide. But *some* lying is undoubtedly also bullshitting, so Frankfurt's definition of activity-centered bullshit is too narrow.

[13] Few liars care about nothing more than inducing false beliefs: that is the ultimate goal of only one of the eight types of liar distinguished by St. Augustine. See "On Bullshit," 131.

> Dialogue between two travelers on a train from Moscow:
>
> "Where are you going?"
>
> "To Pinsk."
>
> "Liar! You say you are going to Pinsk in order to make me believe you are going to Minsk. But I *know* you are going to Pinsk. So whom are you trying to fool?"[14]

Suppose that the first traveler's diagnosis of the purpose of the second traveler's uttering "To Pinsk" is correct: let us therefore call the second traveler Pavel (because of the "P" in Pinsk), and let us call the first traveler Trofim. On the indicated supposition, Trofim is right to call Pinsk-bound Pavel a liar, since, as Frankfurt says, the liar is someone who tries "to lead us away from a correct apprehension of reality" (p. 130), and that's what Pavel is trying to do to Trofim. The peculiarity of the present example is that Pavel here seeks to deceive by telling the truth. Pavel does not, in my view, lie, on this occasion, but he nevertheless proves himself to be a liar. Pavel's goal is the standard goal of the liar, but his tactic, here, is to speak the truth. (The important and entirely nonverbal point is that the standard goal and the standard tactic of lying lose their normal association here, not whether Pavel is lying, or telling a lie, etc.)

A converse case, in which the standard tactic subserves a nonstandard goal, would go as follows. Pavel knows that Trofim knows that Pavel habitually lies, at any rate when it comes to disclosing his intended destinations. But, on the present occasion, it is very important to Pavel that Trofim should believe the truth about where Pavel is going. So Pavel, once again traveling to Pinsk, says that he is going to Minsk, precisely because he wants Trofim to believe the truth, which is that Pavel is going to Pinsk. I don't know, or very much care, whether Pavel thereby lies, but he is not here "attempting to lead [Trofim] away from a correct apprehension of reality," save with respect to his own state of mind: he wants him to think he's trying to get Trofim to believe something false, when he's not.

We must, accordingly, distinguish two respects in which liars characteristically traffic in falsehood. Liars usually intend to utter falsehoods, while intending that they be thought to be speaking truthfully; but that is quite separate from their standard goal, which is to cause a misrepresentation of reality in the listener's mind.

What is the bearing, if any, of this distinction on Frankfurt's distinction between lying and bullshitting?

The root difficulty for Frankfurt's bullshitting/lying distinction, the difficulty underlying the problem with his advertiser example, is that, while Frankfurt identifies the liar by his goal, which is to mislead with respect to reality, he assigns no distinctive goal to the bullshitter, but, instead, identifies the bullshitter's

[14] See Sigmund Freud, *Jokes and Their Relation to the Unconscious.*

activity at the level that corresponds to what I have called the liar's tactic. The standard liar pursues his distinctive goal by asserting what he believes to be false and concealing that fact. Frankfurt's bullshitter asserts statements whose truth-values are of no interest to him, and he conceals *that* fact. But Frankfurt assigns no distinctive goal to the bullshitter that would distinguish him from the liar. And, in fact, Frankfurt's bullshitters, as he identifies them, have no distinguishing goal: they have a variety of goals, one of which can be precisely to mislead with respect to reality, and that, indeed, is the goal of bullshit advertising.[15] Advertisers and politicians spew a lot of bullshit, and they indeed seek to induce false beliefs about reality, but those are not, as Frankfurt must have it, separate but, typically, coincident activities on their parts.

The failure to distinguish the level of tactic from the level of goal runs throughout the discussion. Frankfurt writes at p. 128:

> Bluffing too is typically devoted to conveying something false. Unlike plain lying, however, it is more especially a matter not of falsity but of fakery. This is what accounts for its nearness to bullshit. For the essence of bullshit is not that it is *false* but that it is *phony*. (my emphases)

The problem is that this falsehood is at the level of tactic, whereas phoniness is at the level of goal. If bluffing is like bullshit, that is partly because bullshitting, too, is often devoted to conveying something false—although often not by saying that false thing itself.

As Frankfurt says, the bullshitter may not care whether or not what he says is true. But Frankfurt has confused that with the bullshitter's not caring whether his audience is caused to believe something true or false. That explains an error that Frankfurt makes about the Fourth of July orator whom he describes at pp. 120–21:[16]

> Consider a Fourth of July orator, who goes on bombastically about "our great and blessed country, whose Founding Fathers under divine guidance created a new beginning for mankind." This is surely humbug. … [T]he orator is not lying. He would be lying only if it were his intention to bring about in his audience beliefs which he himself regards as false, concerning such matters as whether our country is great, whether it is blessed, whether the Founders had divine guidance, and whether what they did was in fact to create a new beginning for mankind. But the orator does not really care what his audience thinks about the Founding Fathers, or about the role

[15] It is not, of course, the ultimate goal of that advertising, which is to cause (some of) its audience to buy what's advertised.

[16] Strictly, the orator's oration is presented as an example of humbug, rather than bullshit. But it's clear that Frankfurt would also say that he is a bullshitter, precisely in virtue of what makes him a purveyor of humbug, whatever difference between humbug and bullshit Frankfurt might want to affirm.

> of the deity in our country's history, or the like. At least, it is not an interest in what anyone thinks about these matters that motivates his speech.
>
> It is clear that what makes Fourth of July oration humbug is not fundamentally that *the speaker regards his statement as false*. Rather ... the orator intends these statements to convey a certain impression of himself. *He is not trying to deceive anyone concerning American history*. (my emphases)

The orator's unconcern about truth is, mistakenly, identified at the level of his goal, rather than, in line with p. 130, merely at the level of his immediate tactic. For the bullshitting orator, as Frankfurt describes him, might well care a lot about what the audience thinks about the Founding Fathers.[17] If the orator had been Joseph McCarthy, he would have wanted the audience to think that the "new beginning" that the Founding Fathers "created" should persuade the audience to oppose the tyranny supposedly threatened by American communism. The fact that it is not "fundamental" that "the speaker regards his statements as false" in no way implies that "he is not trying to deceive anyone concerning American history." (Similarly, advertisers may not care whether or not what they say is true, but they do care about what their audience is caused to believe, or, rather, more generally, about the thought-processes that they seek to induce in people.)[18]

4. Unlike Frankfurt's bullshitting, lying is identified in terms of the defect at which it aims, namely, falsehood. We clarify what a liar is by reference to falsehood, rather than the other way around; we do not, that is, when asked to characterize what falsehood is, say that falsehood is what a liar aims to say. In parallel, we might, unlike Frankfurt, seek to clarify what a bullshitter is by reference to what he aims at, to wit, bullshit. We might start with the shit, not with the bull. And that would induce us to consider *OED* definition 1 ("nonsense, rubbish") the one that fits the bullshit that interests me, rather than the bullshit that interests Frankfurt. My bullshit belongs to the category of *statement* or *text*. It is not primarily an activity but the result of an activity (whether or not *that* activity always qualifies as an activity of bullshitting).[19]

A liar who tries to say something false may inadvertently speak the truth, whether or not he is then lying, and whether or not what he then says is a lie. And there is also the opposite case in which an honest person, by mistake, speaks falsely. The bullshit that interests me is relevantly parallel. I countenance a bullshitter who has tried, but failed, to produce bullshit—what comes out,

[17] I do not think Frankfurt means to be *stipulating* otherwise: we are meant to agree with what he says about the orator on the basis of his initial, first-sentence-of-the-passage description of him. "Surely," in the second sentence, would otherwise make no sense.

[18] Although this is not, again (see the text to n. 13 above), their ultimate goal.

[19] See the final paragraph of this section.

by accident, is good sense—and I also countenance a lover of truth who utters what he does not realize is bullshit. A person may avow, in full honesty, "I'm not sure whether what I'm about to say is bullshit." These are not possibilities for the bullshit that interests Frankfurt. But they are possibilities. So the bullshit that interests Frankfurt doesn't cover the waterfront.

A person who speaks with Frankfurtian indifference to the truth might do so yet *happen* to say something true, and, in at least one sense of the term, the one that interests me, what he says could not then be bullshit.[20] And, oppositely, an honest person might read some bullshit that a Frankfurt-bullshitter wrote, believe it to be the truth, and affirm it. When that honest person utters bullshit, *she*'s not showing a disregard for truth. So it is neither necessary nor sufficient for every kind of bullshit that it be produced by one who is informed by indifference to the truth, or, indeed, by any other distinctive intentional state.

The honest follower, or the honest confused producer of bullshit, may or may not count as a bullshitter,[21] but she is certainly honest, and she certainly utters (one kind of) bullshit. There exists bullshit as a feature of utterances that does not qualify as bullshit by virtue of the intentional state of the utterance's producer (although that state may, of course, causally explain why the bullshit is there, and/or why what's there is bullshit).

But what *is* that feature of utterances? *One thing it can be*, at least to a first approximation, is what the *OED* calls it, to wit, *nonsense*. But what particularly interests me is a certain variety of nonsense, namely, that which is found in discourse that is by nature *unclarifiable*, discourse, that is, that is not only obscure but which cannot be rendered unobscure, where any apparent success in rendering it unobscure creates something that isn't recognizable as a version of what was said. That is why it is frequently an appropriate response to a charge of bullshit to set about trying to clarify what was said. (Think of attempts to vindicate Heidegger, or Hegel. The way to show that they weren't bullshitters is not by showing that they cared about the truth, but by showing that what they said, resourcefully construed, makes sense. Those who call them bullshitters do not doubt that they cared about the truth, or, at any rate, it is not *because* of any such doubt that they think Hegel and Heidegger were bullshitters.[22] That Frankfurt issue isn't the issue here.)

[20] Perhaps in contrast with Frankfurt's sense, and certainly in contrast with what Frankfurt says about that sense (see p. 129).

[21] That question is addressed in the penultimate paragraph of this section.

[22] For the record, I do not believe that Hegel was a bullshitter, and I am too ignorant of the work of Heidegger to say whether or not he was a bullshitter. But I agree with my late supervisor Gilbert Ryle that Heidegger was a *shit*. I once asked Ryle whether he had continued to study Heidegger after he had written a long review of *Being and Time* in *Mind*. Ryle's reply: "No, because when the Nazis came to power, Heidegger showed that he was a shit, from the heels up, and a shit from the heels up can't do good philosophy." (Experience has, alas, induced me to disagree with the stated Rylean generalization.)

Something is unclarifiable if and only if it cannot be made clear, but I shall not try to say what "clear" means in this essay. (I'm inclined to think it's not possible to do so, in an illuminating way.) Note, however, that there are relevantly different forms of unclarity, all of which have bearing here. There is the unclarity of a sentence itself, and then there is the unclarity as to why a certain (possibly perfectly clear) sentence is uttered in a given context. So, for example, the meaning of Wittgenstein's "If a lion could speak, we would not understand him" is in one way perfectly clear, but it might nevertheless be judged obscure, and unclarifiably obscure, by one who doubts that it carries, in context, a graspable point. There is also the unclarity of why one statement should be taken to lend credence to another statement. And there are no doubt other pertinent unclarities too.

Note that it is not an objection to the proposed sufficient condition of bullshit that different people might, in the light of different background beliefs, impose different standards of clarity, and, therefore, identify different pieces of texts as bullshit. Some of the people might, of course, be wrong.

I emphasized "one thing it can be" three paragraphs back because defects other than unclarifiable unclarity can suffice to stigmatize a text as bullshit. I focus on this variety of the phenomenon because it commands a greater academic following than other varieties do. In the various varieties of bullshit, what is wanting, speaking very generally, is an appropriate connection to truth, but not, as in Frankfurt's bullshit, as far as the state of mind of the producer is concerned, but with respect to features of the piece of text itself. Unclarifiable unclarity is one such feature. Rubbish, in the sense of arguments that are grossly deficient either in logic or in sensitivity to empirical evidence, is another. A third is irretrievably speculative comment, which is neither unclear nor wanting in logic, such as David Miller's excellent example, "Of course, everyone spends much more time thinking about sex now than people did a hundred years ago."

I focus on unclarifiable unclarity in particular in preparation for a further inquiry into bullshit that addresses the question why so much of that particular kind of bullshit is produced in France. This kind of academic bullshit, unlike the two contrasting types of bullshit, be they academic or not, mentioned in the previous paragraph, comes close to being celebrated for its very unclarity by some of its producers and consumers. What some of them certainly celebrate is a disconnection with truth: in what perhaps ranks as the consummation of the development of unclarity-type bullshit, a consummation that Hegel might have called "bullshit risen to consciousness of itself," truth is, in much postmodernism, *expressly* disparaged.

Although I forswear a definition of "clarity," I can offer a sufficient condition of unclarity. It is that adding or subtracting (if it has one) a negation sign from a text makes no difference to its level of plausibility:[23] no force in a statement has

[23] This criterion of bullshit was devised by Professor Arthur J. Brown, to whom I am indebted.

been grasped if its putative grasper would react no differently to its negation from how he reacts to the original statement. The deliberate bullshit published by Alan Sokal no doubt comes out as unclarifiable, by that criterion.[24] Note that this test does not apply to the different sorts of bullshit reviewed a couple of paragraphs back, and, being a merely sufficient condition of unclarifiability, it does not characterize *all* cases of the latter either.

An objection that faces my account is that it appears to classify good poetry that isn't bullshit as bullshit, since a piece of good poetry may be unclarifiable. A tempting way of acquitting such poetry of the charge of bullshit is by reference to its designation *as* poetry, rather than *as* some sort of contribution to knowledge in a more straightforward sense. But then the same text would be bullshit or not according, Frankfurt-like, to its, as it were, intentional encasement, and I am trying to characterize an intention-independent sense of the term.

An unclarifiable text can be valuable because of its suggestiveness: it can stimulate thought; it can be worthwhile seeking to interpret it in a spirit which tolerates multiplicity of interpretation, and which therefore denies that it means some one given thing, as a clarifiable piece of text does. So let us say, to spare good poetry, that the bullshit that concerns me is not only unclarifiable but also lacks this virtue of suggestiveness.[25] (I am sure that many academic bullshitters get away with a lot of bullshit because *some* of their unclarifiabilia are valuably suggestive, and therefore not bullshit. Their readers then mistakenly expect more, or most, of it to be so.)

So much by way of a preliminary attempt to identify the *bullshit* that interests me. But what reading of "bullshitter," if any, corresponds to the bullshit that I have tried to identify? Producers of Cohen-bullshit are clearly not by nature bullshitters, in Frankfurt's sense, though Frankfurt-bullshitters often produce Cohen-bullshit, at least in the academy. Rather, I would say that the word "bullshitter" that corresponds to my bullshit has two readings. In one of its readings, a bullshitter is a person who is *disposed* to bullshit: he tends, *for whatever reason*, to produce a lot of unclarifiable stuff. In a second acceptable reading of the term, a bullshitter is a person who *aims* at bullshit, however frequently or infrequently he hits his target.[26] (Notice that other nouns that signify that their

[24] In his wonderful spoof "Transgressing the Boundaries" (which was published as a nonspoof in the thereby self-condemning *Social Text*).

[25] I am allowing that the unclarifiable may be productively suggestive, but I would not go as far as Fung Yu-lan does: "Aphorisms, allusions, and illustrations are … not articulate enough. Their insufficiency in articulateness is compensated for, however, by their suggestiveness. Articulateness and suggestiveness are, of course, incompatible. The more an expression is articulate, the less it is suggestive—just as the more an expression is prosaic, the less it is poetic. The sayings and writings of the Chinese philosophers are so inarticulate that their suggestiveness is almost boundless." *A Short History of Chinese Philosophy*, p. 12.

[26] Michael Otsuka comments insightfully on a familiar academic "case in which the two come apart: i.e., in which someone is disposed to unclarifiable unclarity without aiming at it. Many academics (including perhaps an especially high proportion of graduate students) are disposed to pro-

denotations engage in a certain activity display a similar pair of readings: a killer may be a being that tends to kill, with whatever intention or lack of it [a weed-killer, for example, is a killer, and a merely careless human stomper on flowers is a (flower-)killer]; or he may be a being who intends to kill, whether or not he ever does.) Aim-(Cohen)-bullshitters *seek* and *rely* on unclarifiability, whereas innocent speakers of bullshit are merely victims of it. Aim-bullshitters resort to bullshit when they have reason to want what they say to be unintelligible, for example, in order to impress, or in order to give spurious support to a claim: the motives for producing bullshit vary. (And just as a person might sometimes kill, without being a killer in either of the senses I distinguished, so a person who is in neither of the senses I distinguished a bullshitter might, on occasion, produce bullshit.)

What about the verb, "to bullshit"? Does the producer of my bullshit, always bullshit when she produces bullshit, as Frankfurt's does? I see no reason for saying that an innocent does, especially if she's not even a disposition-bullshitter. But an aim-bullshitter who produces bullshit indeed bullshits.[27]

5. It matters that bullshit can come in the non-intention-freighted form by which I am exercised. For there is, today, a great deal of my kind of bullshit in certain areas of philosophical and semiphilosophical culture, and if, as we should, we are to conduct a struggle against it, the sort of struggle that, so one might say, Alan Sokal has inaugurated,[28] then it is important not to make false accusations, and not, therefore, for example, to charge possibly innocent traffickers in bullshit with lacking a concern for truth, or with deliberately conniv-

---

duce the unclarifiable unclarity that is bullshit, not because they are aiming at unclarifiable unclarity, but rather because they are aiming at profundity. Their lucid utterances are manifestly unprofound, even to them. Their clarifiable unclear utterances can be rendered manifestly not profound through clarification. But their unclarifiably unclear utterances are unmanifestly not profound. Hence it is safe for them to think that they are profound. These utterances are not profound either because they are meaningful (in some subtle way, should there be one, that is consistent with their unclarifiable unclarity) but unprofound or because they are meaningless. They are *unmanifestly* not profound because it is hard to demonstrate that they are not profound, given their unclarifiability. By aiming at profundity, these academics tend to produce obscurity, But they do not aim at obscurity, not even as a means of generating profundity" (private communication, September 2, 1999).

[27] Let me now list some central differences between the two kinds of bullshit that I have distinguished:

	Typical context of utterance	*Corresponding OED definition*	*Primary locus*	*Essence*
Frankfurt's bullshit	everyday life	2	activity	indifference to truth
Cohen's bullshit	the academy	1	output	unclarifiability

[28] Initially in the article referenced in n. 24, and then more comprehensively in *Intellectual Impostures*, which he wrote with Jean Bricmont.

ing at obscurity.[29] Our proper polemical target is bullshit, and not bullshitters, or producers of bullshit, as such. So while it's lots of fun for people like me, who have a developed infantile streak, to talk about bullshit, and even just to write "bullshit" over and over again, in an academic essay, there is nevertheless, in my opinion, something important at stake here, and the character of what is at stake makes the bullshitter/bullshit distinction important.

To prevent misunderstanding, let me add that I do believe that there is quite a lot of *aiming* at obscurity in the production of philosophical bullshit, and a lot, to boot, in this region, of lack of concern with truth.[30] But these moral faults should not be our primary focus. For reasons of courtesy, strategy, and good evidence, we should criticize the product, which is visible, and not the process, which is not.[31]

II. WHY ONE KIND OF BULLSHIT FLOURISHES IN FRANCE

6. Whatever may be the relationship between (unclarifiably unclear) bullshit and intentional states, such as the will to conceal a lack of concern for truth, the philosophical culture which, since the Second World War, has been, so I believe, the most successful producer of bullshit, both in respect of the volume of bullshit that it has produced and in respect of the warmth with which that bullshit has been received, is Francophone philosophical culture.[32]

I have views about the explanation of this fact,[33] but I am neither a historian nor a sociologist, and I shall therefore probably say a number of ill-judged things in my attempt to explain it. I think that the question of how the flores-

[29] Consider this sentence from the work of Étienne Balibar: "This is precisely the first meaning we can give to the idea of dialectic: a logic or form of explanation specifically adapted to the determinant intervention of class struggle in the very fabric of history" (*The Philosophy of Marx*, p. 97). If you read that sentence quickly, it can sound pretty good. The remedy is to read it more slowly, and you will then recognize it to be a wonderful paradigm of bullshit: yet I know Balibar to be an honest thinker.

[30] The evidence assembled in Sokal and Bricmont's *Intellectual Impostures* proves, so I think, the truth of those beliefs.

[31] We may hope that success in discrediting the product will contribute to extinguishing the process. I try to contribute to the project of discrediting the product in an unpublished discussion of "Why One Kind of Bullshit Flourishes in France" [published as Part II of this chapter—Ed].

[32] I cannot claim to have read a great deal of what I consider to be French bullshit, since, perforce, I have experienced no incentive to pursue it deeply. But what I have read of Jacques Derrida, Gilles Deleuze, Jacques Lacan, and Julia Kristeva leads me to think that there is a great deal of bullshit in their work.

[33] Of, that is, the fact that France has produced so much bullshit. That French bullshit has been well received in certain academic quarters outside France is not something I shall offer to explain here, largely because it is not very puzzling. (Someone has said: "Fashions in ideas, like *haute couture*, are invented in France and sell in America." But French bullshit does not sell well in philosophically advanced American places.)

cence of bullshit in French philosophy is to be explained is a fascinating one, and I want to get my attempt at explanation into the public domain, so that others can criticize it, and do better. I am conscious that much of what I shall say can be challenged (≠ refuted), through, for example, citation of discrepant parallel instances, cases, that is, where one or two (or more) of the features that I think explain French bullshit are present outside France yet bullshit is not, and cases where bullshit is present, but, as it were, Frenchness, or the French cultural features that I shall adduce, is or are not. I welcome the discussion that, so I hope, the cases that create difficulty for my view will stimulate.

Despite my unprofessionality in empirical matters, I am confident that three features of French intellectual culture dominate the explanation of the fact that France has produced so much bullshit,[34] although I am quite uncertain about how they figure in that explanation. I shall describe the three features, in no particular order, and I shall then cite, for good measure, some further possibly explanatory features.

The first feature is that within French culture only one place, Paris, is authoritative with respect to the endorsement and rejection of intellectual claims. Anglophone culture is, by contrast, multipolar. It matters what is thought about an intellectual claim in Oxford, in New York, in at least two Cambridges, in Los Angeles, in Berkeley, in Sydney, and so on. It seems to me evident that a plurality of authoritative judging centers encourages the exposure of intellectual fraud, of which bullshit is one type; and that, contrapositively, the existence of only one authoritative judging center makes it easier for fraud to flourish (whatever may be the right conjecture about how this feature, that is, French culture's unipolarity, combines with the others that I shall mention in my attempt to explain why so much bullshit is produced in France).[35]

The fateful unipolarity is not essentially a matter of *one city*, but of a unified national academic structure,[36] and the location of the pinnacle of that structure

[34] The features that I shall list characterized French culture before the Second World War. So they certainly don't explain the *timing* of the French bullshit explosion, which postdates that war. I have no speculations about what *triggered* that explosion. I seek to identify features that made such an explosion more likely to occur in France than in other places.

[35] Unipolarity is not a necessary condition of lots of bullshit. Otherwise, as Diego Gambetta has remarked to me, Italy could not, as it does, foam with bullshit, since Italian intellectual life is not unipolar. Perhaps, for multipolarity to do its cleansing work, some well-formed notion of objective criteria must be around, one that is sufficiently clear to be enforced. And that is lacking in Italy. (See, further, n. 47 below, for a conjecture that the lack of objective criteria enjoys a certain explanatory primacy.)

[36] Cécile Fabre writes: "To be sure, Parisian academic institutions set the tone, but what I think is more relevantly unipolar is the way academics are appointed, and the qualifications they all must have, in order to be appointed, foremost of which is the *agrégation*—in short, the uniformity of career paths. Nowadays, candidates for university lectureships, before they can apply to a university, must be vetted by a national committee: once they are so vetted, they can apply to universities for four years in a row; if they are unsuccessful, they have to be vetted by the national committee

in what is in every respect the dominating center of the culture, which helps to make "intellectual activity both highly politically charged (Paris is also where politics is) and a form of cultural commodity,"[37] to the detriment, for both reasons, of dedication to truth.

The second relevant feature of French culture, manifest in its painting, its architecture, its buildings, its couture, its automobiles, even, indeed, in the very posture, both physical and mental, of the French, is a concern with, and a capacity for, style. French artifacts, both material and social, are arresting and, frequently, brilliant.

We must distinguish conditions that promote a propensity and/or an ability to *produce* bullshit, from conditions that promote the *spread* of bullshit. Style operates on both sides of that distinction, because it encourages bullshit as a form of art (we speak, indeed, of bullshit artists), and because style helps to conceal the fact that bullshit is bullshit, thus facilitating its spread. For, to spread, to gain acceptance, bullshit must be good at concealing its status as such. (Italian bullshit is so patently bullshit that no one, outside small circles, buys it.[38] Bullshitters must have the gift to make what they say credible, and the peculiarities of French style help here.)

There is, of course, also a chic style in British culture: there is Britpop, Britart, and so forth. But I believe that it is less accomplished, and in any case the overwhelmingly important fact, here, is that such style has very little academic penetration, no doubt because of the absence in Britain of what I believe to be the third pertinent feature of French intellectual culture, which is that there is a large lay audience for intellectual products in France. Being lay, that audience will read philosophy only if it is *interesting*, and being interested in interestingness is quite different from being interested in truth. (Professionals are paid to be bored, if necessary, so, when they represent the whole audience, the boringness that sometimes accompanies the exposition of truth is more acceptable). The difference between how a philosopher writes in the *Journal of Philosophy* and how she writes in the *New York Review of Books* is greater than the difference between how a philosopher writes in a French academic journal and how

---

again. That makes for great intellectual homogeneity: even though the national committee will not usually turn down someone who is already strongly wanted by a university, it has quite a lot of leeway to decide who, in fact, will become a lecturer. If there were several cities in France that were thought to be a judging centre (in fact Lyon is becoming one), but if the members of the academic institutions in all cities were all from the same intellectual mould, the system would still be unipolar. Contrast the Anglophone world: what makes it multipolar is not the fact that there are several *geographical* centres of excellence, but the fact that these centers differ: an undergraduate at Harvard does not work in the same way as his Oxford counterpart, or, indeed his Cambridge (UK) counterpart; the academic culture in the US is different from the British one, and so on" (private communication, August 30, 1999).

[37] Mark Philp, private communication, October 16, 1999.

[38] Perhaps Italian bullshit fails because of the prominence of what Diego Gambetta calls "discursive machismo" in Italian culture: see his " 'Claro.' "

she writes in *Le Monde*. The existence of a large lay audience for philosophy in France reflects the fact that all French *lycée* students study philosophy,[39] whereas very few high school students do so in English-speaking countries.[40] This makes educated French people expect to be *engaged* by philosophy, and status-seeking intellectuals gladly cater to that expectation.

Those are the three features that I believe to be central. But certain other features of French culture may also play a role.

Fourth (to continue the count) there is the consideration that French universities lack the tutorial system, which enables students to grill their teachers. Take it from me: it is easier to sustain the flow of bullshit in a lecture hall in front of five hundred students than in a semidomestic Oxbridge setting, when you are asked, over tea, or sherry, what you *really* mean. And the bullshit-eliminating effect of tutorials may be more pronounced for students than for teachers, since there is much more grilling of students than of teachers in tutorials. The proportion of British academics who were tutored is much higher than the proportion who tutor, since a much higher proportion were taught at, than teach at, Oxbridge, and most British universities lack a developed tutorial system.

Fifth, and evidently helping to consolidate the popular audience for philosophy, there is a long tradition of works of literature with philosophical content, on the Continent in general and in France in particular: think of Dante, Goethe, Unamuno, Thomas Mann, and, for France, Rousseau, Sartre, and Camus.[41] The legitimacy of philosophy in literature renders literature legitimate in philosophy: people are accustomed to the mix—they expect it. And because literature is beyond the reach of the sort of criticism repeated doses of which render philosophy rigorous (think of what analytical criticism would [inappropriately] do to Keats's identification of truth and beauty, or to Sartre's identification of hell with other people), there is less tendency for philosophy to become rigorous in a culture that conjoins philosophy and literature. (Think of Montaigne and Pascal, who enjoy high philosophical *and* literary status.) A related point is that, while

[39] Cécile Fabre tells me "that the Philosophy paper of the *baccalauréat* is often discussed the day of the exam on TV, and the day after the exam in *Le Monde* and other dailies."

[40] Note, moreover, that French students encounter philosophy at an age when people are inclined to be less critical and more deferential than they are at the age at which Anglophone students first encounter philosophy. Those who regard themselves as unprofessional incompetents are inclined to take bullshitters on trust. And since they think they're incompetent, they believe that what is immediately intelligible to them, and, therefore, what lacks an element of obscurity, cannot be valuable and important. (As Diego Gambetta explains in his " 'Claro'," in some cultures, such as Italy, Latin America, and, to a lesser extent, France, if you say something utterly clear, your audience may feel slighted, almost as though obscurity is a necessary condition of a worthwhile theoretical utterance. [In section 3 of his foreword to *Karl Marx's Theory of History*, Cohen remarks that in Britain, by contrast to Paris, "it is not generally supposed that a theoretical statement, to be one, must be hard to comprehend."—Ed.])

[41] I do not consider these writers to be bullshitters, but the present point does not require that I do so.

British philosophy emancipated itself from religion hundreds of years ago, Continental philosophy remained closer to religion, and, therefore, to its rhetorical style, which persisted even in antireligious writing by, for example, communist philosophers. And the particular religion of France is, of course, the strain in Christianity, to wit, Roman Catholicism, which is particularly unfriendly to debate that challenges fundamental doctrine.

The reference above to rhetoric suggests a sixth relevant feature, which is

> that many continentals are proud of not being British 'cold fish'. Writing passionately and responding to passionate writings, [caring], is looked on less condescendingly than [in Britain]. Writing passionately often involves being unfair, inaccurate, rhetorical, or exaggerated. Under such conditions, it is easier to sell something that is bullshit but sounds left-wing and radical to people who are left-wing and radical. ... Being rebellious, radical, spontaneous, non conformist, defying authority and tradition, not being as law-abiding as the British is also seen as cool, more often than in Britain.[42]

Finally, one may cite a potent seventh feature, namely, the authoritarian ethos of French intellectual life, which combines balefully with the first feature (unipolarity): unipolarity buttresses the intellectual authoritarianism, although it is logically distinct from it. The authoritarian ethos no doubt also connects with the fourth feature, that is, the *de haut en bas* teaching style, and also with the Roman Catholic tradition.

7. It might be thought that the discussion of Section 6 violates the precept affirmed in Section 5, that we should criticize the bullshit, not the bullshitters. But the suggested explanatory elements, while indeed referring to people's interests, and habits, are pretty neutral vis-à-vis the intentions and goals of French bullshit producers. I need take no stand on how much they *aim* at bullshit: I am examining cultural and social circumstances that reinforce a propensity to bullshit, whatever may hold at the level of individual psychology.

That said, let us consider the difficult question of how the elements that I have isolated might be thought to interact.

Each feature would, on its own, threaten fidelity to truth, and, so I believe, they interact to produce an interest in interestingness rather than in truth. But *how* do they interact? Which ones support which other ones? And which ones act jointly with others, and with what synergy, relative to the production of bullshit? I can only offer speculations here.

A premium on style in philosophy and the presence of a lay audience certainly support one another: it is hard to say which (if either) underlies the other. But how does unipolarity affect those two? Paris is the center not only of intel-

[42] Paula Casal, private communication.

lectual, but also, of course, of social life; it therefore matters, disproportionately, for intellectual life what is and what is not boring at Parisian cocktail parties and similar nonacademic occasions, with consequences for what gets into, and is there to be taken out of, journals and books.

As I have said, the features, singly, and (more so) together, put a premium on interestingness, and such a premium is dangerous in the domain of science and philosophy, where the premium should always be on truth. Within French culture, theories tend to be selected and rejected because of their interestingness and their boringness. Too much value is put on the new, as such, and too much disvalue is put on the old, as such. Theories go not because they are refuted[43] but because they are passé.[44] The truth might be boring, and it might be old and all too familiar, and the truth can be shunned in France for these bad reasons.

I do not say that nothing's boring in the massive output of French intellectual culture. On the contrary: it's full of boring stuff, partly *because* it's full of bullshit, and the elaboration of a bullshit idea tends to be boring. Truth and evidence do not control elaboration of the idea, so there is, as it were, no creative tension that draws one on when one reads the relevant texts. But the boredom is (to a degree) tolerated, because of the arrestingness of the idea under elaboration. One may wonder, moreover, how many people actually *read* the big boring books that they display on their shelves. Books produce academic legitimation, even when they are not read.

In one way or another, the features conspire to make authors go for something novel, and interesting, and, if possible, shocking,[45] rather than for what increases contact with the truth. In what perhaps ranks as the consummation

[43] This is not to say that there is no debate in French bullshit, but it tends to be debate of a truth-disregarding kind. Malcolm Anderson advises: "You might mention the fragmented character of French political culture as a result of catastrophic political divisions from the Revolution to the Vichy regime. This has had two effects which contribute to bullshitting—the first is that ideas and intellectual positions are regarded instrumentally (as useful or not useful in political combat, regardless as to whether or not they are true); the second is that people do not genuinely engage in debate with one another in an attempt to discover whether a position is valid or not. This leads to scholarly (and other) periodicals being under the control of particular political-intellectual tendencies and one publishes in those periodicals with which one is generally in sympathy on the grounds that 'one does not shout the truth from the wrong windows'. People are incredibly dismissive of those belonging to other intellectual-political strands. This leads to the erroneous impression that the French are highly critical" (private communication, September 5, 1999).

[44] One might suppose, after Thomas Kuhn, that this is true of theories in general. But I believe that Kuhn's diagnosis of the dynamics of theory change was incorrect, and that, even if he was right, in France theories go because they are passé in a cruder sense than Kuhn's. For Kuhn, theories go when enough "anomalies" have accumulated. It is not merely a matter of growing tired of hearing something and coming to want to hear something else.

[45] Reflecting on an earlier draft of this paper, Tracy Strong remarked, not unfairly, that to a certain extent I am saying that bullshit comes from the desire of an intellectual class to *épater* and the wishes of a bourgeoisie to be *épatée*.

of the development of bullshit, a consummation that Hegel might have called "bullshit risen to consciousness of itself," truth is (as it is in much postmodernism) *expressly* disparaged.[46] Partly because truth is not even aimed at, false, or, rather, untrue theses, abound, and they are protected against exposure by obscure statement and/or by obscure defense when they are challenged: so bullshit, too, abounds.[47,48]

[46] As logic itself was by Jean-Paul Sartre, who responded to A. J. Ayer's criticism of his discussion of nothingness by announcing, "Je ne me place pas sur le plan de la logique."

[47] Perhaps, there is also, to some extent, a reverse moment. Perhaps, that is, the lack of objective criteria in the philosophical culture *allows* Paris, and chic, to dominate it, and enables high intellectual life to reach a semi-intellectual wide public. The lack of objective criteria encourages the confident, institutionally well-established, bluffer. Developing this point, Paula Casal writes: "Since even a [junior, not well-connected teacher in Clermont-Ferrand] is capable of coming up with a good comment or objection, more objectivity gives non-dominant groups more of a chance. This is combined with the general phenomenon that people tend to see genius where they expect it. Those who expect to find in Plato the deepest thoughts are more likely to find them than those who don't. People's expectations cause them to make greater efforts to see the point, the importance or the originality of something ... The more such faith is required the more confidence and reputation counts. Faith tends to be more important when something is difficult or appears to be unintelligible or implausible (perhaps because it is)" (private communication).

[48] For comments on an earlier draft [of the material that constitutes this chapter—Ed.], I thank Malcolm Anderson, Annette Barnes, Jerry Barnes, Sarah Buss, Paula Casal, John Davis, Jon Elster, Cécile Fabre, Diego Gambetta, Grahame Lock, Ian Maclean, David Miller, Alan Montefiore, Michael Otsuka, Lee Overton, Derek Parfit, Rodney Peffer, Mark Philp, Saul Smilansky, Alan Sokal, Hillel Steiner, Tracy Strong, and Arnold Zuboff.

Chapter Six

CASTING THE FIRST STONE: WHO CAN, AND WHO CAN'T, CONDEMN THE TERRORISTS?

> No matter what the grievance, and I'm sure that the Palestinians have some legitimate grievances, nothing can justify the deliberate targeting of innocent civilians. If they were attacking our soldiers it would be a different matter.
>
> —Dr. Zvi Shtauber, Israeli ambassador to the United Kingdom, BBC Radio 4, May 1, 2003

1. PRELIMINARIES

In April 1997 my son Gideon was dining out with his then wife-to-be in the Blue Tops restaurant in the center of Addis Ababa. Suddenly, a hand grenade sailed into the room. The explosion killed one woman and it severely injured other people, but Gideon and Carol protected themselves by pushing their table over and crouching behind it. While Carol was physically unharmed, shrapnel hit and entered Gideon's right temple. It was removed three and a half years later, after it had caused bad headaches. Not only the identity but even the inspiration of the Blue Tops terrorists remains, up to now, unknown.

One year later and one country away, in Sudan in 1998, my daughter Sarah was less anonymously menaced. For she was one mile from the Khartoum factory that was said by President Clinton to be producing chemical weapons and that was bombed by Clinton in what was presented as an appropriate response to then recent anti-American terrorism in Africa. Whatever may have been the motive, or mix of motives, behind Clinton's action, the bombing of the pharmaceutical facility (which was merely *maybe also* a weapons factory) with Sarah nearby enabled me to identify with the victims of superpower military force more than a Western person normally might. Hundreds of miles away, I could fear for Sarah's fate under possible further Khartoum bombing.

These experiences caused me to ruminate more than I otherwise would have done on the similarities and differences between the little bombs of the underdog and the big bombs of the overdog,[1] and I thank you for allowing me to present some of that rumination to you today.

On May the 1st, 2003, Dr. Zvi Shtauber, who was then Israel's ambassador to Britain, said this on British radio:[2]

> No matter what the grievance, and I'm sure that the Palestinians have some legitimate grievances, nothing can justify the deliberate targeting of innocent civilians. If they were attacking our soldiers it would be a different matter.

Shtauber's statement made me angry, and I want to explain why it did so. I was not angry because I disagreed with what he said, and I shall not challenge the truth of what he said in this paper: I shall neither deny it nor affirm it, and everything that I shall say is intended to be consistent with the claim that the deliberate targeting of innocent civilians is never justified. Yet while I shall not deny what the ambassador said, I shall raise some questions about his right to say it, with the vehemence and indignation that he displayed, and in the posture of judgment that he struck.[3] A lot of people who think it impossible to justify terrorism nevertheless find condemnations of terrorism by some Westerners, and by some Israelis, repugnant. Yet if terrorism is impossible to justify, why can't just anybody at all condemn any terrorism whatsoever? I try to answer that question here.

There has been a certain amount of discussion in the literature about how to define the word 'terrorism.' But my topic is not the definition of the word. For my purposes, we can let terrorism be what Shtauber objected to, namely, the deliberate targeting of innocent civilians, for military and/or political purposes. If that is not what terrorism *is*, it is certainly what most people object to when they object to what they call 'terrorism.' And most people think, as Shtauber manifestly does, and as I do too, that deliberately targeting innocent civilians is, other things equal, morally worse than deliberately targeting soldiers.[4]

[1] Perhaps I should define the word 'overdog.' On September 4, 2003, just before 1:30 P.M., U.K. time, *The World at One*, a British news program, interviewed a spokesperson for the British arms industry (whose name I did not catch) about the then current International Arms Fair in London. The spokesperson was asked whether he did not agree that, although arms exports made money for Britain, and British people might welcome that, they would nevertheless be happier still if the same amount of money were being made through some form of *non*-arms export. He replied more or less as follows: "Not at all. British people are proud when they see Harriers and Tornadoes being used in far-flung places. Of course, if we were selling small arms, like Kalashnikovs, that would be a different matter." That man was a spokesperson for overdogs.

[2] To his *Today* program interviewer, John Humphrys, at 8:15 A.M., U.K. time.

[3] Voltaire famously said, "I disagree with what you say, but I shall defend to the death your right to say it." I am saying something closer to "I agree with what you say, but I shall attack your right to say it." OK, maybe not to the *death*.

[4] You might nevertheless have wanted me to say what I think terrorism actually is. But there is, in a sense, nothing that I think terrorism is, where 'is' is the 'is' of identity: I would affirm no

A final preliminary point. I shall assume throughout that terrorism, or at any rate the terrorism that concerns us here, effectively serves the terrorists' aims. If terrorism, or a given case of terrorism, is *anyhow* counterproductive, with respect to the aims of the terrorists themselves, then, for *practical* purposes, no questions of principle arise, since no sane person, or anyway nobody that I want to argue with, would say that some principle justifies *counterproductive* terrorism. But note that anybody who condemns terrorism *only* on the ground that it is counterproductive has conceded a large point of principle to the terrorists. The criticism that terror is counterproductive doesn't criticize it *as* terror.[5] More approved forms of violence are also sometimes counterproductive, and Shtauber's complaint was not that a course of action that includes terrorism[6] will not succeed, or that terrorism makes it harder for Israel to agree peace terms, though he would no doubt have *added* such claims, had the distinct question of the *efficacy* of Palestinian terror been raised. Shtauber's judgment was one of principle, and it is issues of principle, not difficult questions of fact, that fall under my inspection here.

The rest of my discussion is inspired by reflection on the Israeli-Palestinian conflict, although some of it has application to the confrontation between the United States and Al-Qaeda. As a left-wing Jew whose Jewishness matters to him, I am exercised, indeed, I am agonized, in the particular way that many left-wing Jews whose Jewishness matters to them are agonized, by the Israeli-Palestinian conflict. But although what I shall say is a response to the Israeli-Palestinian conflict, I offer no conclusions about that conflict: people who agree with my observations would apply them in different ways, according to their divergent further convictions. I model certain aspects of the conflict, more particularly, some aspects of the discourse that surrounds it, for the sake of philosophical discussion. But the further significance of what I have to say will depend on the answers to controversial questions of fact and principle about which I shall say nothing. I have in mind controversial factual questions about

---

English sentence of the form "Terrorism is …" of which I would say that anybody who denies that *that* is what terrorism ('is' of identity) *is* says something false. The behavior of the word 'terrorism' is too disorderly for us to be able to identify a range of its uses that could serve as canonical tests of proposed definitions of the term.

[5] It is, moreover, false that terrorism is never productive, as Michael Ignatieff economically shows: "As for the futility of terrorism itself, who could say with confidence that Jewish terrorism—the assassination of Lord Moyne and then of Count Bernadotte, the bombing of the King David Hotel, followed by selective massacres in a few Palestinian villages in order to secure the flight of all Palestinians—did not succeed in dislodging the British and consolidating Jewish control of the new state? Though terror alone did not create the state of Israel—the moral legitimacy of the claim of the Holocaust survivors counted even more—terror was instrumental, and terror worked" ("The Lessons of Terror: All War against Civilians Is Equal," *New York Times Book Review*, February 17, 2002).

[6] Note that the proper object of assessment is not terrorism but a course of action that includes terrorism, which covers courses that also include negotiation. Pure negotiation is not the only alternative to terror: the efficacy of the good cop/bad cop strategy is well understood.

what happened in 1948 and in 1967 and earlier, and later, and other factual questions about what the intentions of various parties to the conflict are now. I also have in mind difficult questions of principle, such as whether a people, or, at any rate, a massively abused people, has a right to a state, and, if so, at whose expense, and at how much of their expense. All that will be set aside here. What will not be set aside—it is crucial to the case that I shall build—is that the rights and wrongs of the Israeli-Palestinian conflict are deeply controversial: that much is surely *un*controversial. If you disagree with that assessment, if, in particular, you think that the Israeli position, on all the major issues, is uncontroversially correct, then you will find it difficult to sympathize with the line of argument in this paper.

2. WHO CAN CRITICIZE WHOM: "LOOK WHO'S TALKING"

Before we think hard about the implications of what we are saying, we may be disposed to affirm that certain conditions of extreme injustice need not be tolerated, that people may do everything within their power to remove them, or, at any rate, that the sufferers of that extreme injustice may themselves do anything that *they* can do to remove them.[7] But we are also inclined to affirm that certain means of fighting injustice should never under any circumstances be used. Yet what can we then say when our two inclinations come together because we are asked to consider circumstances that display the contemplated conditions of extreme injustice, in which the forbidden means are the *only* means available? When we acknowledge that such circumstances are possible, we are forced to *revise* some of our convictions about what morality says.

And, in what turn out to be the convictions about morality upon which we come to settle, morality might say, to some victims: "Sorry. Your cause is just, but you are so effectively deprived of all decent means of resistance by your oppressor that the only means of resistance that remain open to you are morally forbidden means." Morality might say that, because that might happen to be the sad moral truth of the matter. But can just anyone at all say that on morality's behalf, *in a posture of moral admonition*? Can the oppressor herself strike that posture? Can the oppressor, whoever that may be, and I make no assumptions about who qualifies as an oppressor here, can the oppressor get away with saying: "I am sorry. Your cause is just, but you are so effectively deprived (as it happens, by me) of all decent means of resistance that the only means open to you are morally forbidden?"

[7] The implications of the proposition would make most people recoil from it. Andrew Williams spells them out: "The view contemplated here seems to me to imply that there is an injustice so burdensome that if the only way in which I can escape it is by imposing it on others, then it is permissible for me to do so *no matter how many individuals I might have to sacrifice and how little threat they pose to me*" (private communication).

As the example of the oppressor suggests, the force, the effect, of a moral admonition varies according to who's speaking and who's listening.[8] Admonition may be sound, and in place, but some may be poorly placed to offer it. When a person replies to a critic by saying: "Where do *you* get off criticizing *me* for *that*?," she is not denying (or, of course, affirming) the inherent soundness of the critic's criticism. She is denying her critic's right to make that criticism, in a posture of judgment. Her rejoinder achieves its effect without confronting the *content* of her critic's judgment. She challenges, instead, her critic's right to *sit* in judgment, and to *pass* judgment. She could not similarly challenge a critic whom she had overheard saying, to a third party: "I of course agree that what she did was morally wrong, but I'm not myself in a position to criticize her. (It's not for me to cast the first stone.)"

Let me step back a bit. We can distinguish three ways in which a person may seek to silence, or to blunt the edge of, a critic's condemnation. First, she may seek to show that she did not, in fact, perform the action under criticism. Second, and without denying that she performed that action, she may claim that the action does not warrant moral condemnation, because there was an adequate justification for it, or at least a legitimate excuse for performing it. Third, while not denying that the action was performed, and that it is to be condemned (which is not to say: while *agreeing* that it is to be condemned), she can seek to discredit her critic's assertion of her standing as a good faith condemner of the relevant action.

I should make clear what I am not claiming, when I say that a critic may be disabled from condemning, and, therefore, in the relevant sense, may be *un*able

[8] The question, "Who can say what to whom?," goes largely unexplored in contemporary moral philosophy. To be sure, if all that moral philosophy were interested in were which acts are right and which wrong, then this phenomenon *might* deserve little attention. ("*Might*": I do not myself believe that the phenomenon carries no lessons as to what is morally right, because I believe that what, on pp. 280ff. of "Incentives," I call the "interpersonal test"—which is not employed in the present paper—has noninterpersonal moral implications.) But, insofar as moral philosophy seeks to reconstruct actual moral discourse, the widespread neglect by moral philosophy of the phenomenon described in the sentence to which this footnote is attached is unjustified, since it looms very large in moral discourse.

I myself began to examine the interpersonal dimension of moral utterances in "Incentives," and the theme was subjected to further study by Jerry Dworkin in an article called "Morally Speaking." As I said: "A [moral] argument will often wear a particular aspect because of who is offering it and/or to whom it is being addressed. When reasons are given for performing an action or endorsing a policy or adopting an attitude, the appropriate response by the person(s) asked so to act or approve or feel, and the reaction of variously placed observers of the interchange, may depend on who is speaking and who is listening. The form, and the explanation, of that dependence vary considerably across different kinds of case. But the general point is that there are many ways, some more interesting than others, in which an argument's persuasive value can be speaker-and/or-audience-relative, and there are many reasons of, once again, different degrees of interest, why that should be so" ("Incentives," p. 273: a number of illustrations of the "general point" follow the quoted paragraph).

I hope to say more about these matters in a paper called "Ways of Silencing Critics" [published as Chapter 7 of this volume—Ed.].

to condemn, the agent under judgment. I do not mean that the critic cannot be speaking the truth when she condemns the agent: it is central to the interest of the phenomenon under exploration here that she might well be speaking the truth. Nor do I mean that the critic should be forbidden, under whatever sanction, to make the relevant utterance. Whether there ought to be a legal prohibition, even whether there is a moral prohibition, on the utterance, is a somewhat separate matter.[9] What I mean is that there are facts about the critic that compromise her utterance considered as, what it purports to be, a *condemnation*: the focus is on that intended role, or illocutionary force,[10] of the utterance. If Shtauber had said, "By the way, I think what the Palestinians are doing is morally horrendous," then what I shall say about his actual and differently toned utterance would not apply. It is material to the contention that I shall lay before you that Shtauber was not merely seeking to speak the moral truth, but, precisely, to condemn, and the question is: was he well placed, as a spokesperson for Israel, to engage in that particular speech-act of condemnation? Did he have the right, the requisite standing, to condemn the Palestinian terrorists, in the terms in which he did?

This *third* way of deflecting criticism, that is, by impugning the right of the critic to condemn, is of great importance in the political world, where it matters enormously who can say what to whom, credibly and sincerely: that consideration helps to determine the fate of would-be critical political interventions. The world of politics is not populated by saints with spotless track records, but by nonsaints who have a better hope of deflecting criticism not by trying to justify what they themselves did, but by implicating their criticizing fellow nonsaints in the same or similar charges.

We often implicitly acknowledge the force of the third form of response to criticism. When someone says, "I'm not in a position to criticize him," and cites some relevant disabling fact about herself, people do not say: "But anyone can

[9] My topic is not when it's morally permissible or obligatory to condemn, and it is not part of my view that it is always bad or wrong for someone who is not in a position to condemn to condemn. I could agree with a person who said: "I really wasn't in a position to condemn him, but issuing that savage condemnation was the only way to rally others and/or to get him to stop, and that was more important than making sure that my speech-acts were in accord with my 'standing.'"

I believe that lying is in itself wrong, and that it therefore counts against an act that it is a lie, which is to say that there is something wrong with lying because of its nature, whatever its typical, or unusual-case, consequences may be. But sometimes those consequences can make it all right, or even imperative, to lie. So, similarly, here: I believe that there is something wrong with condemning unless certain presuppositions are fulfilled, but if dodgy condemning is going to save the children, then I say: "Condemn away!" It may be better that villainous superpowers condemn one another's villainies than that they remain silent about them, because that way we learn about the villainies on both sides (and, hence, *inter alia*, how poorly placed the superpowers are to condemn each other). I think one can say: "He has no right to condemn, but let us hope he does condemn," and maybe even "but he ought to do so . . ."

[10] The phrase 'illocutionary force' is J. L. Austin's: see his *How to Do Things with Words*, Lectures VII–XII.

criticize anyone, regardless of their *own* track record." If you, reader, are indeed disposed to say the latter, then you disagree with me at a very fundamental level. If you do not recognize a difference between expressing a negative moral belief and condemning, then I do not know how you would account for the peculiar force of the disavowal that is expressed by the words "I'm not in a position to criticize her."[11]

An ambiguity in the word 'criticize' may cause you to resist the distinction that I have sought to substantiate. There is certainly *a* sense of 'criticize' in which, if I express a negative moral opinion about some person, then I count as criticizing that person: the word 'criticism' can be used to name a form of opinion. But it can also be used to denote speech-acts that are, or are akin to, acts of condemnation; otherwise, so I claim, it would not make sense to say, "I think," or, indeed, "I *know*," "that what he did was wrong, but I'm not in a position to criticize him." The key point is that, when the moral capacity to criticize or condemn is undermined, the capacity to perceive and register and speak the truth is not undermined with it, from which it follows—this is, roughly speaking, the contrapositive of the key point—that being in a position to utter a well-grounded truth does not suffice for being in a good position to condemn. *Exactly* what "I am not in a position to criticize" means I do not (yet) know: I have not to date produced an explication that specifies, with satisfying precision, and in general terms, the nature of the defect in speech-acts of condemnation that is my topic, but I am confident that the quoted words signify an *explicandum* that is eminently worth explicating.[12]

Two ways of discrediting a condemning critic's standing will concern me here. They both occur widely in moral discourse, and they occur saliently in exchanges of condemnation about terrorism, and, in particular, in exchanges between Israelis and their supporters on the one hand and Palestinians and their supporters on the other.

The first of these techniques for compromising a critic's voice was signaled in my childhood by the retort "Look who's talking!" Shapiro might say, "Hey, Goldstein, how come you didn't come to the club last night? All the guys were expecting you." And Goldstein might reply: "Look who's talking. *Twice* last week, *you* didn't show up." Unless Shapiro could now point to some relevant difference, his power to condemn was compromised, whether or not the criticism he originally

[11] It may be worthwhile to distinguish some distinct ways of resisting the claims of this paper. You disagree with me most fundamentally if, as I have said, you deny the very existence of the sort of transgression of which I accuse Shtauber, if, that is, you deny that the capacity to engage in good-faith condemnation is relative to the record and/or posture of the would-be condemner. But you might accept that relativity thesis yet insist, against what I have said, that absolutely excluded acts *can* be condemned by anyone: Shtauber might then be immune to my critique. And he might also be thought immune to it for some other reason, even if one's standing *does* bear on one's capacity to condemn absolutely excluded acts.

[12] For some further attempts at explication, see my "Ways of Silencing Critics."

made of Goldstein was sound.[13] In places that are more genteel than the immigrant streets of postwar Montreal where I grew up, people do not say, "Look who's talking," but "That's the pot calling the kettle black." If I, the putatively black kettle, make that reply, under criticism, to the putative black pot, I am not denying (or, necessarily, accepting) that I am tarnished. I am saying that, since the pot is even more *whatever* it is that leads it to condemn me than I am, the pot, on its own express view of the matter, should look upon on its own hue rather than on mine.[14]

And a still more elevated epithet that occurs in the contemplated range of disabling replies is more elevated still because it is in Latin. I have in mind the sentence, "*Tu quoque*," which means, "You, too."

When Jesus said, "Judge not, that ye be not judged," and when he allowed only the sinless to cast the first stone,[15] he was invoking *tu quoque* in an extreme form. But he was not saying that the compromised judgment would be mistaken. He was, on the contrary, implying that the judgment he was forbidding would indeed be correct, yet one that *you* are not well placed to make, because it also applies to, and against, you. "Judge not, that ye be not judged" is extreme because it disempowers me as a critic as long as I am not *entirely* sinless. Contrast the other Jesus statement, about not pointing out the mote in my brother's eye when there is a beam in my own eye. Beams are larger than motes, so if, somewhat unrealistically, we take the beam/mote statement *au pied de la lettre*, then we may say that the beam/mote statement relaxes the Jesus view a bit, because it condemns judgment only from judges whose sins are *worse* than the sins of those whom they seek to judge.[16]

[13] Yet both Goldstein and Shapiro could, of course, be condemned by the conscientious club-attender Hockenstein.

[14] This is not to deny that what the pot says is true, and in some contexts, its truth will be all that matters. If the kettle had said that it was clean, what the pot says to the kettle might pass muster. But in political contexts, in contexts of political enmity, what the pot says is often discredited *even if* it is preceded by a rosy and false self-appraisal on the part of the kettle.

Compare Christopher Ricks's quip about T. S. Eliot: ". . . Ricks said Eliot's clearing Wyndham Lewis of having fascist sympathies was like the pot calling the kettle white. 'I was right and wrong to make the joke, which was quite a good joke,' says Ricks. 'If you follow it remorselessly it suggests Eliot was a fascist which I don't think he was. But he also wasn't in a position to clear other people of the accusation. There is too much that Eliot is associated with that is not without its links to fascism'" (profile of Christopher Ricks by Nicholas Wroe, *Guardian*, January 29, 2005).

Worthy of narration here is the following joke: The rabbi has left the synagogue to do some shopping, and the shammes, or, if you must, the verger, is in charge. The rabbi returns unexpectedly early, and, entering the synagogue, finds the shammes on the floor, in prayer: "Oh, Lord, thou art everything and I am nothing!" Says the rabbi: "Hah! Look who says he's nothing!"

Nietzsche said it quicker: "He who despises himself still esteems the despiser within himself."

[15] I presume here that, despite the context of that remark, Jesus intended it as advice not only about literal but also about metaphorical stone throwing.

[16] Would Jesus have allowed you to cast a stone if you first signed up for being the next victim of stone casting? Consider monks who flagellate each other. Why shouldn't the fact that we are all sinners mean that we should all criticize each other, rather than, as Jesus says, that no one should criti-

For that first type of would-be discrediting response I have three good labels: "look who's talking," "pot calling the kettle black," and "*tu quoque*." For my contrasting second type I have no good vernacular or Latin tag. But I will point you in the right direction by reminding you of retorts to criticism like "You made me do it," and "You started it," even though those phrases don't cover all the variants of the second type. I shall name the second type "You're involved in it yourself," but if anybody can think of a better name, then suggestions are welcome.

In this second type of silencing response you are disabled from condemning me not because you are responsible for something *similar* or worse yourself but because you bear at least some responsibility for the *very thing* that you seek to criticize. My Nazi superior cannot condemn me for doing what he orders me on pain of death to do, even if I *should* disobey, and accept death. I return to the second type of silencing in Section 3.

The first type, *tu quoque*, clearly plays a large role in Palestinian responses to Israeli criticism of Palestinian terrorism, and also some role in Israeli responses to Palestinian criticism of Israelis. Was I angered by Ambassador Shtauber's statement because it is vulnerable to the "look who's talking" reply? In part yes, not because I am confident that what Israel does is *as* bad as terrorism is, but because Israel so clearly has a case to answer under *tu quoque* that setting aside possible comparisons with Israeli behavior, as Shtauber sought to do, is unacceptable. He was saying to us: "*Join me*[17] in condemning them regardless of whether we're just as bad as, or worse than, they are," and that is not an invitation that anyone should accept.

The Israelis have a *tu quoque* case to answer, because they kill and maim many more people, and deprive many more still of their homes and livelihoods, than Palestinian terrorists do. To be sure, there are Israelis who are oppressed by that fact and who are highly critical of their own government, but who believe that that government may nevertheless credibly condemn Palestinian terror-

---

cize anybody? (I thank Marshall Berman for that pregnant countersuggestion.) Compare the discussion of the "inconsistency explanation" of *tu quoque* in Section 2 of my "Ways of Silencing Critics."

There is some further investigation of *tu quoque* in my "Ways of Silencing Critics." And we should also consider what might be called *counterfactual tu quoque*: "You'd do this, or worse, if you were in my shoes." Can American neocons put their hands on their hearts and declare that if their own weapons of mass destruction were somehow immobilized, say, by computer hackers, then they would nevertheless refrain from using terrorist means against their opponents, even if they thought them effective? (I set aside the claim that they have noncounterfactually used, and nourished the use of, such means in Latin America.) Can they deny that what are now terrorists might prefer to use approved weapons of mass destruction, in acceptable ways, as the United States may be presumed to have done (in discussions with terror-condemning Americans who do not condemn the United States) at Hiroshima and Nagasaki?

[17] I italicize those words, because they point to a theme that occurred to me late in the course of my work on this paper, and that needs further development. In some fashion condemners invite third parties to *join* them in condemning the condemnable, but when *tu quoque* applies to condemners, there are reasons for third parties to refuse to join them.

ism because terrorism is morally much worse than any violence that the Israeli government *itself* commits. In response to the claim that Israeli condemnation of Palestinian terror is silenced by the fact that Israelis kill many more Palestinians, and a lot more children, these Israelis argue that Israeli killing is not as bad as Palestinian killing.

Some of these Israelis invoke the principle of double effect, which distinguishes between killing innocent people as an unintended but foreseeable *side effect* of *otherwise* targeted action, and killing innocent people who *are* your target, people, that is, whom you hope and intend to kill. "Our government can condemn them," these Israelis might say, "because although our government kills *more* innocent people than they do, our government does not *aim* to kill innocent people."

Now I myself believe in the principle of double effect, or at any rate in the judgments about cases that are meant to illustrate that principle.[18] But I also believe that the only sane form of the principle of double effect is comparative, rather than absolute. I believe, for example, that, holding everything else equal, such as, for instance, the amount of justice that there is in the motivating cause, killing two hundred innocents through foreseeable side effect is actually *worse* than killing one innocent who is your target. It seems to me ludicrous for us to say that *you* committed an outrage when you set your sights on, and killed, *a* civilian with your petrol bomb, but that we did not commit an outrage when our bombing destroyed not only the Hamas leader that we were aiming at but also fifteen people that lived near him, because we merely *foresaw* that effect, without intending it. And we also have to take into account how careful combatants are to avoid killing civilians. It is possible not to *aim* at killing them yet to be utterly reckless of their safety, and it seems pretty clear that Israeli soldiers have become more reckless, in some cases willfully reckless, as the conflict has deepened.[19] And worse still than (merely) reckless side-effect killing is side-effect killing that is still not aimed at, that remains "mere" side effect, but that is expected and welcomed, because it deters potential terrorists who care about their families and their neighbors.

So it is not at all clear that Israeli criticism of Palestinian terrorism can escape the *tu quoque* rebuke by sheltering under the doctrine of double effect. But Palestinian terrorists and their apologists also face a powerful *tu quoque* challenge.

Palestinians complain that they lack a state. They complain that their rights are denied. But how can they then justify a terror that denies the right to life of innocent others? Is not the right to life more precious still than the right to a state?

[18] The diagnosis of those judgments, and whether or not they really support double effect, is controversial.

[19] If some amount of side-effect killing n is just as bad as some lesser amount of aimed-at killing m, then some amount of side-effect killing p ($m < p < n$) where recklessness is displayed would surely be just as bad as *that* amount (m) of aimed-at killing.

Palestinians might protest that they do not *aim* at innocents but only at Israelis who are complicit in causing their grievance. But no defensible doctrine of complicity, however wide may be the criteria for complicity that it proposes, will cover everybody in those Tel Aviv cafés, including the children, and the noncitizens of Israel. In face of that fact, can Palestinians claim that they are *aiming* only at the *complicit* citizens in the Tel Aviv bars, and that the other deaths are side effects? I, for one, do not find that posture credible. But how does it differ from the posture of Israeli assassination squads who blow up houses because Hamas supporters live there even when they know that innocent people who also live there will lose their homes and their livelihoods and even their lives?

In sum: I'm not sure who can point the finger at whom here, but I'm sure that it's absurd, given the uncontested facts, for either to point the finger at the other with no comment on his own glass house: and that was undoubtedly one provocation to the anger that I felt when I heard Shtauber's statement. (I should also have been angry if a Hamas leader had accused Israeli soldier-killers of a callous disregard for human life: but that isn't the example on the table.)

3. WHO CAN CRITICIZE WHOM: "YOU'RE INVOLVED IN IT YOURSELF"

So much for the case to answer that faces Shtauber under *tu quoque*: that case puts his right to condemn in question. But he has two further cases to answer under the contrasting "You're involved in it yourself" challenge. Let me first say something about "You're involved in it yourself" in general terms. After that, I'll return to Shtauber, and the two subtypes of this second type of silencing that I want to distinguish.

I said earlier that among the variants of this second way of deflecting criticism (*tu quoque* was the first) are "You started it" and "You made me do it": the reply has many variants, with "It's your fault that I did it" at one kind of extreme and "You helped me to do it" at another. And note that if it's your fault, in whole or in part, that I did it, then it can be your fault for structurally different reasons. Here's part of the relevant wide array: you ordered me to do it, you asked me to do it, you forced me to do it, you left me with no reasonable alternative, you gave me the means to do it (perhaps by selling me the arms that I needed). When such responses from a criticized agent are in place, they compromise criticism that comes from the now impugned critic, while leaving third parties entirely free to criticize that agent. The functionary who obeys Nazi orders can't be condemned for obeying those orders by the superior who issues the orders;[20] he can

[20] Note the present tense: I do not say that a reformed Nazi superior cannot condemn an unreformed lesser functionary for having obeyed him.

nevertheless be condemned by us. (When, as a child, I tried to excuse an action on the ground that someone else had *told* me to perform it, my mother, a third party, could and did reply: "So, if they told you to jump off the Empire State Building, you would do that too?")

Note, now, how this second type of challenge, "You're involved in it yourself," differs from "Look who's talking." "Look who's talking" says: "How can you condemn *me* when you are *yourself* responsible for something similar, or worse?"[21] In "You're involved in it yourself" the responding criticized person need make no judgment about whether her critic has *herself* done something similar or worse. Instead, "You're involved in it yourself" says: "How can you condemn me when you are *yourself* responsible, or at least coresponsible, for the very thing that you are condemning?" That responsibility can run from physically forcing at one end to merely abetting at the other. "You criticize me for robbing the bank, but why, then, did you willingly give me the number on the lock on the safe?"[22]

The general form of "You're involved in it yourself" is this: you are implicated in the commission of *this* very act, as its coresponsible stimulus, commander, coercer, guard, assistant, or whatever (whether or not what you did was wrong, or similar to what I did, or worse than what I did).

Let me now consider Ambassador Shtauber's statement within the "You're involved in it yourself" framework. I focus first on the concession at the opening of Shtauber's statement, the concession which says, "Your *grievance* may be just." That concession is often heard from Israelis who speak about Palestinian terror. But I believe that there can be a problem about proceeding to condemn the terrorist means after you have expressed a willingness, in principle, to concede just grievance, when you, the critic, are the *source* of the grievance, *if* there is one. I believe that whether or not the Palestinians *have* a legitimate grievance, and whether or not those Palestinians who use terrorism in pursuit of a supposed grievance are justified in doing so, Shtauber's statement is indefensible, on *his* lips, because they are the lips of a spokesperson for Israel: an Israeli spokesperson is not morally qualified to make the "no matter what the grievance" concession when it is followed by the "nothing can justify" condemnation. For you are yourself more or less implicated in the act you seek to condemn if you caused a *legitimate* grievance to which the act is a response. And how, therefore, can you reasonably expect your condemnation of the act to be received as made in good faith, unless you address the grievance of those you condemn? How can you suppose yourself to be free to set aside the size and character of that grievance,

[21] On "similar *or* worse," see "Ways of Silencing Critics," Section 1*b*.

[22] Also worthy of exploration is how and under what circumstances your involvement imposes on you a *duty* to condemn. And there may be cases in which you have both a duty to condemn and no right to do so.

and your putative role in causing it, and proceed to condemn the responsive terrorist act, as a third party freely might? If the Palestinian grievance is large, and Palestinians have no effective way of pursuing it save through a strategy that includes terror, then, even if it is not Israel that thus constrains their practical options, the putative Israeli responsibility for the grievance itself compromises what Shtauber says after he has made his concession.

One might mount the following objection to what I have claimed. Someone who imposes a grievance and thereby induces a violent response might not be able to complain that there was some sort of aggressive response, but could still condemn a particular response as *disproportionate.* If, in response to my callous snub, you shoot me in the foot, that your shooting is a response to my callous snub does not disable me from condemning it. And one might say that terrorism, because always wrong, is *a fortiori* always disproportionate, and therefore condemnable by anyone.

To this objection I have two replies. First, that the objection overgeneralizes. For, if the grievance I impose is spectacular, one that is as absolutely condemnable as is the terrorist response to it, then the fact that the latter is morally excluded does not seem to me to show that it is, in particular, a *disproportionate* response. (Suppose, for example, the imposing of the grievance is *itself* a disproportionate response to a still previous insult: the power of *tu quoque* then joins the present different disabling fact to condemn the condemnation.)

And a further reply to the objection is that some sort of discount rate applies here. Suppose responses can be calibrated on a scale of severity which runs from 1 to 10, and, in a particular case, anything over 5 would be disproportionate, and the response under examination is 6 or 7. Then a third party can, *ex hypothesi*, condemn that response, but one might nevertheless think that it needs to be, say, 8, for the provoker *herself* to condemn it. For this further reason, I do not bow to the suggested vindication of Shtauber's right to say what he did that I sketched two paragraphs back.

But there is a second and distinct way in which Israelis might be thought implicated in the terrorism that they seek to condemn. For whoever caused a particular grievance, and whatever the weight of that grievance may be, an agent who unjustifiably constrains the practical options that are available to the putatively aggrieved is not well placed to condemn the choice of an option (in our case, terrorism) that he, the constrainer, makes particularly eligible, from the point of view of the aims of the constrained. (Recall that we have legitimately supposed—see my "final preliminary point" in the paragraph accompanying n. 5 above—that the terrorist option is a particularly good one for Palestinians).

Consider a Wild West parallel. A certain varmint is deprived of his gun, when everybody else has one, because guns are standard equipment for wild westerners. Suppose it was Cal who removed the varmint's gun. If Cal now seeks to condemn the varmint's recourse to whatever it is that is worse than a gun—maybe a hand grenade—that the varmint perforce uses instead, then Cal must either justify his removal of the varmint's gun or show that its removal, even if unjustified, didn't effectively *drive* the varmint to his alternative course. If you've got somebody up against the wall, don't complain if he kicks you in the balls, unless you are prepared to say something about your own act of putting him up against the wall. (You *can* protest when a homicidal criminal that you have disarmed tries to strangle you, but that is because disarming him was justified. After all, he made you do it.)

Let me now pursue the putative—putative is enough—parallel between Cal and the varmint on the one hand and Israel and the Palestinians on the other. If you rule over a people who have no citizenship in your country, and whom you therefore deny civil democratic means of redress, if it is you, moreover, who disarmed them, and you who deprive them of weaponry that is effective against your soldiers, or at least ensure that they cannot get such weaponry, then *you* in particular cannot complain if they use unconventional weaponry against nonsoldiers, *unless* you can justify your constraining action, or show that the constraint was not substantial enough to make their action understandable. Israelis ensure that Palestinians cannot acquire conventional means of combating Israeli forces, and they therefore cannot complain that the Palestinians use other ones, *if* the Palestinians have a legitimate and sufficiently substantial grievance. If *B* claims to have a legitimate grievance, and *A*, who may not have caused that grievance, leaves *B* no effective recourse except horrible violence, or even if *A* makes such violence a strategically attractive recourse, then how can *A* in particular complain about that horrible violence, without commenting on the justifiability of his, *A*'s, constraining *B*'s options, and therefore on the status of *B*'s putative grievance (again, whether or not it was *A* himself who *caused* that grievance)? Because other people routinely carry guns, Cal has to explain why he removed the varmint's, if he wants to condemn the varmint's use of a hand grenade. And when other peoples, Israelis, Americans, British, and so forth, have "superguns," true weapons of mass destruction, then those who deprive the Palestinian people of the capacity to acquire similar weaponry must explain why they did so if they seek to condemn the Palestinian recourse to unsimilar weaponry.

Thus, and for two reasons: *even if* it is the moral truth that one should never attack civilians, in terrorist fashion, the Israelis in particular can't condemn Palestinians for attacking civilians, *regardless* of the justice of their grievance. Even if terrorism is always wrong, Shtauber's stance in condemnation of Palestinian terror is unsustainable, in the absence of an argued case against the Palestinian grievance, not because their grievance might justify terrorism (that being excluded by the *protasis* of this sentence), but because, if the Palestinians have a legitimate grievance, then it is against an Israel that *both* created their grievance *and* restricts their practical options of response.[23] Accordingly, the question of the justice of the Palestinian grievance cannot be set aside by those who deprive them of conventional means of redress in a discussion of the particular unconventional means that they use to pursue their grievance, *especially* (but not only) if those who deprive them of conventional means are *also* the unjust causers of that grievance.

The two charges against Shtauber that belong under the "You're involved in it yourself" heading—"You caused our grievance" and "You forced us to use terrorist means"—do not simply lie side by side. Though logically and practically independent, in the general case,[24] they are, in a certain manner, fused here. For consider. If the Palestinians had normal democratic sovereignty and normal civil liberty they would have a normal army which is not equipped merely to police its own people.[25] It is central to their grievance that they lack a *state*,[26] and, therefore, among other things, the approved means of violence that a state possesses. But the lack of what they would have, if they had a proper state, to wit, just such an army, contributes strongly to the explanation of their mode of pursuing their grievance. For it is only by *un*conventional means that you can pursue any grievance which includes the grievance that you lack conventional means of pursuing grievances.[27]

[23] Suppose some oppressed opponents of a state begin a campaign of liberation by attacking soldiers. But then the state gives its soldiers bulletproof armor, and, needless to say, doesn't also issue such armor to its oppressed opponents. Suppose that, as a result, the oppressed can *now* have an effect only by attacking civilians. Can they not say, tellingly, that their oppressors, in adopting the armor policy, have left them with no other recourse? *We*, the bystanders, may be able to condemn *both* coresponsible sides: the state for its armor policy, the oppressed for now attacking civilians. But how can the state condemn the oppressed, *unless* the state can impugn their grievance?

[24] By that I mean that the grievance-causer need not be the options-restricter, or vice versa: I do not mean that "You caused our grievance" is powerful even if we have many good nonterrorist options, or that "You made terror a good recourse" is powerful even if we have no justified grievance. The force of each consideration is indeed normatively dependent on the force of the other.

[25] An army which they would of course not need to use to seek to achieve an independence that they lack!

[26] Many Israelis would claim that both the Oslo agreement and Camp David offered the Palestinians a state, but that Arafat's venality and incompetence lost it for them. Palestinians counterclaim that what was offered was both constitutionally and geographically inadequate: a set of powers that amount to less than full and rightful sovereignty, within a set of "Bantustans" that did not satisfy the full and rightful Palestinian territorial claim. I take no stand on these matters here. But the Israeli case, even if sound, cannot be pressed against my criticism of Shtauber, since to raise that case is to embark on the enterprise of assessing the Palestinian grievance—and that is what Shtauber thought and sought to avoid.

[27] To be sure, there exist nonviolent unconventional means, and they are sometimes more effective than terrorism, but recall our decision (see paragraph accompanying n. 5 above) to face the challenge of a terrorism that is distinctively productive. In any case, Shtauber wasn't forbidding violence, just violence against nonsoldiers, and violence, to similar effect, against soldiers, is harder for Palestinians to achieve.

Let me expose and defend two conceptual claims that inform my thinking about the "You made it a good choice" part of the case that Shtauber has to answer. Each conceptual claim is a bit surprising, but each is, so it seems to me, incontrovertibly true.

The first truth is that your having left me with no reasonable alternative does not itself entail that I was forced to do whatever it was you left me with no reasonable alternative to, if only because I might nevertheless *not have done* that thing. If you think that sounds peculiar, then consider the following example. Suppose a highwayman credibly says, "Your money or your life," and thereby leaves his victim with no reasonable alternative to giving up his money. It does not follow that the victim will hand over the money: he might, instead, choose death, for example, out of defiance. *If* he hands over the money, then he does so because he is forced to, because he had no reasonable alternative. But he cannot be said to be forced to do it if he does not actually do it. Therefore having no acceptable alternative to doing something does not entail being forced to do that thing.

The second truth is that having no reasonable alternative to doing a certain thing does not entail being *justified* in doing that thing,[28] supposing that one *did* do it. Having no acceptable alternative to using terror may be a necessary condition of being justified in using terror, but it does not follow that it is a sufficient condition of being justified in using terror. For it might be true, I might be in the parlous position that, while I have no acceptable alternative to terrorism, terrorism is nevertheless *more* unacceptable than one or more of my *other* unacceptable courses. I might have to choose between disaster for me and a course so morally horrible that the only decent thing I can do is to choose disaster for me. But how can *you in particular* condemn me if I refuse to choose disaster for me, when it was you who deprived me of all acceptable alternatives, unless you can justify your having done so? If someone has no acceptable alternative, then there is a case to answer against whoever made that true. If the sad moral truth is that, although all of my alternatives to terrorism are unacceptable, my terrorism is nevertheless unjustified, then how, even so, can the person who deprived me of acceptable alternatives, and so drove me to admittedly unjustifiable terrorism, condemn that resort, without justifying the action that thus disabled me? That person must respond to my grievance that he left me with no acceptable alternative to a morally heinous and forbidden action. That my only way out is forbidden does not forbid me to reject *his* condemnation of me if I take that way out.

[28] I think that one reason why colossal terrorism in response to colossal injustice perplexes us is that we commonly take a person's lacking any reasonable alternative to an action *A* as justifying her doing *A*. It usually does. But not always. And realizing that helps us to think more clearly about terrorism.

Shtauber supposes himself entitled to condemn terrorist means *even if* the Israelis have made a course that includes terrorism the best course of a sorely aggrieved people whose grievance, moreover, the Israelis themselves caused. But *if* that is actually so, then he could not condemn them. So he cannot set aside as an irrelevance the question of whether it *is* so, in his bid to condemn them.

The terrorists say: "Your brutal occupation makes us use these methods." The Israelis say: "Your terrorist methods necessitate the continuation of our occupation." And each accuses the other of worse acts than what they themselves commit. These claims raise charges of "You're involved in it yourself" and "*Tu quoque*" that cannot be adjudicated in the absence of some view about who has what sort of justified grievance. But Shtauber affected a right to condemn that prescinded from all that controversial matter, and that, so I have sought to persuade you, is a right that he did not have.

4. ENVOI

Two further remarks.

(i) I have assumed, in order to expose some lines of moral principle, that Palestinian terrorism is an effective strategy. But certain nonterrorist strategies might in fact be more effective. Suicide protests which kill only the protesters might be far more effective, because of the reaction of world opinion.[29] But Shtauber couldn't decently recommend pure suicide as an alternative, even if third parties could do so. Or suppose that the Palestinians retire their anti-Israeli armed struggle and demonstrate wholly peacefully on a mass scale against the semiapartheid-semicolonial status that they are coming to have under Israeli rule. Might this not, in time, produce a potent international, and Israeli, outcry against Israeli rule? Should Ambassador Shtauber recommend that Gandhian course?

(ii) It has been a central claim of this paper that one consequence of the difference between an expression of moral opinion and a condemnation is that it might be true *both* that terrorism is to be condemned (moral opinion) *and* that some particular person is not in a position to condemn it. But equally, so it follows, the fact that someone is not in a position to condemn something does not imply that the thing is not to be condemned. So if some leftist thinks that the present Israeli government cannot condemn the Palestinian terror, then I might agree with him about that, but if, as some leftists seem to think, he also thinks it

[29] But straightforward suicide is forbidden by Islam, whereas suicide that also kills infidels or other legitimate opponents is honorable martyrdom: in which case it would be religious belief, not Israeli action, that blocks this more effective and, judged non-Islamically, more acceptable course. (I owe the suicide-without-homicide suggestion, and the comment on it in this footnote, to Diego Gambetta.)

follows that the Palestinian terrorist response cannot *be* condemned, then I part company with him at that point.

Both Shtauber and the imagined leftist believe, falsely, that, if the terrorist is blamable, then Shtauber can blame him. Shtauber concludes that he can blame the terrorist. The imagined leftist concludes that the terrorist is not blamable. Both make an invalid inference.[30]

APPENDIX—ISRAEL AND ME

I can explain something, quite a lot, of my attitude to Israel by taking you through some of my personal history.

Israel was founded in 1948, when I was seven years old, old enough to understand what it meant that Israel was being founded, young enough[31] to be enthralled by that in a childlike way. My parents were Stalinist communists, but the Soviet Union blessed Israel at its inception, and it was with no ambivalence at all that I walked beside my father, hand in hand, to the Montreal Forum, in the summer of 1948, upon which some fifteen thousand of Montreal's then probably about a hundred thousand Jews were converging, to celebrate the glorious event. "Hatikvah," the Israeli national anthem, was sung in the Forum. It affected me profoundly.

We shift to 1983, my first visit to Israel, now with my son Gideon, who was then sixteen years old. We arrived just a few days after the assassination of Emil Grunzweig, who was the first Jew to be killed (the second was Yitzhak Rabin) by a Jew because assassin and victim held different views of the Palestinian-Israeli conflict, Grunzweig's being to the left of his assailant's. I had been invited by the Van Leer Institute to give a lecture and I was quite unaware when we arrived, I hadn't known, that Grunzweig had been an active member of that institute.

Gideon and I were taken by taxi to our billet, an apartment near the Ramban. We were greeted in the apartment by a young man called "Adeeb." He gave us a note from the director of Van Leer, which said, with real warmth, that we were most welcome, and that he greatly regretted that we were coming at such a terrible time.

[30] After writing this paper, I benefited from reading Tim Scanlon's "Blame," a work in progress that distinguishes three items: blameworthiness, (the attitude of) blame, and the act of blaming. [This has since been published as chapter 4 of Scanlon's *Moral Dimensions*.—Ed.] One might say that I explore above certain contrasts between the first and the third of those. I should therefore note that, as it seems to me, much of what disqualifies the act would also disqualify the attitude, and that, as it also seems to me, a major reason why the act gets disqualified, in the relevant cases, is that it expresses a disqualified attitude.

[31] The end of what the Jesuits consider to be a person's most impressionable age.

We began to talk to Adeeb. I, in my ignorance, one could even say in my stupidity, did not realize that Adeeb was an Arab: his name should have told me that. Adeeb had beard stubble. He explained that he was unshaven because he was in mourning, and that Emil Grunzweig had been his best friend. It dawned on us somehow, or maybe the further conversation implied it, that Adeeb was a Palestinian. This made the whole context of our visit that much more weighty and moving.

The next day there was in the evening an outdoor memorial meeting for Emil Grunzweig which was held near the Knesset. Gideon and I went with Adeeb. At the end of the meeting it was time to sing "Hatikvah," the Israeli national anthem, which I had heard sung so joyously in 1948. I was conflicted. Had Adeeb not been beside me, I would have sung the song with my fellow Jews, and I wanted to sing it, but I also thought that I should not, because how could Adeeb fail to experience the song as celebrating the event that dispossessed his people? I decided it would nevertheless be dishonest not to sing, and I sang.

We come to 1998, in the month of June, when I was traveling in a car with my friends Dani Attas and Avner de-Shalit from Jerusalem to Haifa. We talked about the conflict all the way up to Haifa, and I was shown countless Israeli achievements, and many places that were now Arab-*rein* that had been summarily confiscated, and I learned a lot that I had not known about the treatment of Arabs within the pre-1967 borders. As we traveled up to Haifa I felt swells of pride, and of shame, sometimes about more or less the very same thing.

If I were in Israel today, and there was a demonstration by progressive Jews, and Adeeb and I were side by side at the demonstration, and "Hatikvah" was to be sung, I would not, I could not sing it, I could not dream of singing it.

I have not tried to justify anything here, not any past or present attitude of mine. But I believe that my present attitude is amply justified.[32]

[32] I thank Marshall Berman, Akeel Bilgrami, Paula Casal, Clare Chambers, Miriam Christofidis, Avner de-Shalit, Marcos Dracos, Jon Elster, Nir Eyal, Cécile Fabre, Diego Gambetta, Samia Hurst, Keith Hyams, Natalie Jacottet, Catriona McKinnon, John McMurtry, Avishai Margalit, David Miller, Michael Neumann, Michael Otsuka, Mark Philp, Joseph Raz, Michael Rosen, John Roemer, William Simon, Saul Smilansky, Sarah Song, Hillel Steiner, Andrew Williams, and Arnold Zuboff for illuminating comments, and Gideon and Sarah Cohen for information, and the members of the Non-Bullshit Marxism group for challenging discussion.

Chapter Seven

WAYS OF SILENCING CRITICS

Here are some notes that address two questions: (1) What, exactly, is the scope of *tu quoque*? When does it have force? (2) What *explains* that force? How, exactly, does *tu quoque* disable moral condemnation, in the general case?

1. WHAT IS THE SCOPE OF *TU QUOQUE*?

a. The Strong Jesus View. Tu quoque possesses very wide scope under the doctrine that Jesus affirmed when he said: "Let he who is without sin cast the first stone." By our current lights, that admonition against admonishing, taken literally,[1] disables too indiscriminately. Few of us think that no one can call the kettle black who has committed sin of *any* kind. Most people believe that I could say to you without strain, "I know I'm not perfect, but I wouldn't do a thing like *that*": *pace* Jesus, I could *willingly* expose *myself* to the judgment the prospect of which is supposed by him to deter me from judging you, when he says, "Judge not, that ye be not judged." And maybe I can, in some circumstances, call you a complete swine even when I confess that I'm one too. But it is another matter, and this touches politics, whether I can do so with the vigorous *indignation* that would standardly accompany such a remark. Perhaps I could only say it cynically,[2] and that has a strong bearing on how you could be expected to receive it.

I now consider two ways of narrowing the scope of *tu quoque*, each of which modifies and moderates the strong Jesus view.

[1] I shall interpret Jesus's utterances as literally as possible, within the bounds of reason. That is certainly one traditional way of interpreting him, and in any case what he meant doesn't matter, because I'm not claiming his *authority* for anything. Whether He (or he) was a true (or a false) Messiah is irrelevant to my purposes.

[2] Editor's note: Here Cohen writes, "As Broderick Crawford does, in the last line of *Born Yesterday*." Cohen may instead have had in mind Howard St. John's response to Crawford's last line in that film from the fifties. The exchange is as follows:

> Crawford: How d'ya like that! He could've had a hundred grand. She could've had me. Both wind up with nothin' … Dumb chump! … Crazy broad!
>
> St. John: [raises a glass as a toast] To all the dumb chumps and all the crazy broads, past, present, and future, who thirst for knowledge and search for truth … who fight justice and civilize each other … and make it so tough for crooks like you … [Crawford stares at him angrily] … *and* me.

b. The Modified Jesus View: My Sins Are Smaller. When speaking of casting stones, Jesus said that you must be *sinless* to condemn. The first contraction of the scope of *tu quoque* that I shall consider says that you can condemn only if your sins are smaller, perhaps substantially smaller, than those of the person you seek to condemn. Call that the "less sin" (or the "quantity") view. On the "less sin" view, we shall think that the boss who cheats on his income tax on a grand scale lacks the standing to condemn the secretary who pilfers petty cash insofar as we think of large-scale income tax cheating as *at least as bad* as a little pilfering. The suggested scope of *tu quoque* is formulated in this principle, which is more permissive than the strong Jesus view, namely: criticize only those who sin *more* than you do, do not criticize if you sin more than the person you're criticizing does. If, somewhat unrealistically,[3] we take Jesus literally, we may note (as I did in "Casting" [Chapter 6 of this volume—Ed.]) that he *also* propounds the weaker, quantity, doctrine. For, after he has delivered the "Judge not" (at all) prescription, he says this:

> And why beholdest thou the mote that is in thy brother's eye, but considerest not the beam that is in thine own eye? Or how wilt thou say to thy brother, Let me pull out the mote out of thine eye; and, behold, a beam is in thine own eye. Thou hypocrite, first cast out the beam out of thine own eye; and then shalt thou see clearly to cast out the mote out of thy brother's eye.[4]

c. An un-Jesus View: My Sins Are Different. An alternative narrowing of the don't-cast-stones doctrine says that you can condemn only if your sins are different in character from those of the person under judgment. Call that the "different sin" (or the "quality") view. It says that I am entitled to criticize you as long as I'm not guilty of the *same* sin as you are, even if I commit a graver sin of another kind. On this view, I might credibly say, "Yes, I know that I raped, and I know that's worse, but I nevertheless deplore your shabby pilfering." Defending the quality view, Gerald Dworkin writes: "It is not a matter of one's relative purity, so that what is inappropriate is the less pure criticizing the more pure. What seems crucial is that the fault one is criticizing is the very same fault one has."[5]

I have two comments on Dworkin's proposal. The first comment concerns the individuation of faults: note that, in order to apply Dworkin's proposal, we

[3] See n. 4 below.

[4] Matt. 7: 3–5. I presume, here, that beams are bigger than motes. But Jesus can't mean the mote/beam contrast literally (quite apart from the fact that he is not an ophthalmologist). For he seems to want nobody to condemn anybody, yet he can't think that each person's sins are worse than those of anybody whom he might seek to condemn.

[5] "Morally Speaking," p. 185. [All subsequent parenthetical page references in this chapter are to Dworkin's paper.—Ed.] Dworkin speaks of *faults* (presumably of character) rather than, as I have done, of sinful (or faulty) actions. I ignore this difference for the time being: but see Section 1*d* below.

have to know when to count faults as *different* (in kind).[6] And my second comment, which will be entered under heading (2) below, concerns Dworkin's explanation of *why* fault-similarity generates moral incapacity, which I believe to be inconsistent with his view that identity and difference of fault are of the essence in *tu quoque*.

First, then, by what criterion do we decide that two or more actions display the *very* same fault? Pilfering from petty cash, it might universally be agreed, is the same fault as pilfering from the lunch fund, but are they also the same fault as cheating on income tax, which is pilfering from the public purse? And is pillaging a form of pilfering? Faults count as the same or not depending on the level of generality at which they are described. What's the *right* level of generality, for the purposes of applying Dworkin's same-fault test?

In response to this problem, Dworkin might abandon his claim that the fault has to be the *same* one in favor of a graded version of the "different sin" principle. He might say that the higher the level of generality to which we must recede to affirm sameness of fault, the less damage there is to the critic's capacity to criticize that he commits the same fault. And perhaps that is a satisfactory reply to the individuation problem. It is not out of the question that the disablement that we are trying to characterize should come in degrees.

d. The Scope of Tu Quoque. What, then, is the scope of *tu quoque?* What is the truth of this matter, the quantity view, the quality view, or some hybrid?

Note, first, that sameness of fault, in a merely qualitative sense, can't be the *whole* story. For it surely bears on my capacity to criticize you that I have stolen or caused harm or created mayhem much *less* than you have. Quantity of sin certainly matters *within* a single category of sin. Is it plausible to think that it doesn't matter *at all* across categories?

Whatever the answer to that may be, sameness of sin seems also to play its own separate role. I criticize you for pilfering. You say: "But you're pilfering too." I can't now reply: "Don't change the subject." But if you say: "But you *raped*," maybe I *can* say: "Don't change the subject." If I can, then that supports Dworkin's quality view.

But we have to ask, as we have not done thus far, what *is* the subject that might or might not be changed, by various *tu quoque* ripostes? We have to distinguish, for example, between, on the one hand, a full review of your character (which will look ridiculous if I am sternly critical but also, and beknownst to both of us, a much worse person than you are) and, on the other hand, evalu-

[6] What Dworkin means, by "very same fault," is "very same *kind* of fault" rather than "very same *metaphysically particular* fault": he discusses "*tu quoque*" only, and not also "you're involved in it yourself" [see Sections 2 and 3 of Chapter 6 of this volume—Ed.], where the very same fault, or untoward proceeding, is at issue.

ation of a particular act. I could say, "Look, that's *not* the way to treat a beggar. Whatever the comparison between our characters in general may be, *that's* crass and contemptuous." Can't I say that even if I'm a bank robber who's willing to kill people (for whom I have no contempt) who are in my way?

2. WHAT EXPLAINS THE FORCE OF *TU QUOQUE?*

There is an inconsistency between Dworkin's "different fault" principle and his explanation of that principle. His account of *why* I am disabled from criticizing if I display the same fault seems to defeat the quality view.

Dworkin asks: "Why should moral discourse have this feature? What point or purpose is secured by requiring that the person launching a criticism not be guilty of the same fault?"[7] (p. 185). He answers as follows:

> When the person who calls attention to my character fault suffers from the very same fault, this puts him on a par with me—with respect to this fault at least. If I lose respect in his eyes because of the presence of this fault, he must lose respect in my eyes as well. But this means that I do not care as much whether he disapproves of my conduct. And this means that the criticism cannot be as effective as it normally would have been. (p. 187)

But, whether or not corrosion of respect is indeed the operative mechanism in *tu quoque* disablement, the respect consideration does not go well with the "different fault" account of the scope of that disablement, since a critic's fault need *not* be comparable in character to that of the agent he criticizes for the critic to lose that agent's respect. If you raped, whereas I merely pilfered, I have better reason to lose respect for you than I would have if you, too, had merely pilfered.

There is, then, an inconsistency between Dworkin's answer to his p. 185 question and his denial (see text accompanying n. 5 above) of the relevance of relative purity. The inconsistency is that if I am *less* pure than you, because, for example, I raped and you merely pilfered, then my criticism of your pilfering should fail, even if I haven't pilfered, since, according to Dworkin's explanation of the force of *tu quoque*, the key point is that you have reason not to respect my moral voice. One cannot hold *both* that I may criticize as long as my sins are different *and* that I may criticize only if I can retain your respect. For you may have good reason to disrespect a critic who is *generally* a swine, even if she

[7] I note in passing that Dworkin's second question is posed insufficiently generally, because the *tu quoque* device need not have a particular point or purpose: it might instead be justified by some form of *incoherence* in the stance it condemns. (Note that one would not ask what the point or purpose is of forbidding Mooreanly paradoxical utterances of the form "*P*, but I do not believe that *p*.") And in fact Dworkin's *own* answer to his question seems to me to be of the latter kind: it doesn't purport to identify a purpose that the practice of not accepting criticism from co-offenders serves.

exhibits impeccable behavior within the dimension in which she is criticizing you. *If* the facts about respect that Dworkin cites explain the force of *tu quoque*, then Dworkin's "same fault" account of the scope of *tu quoque* can't be correct.

But now let us ask: *is* respect of the essence? What role does it play in *tu quoque*? Note, first, that if I criticize you for a peccadillo that I, too, commit, it would be disproportionate to say that you should lose your respect for me: we may all respect each other even though we all know we all commit peccadilloes. But it might nevertheless be absurd to criticize you, in a certain style, for committing a peccadillo that I, too, commit.

And does it really disqualify me as a critic of your pilfering that I rape? (What if I'm raping *while* you're doing the pilfering that I'm criticizing?) And if it doesn't disqualify me, is that because disrespect doesn't disqualify or because, *even* if you have raped, you continue to merit my respect *as* a morally evaluating human being? On that view, disrespect of a kind that Dworkin cannot mean might well disqualify, but *such* disrespect is never in place: Dworkin cannot mean by "disrespect" that disrespect which consists in not giving the respect that is due to a person as such, since my moral track record does not affect my title to *that* respect.

Perhaps what explains the force of *tu quoque* is nothing directly to do with respect but something to do with a certain form of inconsistency. Suppose *A* and *B* have both committed the same crime, but I indignantly condemn *A* only. Isn't my condemnation of *A* suspect, unless I can supply a pertinent distinction between *A* and *B*? To what extent is the force of *tu quoque just* the force of rejection of that sort of arbitrary selection, in the special case where I am *B*? Is *tu quoque* forceful in just the way that *illa quoque* is?

For an example of such arbitrary selection, consider the report on the front page of the *Guardian* for September 17, 2004, of the protest by some Tory MPs against the then recent rough handling of pro-fox(etc.)-hunting demonstrators[8] outside the Palace of Westminster and the reply it got from Peter Hain, the Labour Leader of the House of Commons: "Some are angry with what Tory Alan Duncan called the 'lippy, surly, provocative and menacing' way the police handled the pro-hunt demonstration. Sir Nicholas Winterton called the police tactics 'horrific, excessive'. Mr. Hain said that if the protesters had been miners during the 1984–85 strike the MPs would not have condemned the police." No reply from Duncan or Winterton was reported.

The condemnation is rejected because of its motivated selectiveness: a condemnation that displays motivated selection condemns itself. Contrast the effect of such selectiveness when the selfsame utterance is assessed for truth, namely, nil: you do not fail to state the truth by failing to state the whole (relevant) truth.

[8] That is, antifox (etc.) demonstrators.

The "inconsistency" explanation of the force of *tu quoque* locates that force in a certain form of *hypocrisy*. Dworkin calls "making a criticism of another along a dimension on which one is itself at fault" "hypocrisy" (p. 184). But he doesn't specify the kind of hypocrisy that he means, and, whatever the right explanation of the force of *tu quoque* may be, it's not clear that critics vulnerable to *tu quoque* are vulnerable because they display hypocrisy of one central kind, namely, the hypocrisy that approximates, or is cousin to, lying. If hypocrisy in that sense were the issue, if the critic's moral incapacity related to his failure to *avow* that he himself commits a similar or worse sin, then his moral incapacity should disappear, his standing should be restored, if he precedes his criticism with a concession, in which he confesses to a similar and/or greater sin.[9] But does he not *still* fall subject to the *tu quoque* charge if he *admits* his ongoing equivalent or worse sins, and thereby escapes the contemplated charge of hypocrisy? Is his stance now not just more *manifestly* absurd? Or is the disability under discussion indeed eliminated, or at least reduced, where appropriate *self*-criticism precedes (we could call it "preemptive me, or *ego, quoque*") or accompanies criticism of the relevant other? If so, then it is an interesting question whether indignation can then be in place, and if so, against whom, where the possible answers are "nobody," "oneself only," "the other," and "both." At the high tide of Stalinism, Communist Party branch meetings in Montreal (and no doubt elsewhere too, but I'm telling you what I happen to know about) would end with a (usually short) period called, on the agenda, "Criticism and Self-criticism." As a small child I sometimes sat in the corner of such meetings, and I was amazed when, at one of them, a certain J. L. said, with some indignation, that the club had of late been quite bad at recruiting new members, and that he thought he himself in particular was one of the worst offenders. Was I right to be amazed, or should I have been merely surprised?

Whether or not an equal sinner can level criticism laced with an "*ego quoque*" *with indignation*, some will think that a critic like J. L. does indeed presilence the criticized person's *tu quoque* if he says, "I know I'm just as bad, but I do think it was awful of you to do that." Even so, the criticism part is not acceptably utterable *without* the accompanying concessive admission, and that has some *political* relevance: for imagine the effect on politicians' criticisms of each other if politicians routinely *added* the fault-avowing concessive phrases. Such a practice might bring even politicians into disrepute! (Can one say: "Don't be a sinner like me. Don't attack noncombatants"? No Israeli politician could say that.)

[9] Dworkin doesn't seem to address the strategy of concession. He considers additional remarks that might protect the critic against *tu quoque* (see p. 184, 1 through 4), but not that one. In the light of the power of certain remarks to silence a *tu quoque* response, he writes: "A more accurate way of formulating the issue, then, is that there is an initial inappropriateness that calls for some kind of further clarification to remove. My question is what accounts for the initial situation" (p. 184). But are we still in the "initial" situation when the concession ("of course, I'm just as bad") has been added?

3. CONCLUDING REMARKS

My discussion of *tu quoque* has rambled, but we should not expect a compelling account of *tu quoque* to be forthcoming in advance of some measure of debate about this largely undiscussed matter. At this stage, we are in danger of suffering from the philosophical disease that was diagnosed by Ludwig Wittgenstein at paragraph 593 of the *Philosophical Investigations*, the disease that is due to "a one-sided diet: one nourishes one's thinking with only one kind of example." In any case, it requires more imaginations than mine alone to generate the range of examples that we need to have before us if we are to extract good answers to questions (1) and (2). My own prediction is that, after appropriate discussion, a hybrid view, in which each of quantity and quality plays some role, would emerge in answer to question (1), and that both respect and consistency would feature in answer to question (2).

I remark, finally, that a general skepticism about the force of *tu quoque* might fix on the curious utterance "Do as I say, not as I do." But is that really an acceptable thing to say, even when it means neither "Do as I (now) say, not as I did" nor "Our different positions entitle us to different behavior. (I am, after all, your parent)"? Consider the difference between "Do as I say, not as I do" and "I think you ought to do as I say, not as I do." That is more coherent, because I am not now *telling* you to do it. For how can I credibly *tell* you to do it unless I also tell myself to do it, and how can I present myself as telling myself to do it, if I don't do it? By contrast, I might certainly *believe* that I, like you, ought to do it, but fail, akratically, to do it.[10]

APPENDIX—
THE TERRORIST THREAT IN LIBERAL DEMOCRACIES

Many people who live in what are called (albeit, often, optimistically) liberal democracies now ask themselves this question: how much restriction on civil liberty does the threat of terrorism justify? I did not consider that question in "Casting," nor did I consider questions in the neighborhood of that question, questions about the meaning and value of security. Instead, I entered the neighborhood of, without frontally addressing, a different question, one that faces many of those who live in what are uncontroversially *non*liberal *non*democracies. The question they face is not: how much restriction on civil liberty does the threat of terrorism justify, but: how much terrorism does *lack* of civil liberty justify? If you lack civil liberty, and therefore cannot pursue your political goals

[10] An unwillingness to acknowledge the asserted contrast is at the heart of R. M. Hare's metaethics: see, especially, chapter 3 of his *Freedom and Reason*.

by civil means and methods, how uncivil are your means and methods allowed to be? That question arises more sharply for Palestinian people than it does for British people.

Let me now, however, offer some reflections about the unaddressed question, to wit, how much restriction on civil liberty does the threat of terrorism justify?

In order to answer the stated question, in its general form,[11] we have to decide the right rate of exchange, as far as our values are concerned, between amounts of security, at various levels,[12] and amounts of civil liberty. We need at least part of the answer to the general question in order to answer this more particular question: if, before 9/11, we had this much security and that much liberty, and if that constituted the right balance, then how much liberty should we *now* be willing to sacrifice to ensure how much security?

Now, there are three possibilities here. The first possibility is that we can express both the value of liberty and the value of security in the currency of a common further value, or further values, values that will settle the proper exchange rate between liberty and security. Perhaps, for example, each of liberty and security is valuable because it serves the value of human welfare, or the values of human welfare and human self-realization. But it is also, and contrastingly, possible that we *cannot* so reduce the competing values of security and liberty to more fundamental ones, because each of security and liberty is *fundamental* for us. (I ignore other possibilities here, because they raise no issues of independent current interest. One would be that one of liberty and security is fundamental and one is not. Another would be that they are both reducible, but to *different* fundamental values.) If we cannot effect the mooted reduction, then the exchange rates of security and liberty are not only independent of further value but also, and consequently, independent of fact: I say "consequently" because facts settle general trade-off rates between values only in the light of further values.[13] And, after general trade-off rates have been settled independently of fact, the facts *then* weigh in, to determine what is the best *actualizable* package, in the light of those general trade-off judgments that have nothing to do with actuality, just as properly formed indifference curves across bundles of commodities are independent of their prices.[14] If, on the other hand, the first possibility is satisfied, and the contemplated reduction to further value(s) is sound, then facts affect *both* the *general* trade-off judgments between liberty and security, *and*, as before, the actual determinate choice, and the *a priori* component in the judg-

[11] As opposed to in its particularized form, where it asks how much restriction on civil liberty the threat of terrorism justifies here and now.

[12] "At various levels": the phrase is required because the relevant function is pretty certainly not rectilinear, with, for example, one unit of loss of liberty always requiring two units of gain in security, regardless of how much liberty and security we currently have.

[13] See my *Rescuing Justice and Equality*, pp. 269 and 272.

[14] See ibid., p. 272.

ment relocates itself at the level of affirmation of the governing more fundamental value(s) (or some even *ur*-er value(s) that it (or they) reflect).

There is a facile view of these matters of which the following statement is representative, a view that tends towards a denial that a trade-off between liberty and security might be necessary: "The only way to fight terrorism is surely not to become like the states and organisations that seek to destroy us: what good is victory if all we have done is become just like our opponents?"[15] Before the recent prodigious terror, before 9/11, we already had *a* security problem, because we had to protect ourselves against crime, and, for that matter, against the threat of nonprodigious terror, and we consequently already had *less* civil liberty than we might have allowed ourselves if we had had *no* security problem: our rules of civil liberty were already shaped in deference to the need to contain the pre-9/11 less awesome menaces. Now *if* the trade-off that we struck in the pre-9/11 past was right, then it would surely be rational, if the gain in security were sufficiently great, to give up a bit *more* civil liberty now that the threat to security is more severe. Few people could think that we had already in the past reduced liberty to a lexically prior minimum, that is, that we had expanded restrictions on liberty to the maximum that is morally tolerable.

Civil liberty isn't something we either simply have or simply lack. Like security, there can be more or less of it. To be sure, it is possible that the right exchange rate between liberty and security in our present more testing circumstances justifies no *further* reduction in liberty, or even an *enhancement* of it. But that has to be shown by sober judgments of what's worth sacrificing for what, and measured judgments of fact. Yet if Gearty's statement were true, all the difficult questions that 9/11 might be thought to raise could be swept aside.

[15] Conor Gearty, "Cry Freedom," *Guardian*, December 3, 2002. Gearty is a professor of human rights law at LSE.

Chapter Eight

RESCUING CONSERVATISM: A DEFENSE OF EXISTING VALUE

Attributed to Ludwig Wittgenstein: "I don't mind what I eat, as long as it's always the same."

Uttered by Morrie Cohen, and heard by me, many times, from around 1950 to 1985: "It's not like it was."

HEGELIAN PRELUDE

Hegel says that "Spirit" achieves freedom when the subject finds itself in its own object, so that "it is at home with itself in its own otherness as such."[1]

This essay explores modes of finding oneself in the other. I am not here interested in the characterization of that condition as freedom, not because that is an unimportant aspect of Hegel's claim—it *is,* after all, his claim—but just because I fry other fish here. The conservatism that I defend is Hegelian to this extent: in each of three cases that I shall distinguish, namely, that of accepting the given, of valuing the valuable, and of valuing the valued, the subject is at peace with the object.

For me, it is a pregnant moment in the New Testament when Jesus, awaiting his arrest in the Garden of Gethsemane and foreseeing the toils to come, cries out, "Oh, Lord, take away this cup," but then corrects himself: "but not my will, Lord, thine." The motif is abandonment of striving, of seeking a better state, and instead going with the flow, as do the lilies of the field, which are at peace with the world, and therefore with themselves. There is a connection, as yet to be mapped, between the conservatism that I defend, and cherish, and the Gethsemane idea.

[1] [This is a quotation from the beginning of chapter 8 ("Absolute Knowledge") of Hegel's *Phenomenology of Mind.* Cohen slightly altered J. B. Baillie's translation of the passage, by adding "own" before "otherness as such." The original is "in *seinem* Anderssein als solchem bei sich ist."—Ed.]

1. INTRODUCTION

> "Professor Cohen, how many Fellows of All Souls does it take to change a lightbulb?"
>
> "Change?!?"

The present paper defends the attitude that I just expressed in my answer to that question. I have for decades harbored strongly conservative, that is, strongly small-c conservative, opinions, on many matters that are not matters of justice, and I here mount an exposition and the beginnings of a defense of what I believe to be my widely, although perhaps not universally, shared, conservative attitude.

I do not have conservative views about matters of justice. Conservatives like me want to conserve that which has intrinsic value,[2] and injustice lacks intrinsic value[3]—and has, indeed, intrinsic disvalue. I also promote the distinct claims of what I shall call personal value, but I do not endorse the personal valuing of injustice. (I shall say something in Section 7 about the relationship between small-c conservatism and large-C Conservatives, many of whom are indeed devoted to conserving injustice.)

I am a kind of conservative not only in that I have the strong small-c conservative *attitude* that I shall describe, but also in that I endorse certain conservative *factual* assessments according to which a lot of valuable things have been disappearing lately. I join the ranks of the complainers down the ages who say: "Things ain't what they used to be."

Do not suppose that, because that lamentation is perennial, it is misplaced. Anticonservatives say, "But people have always said that things are getting worse," and anticonservatives mean thereby to convey that the conservative lamentation expresses an illusion.[4] But it is entirely possible that at any rate certain *kinds* of things have *always* been worse than they were before. A wise Hungarian was once asked how things were going for him. He replied: "How are things going for me? Oh, you know, things are about average. Not as good as yesterday, better than tomorrow." In fact, I think lots of good *old* things are being lost and lots of good *new* things are arriving. It is the conservative disposition, in the present sense of "conservative," to lament the first fact more than nonconservatives do. But, and as I will explain in Section 3, it does not follow that a person who is conservative in the present sense welcomes the second fact—that lots of good

[2] Which is the value that something has in itself, independently of its consequences, including its consequences for human utility and edification. Not everybody believes that there exists intrinsic value, within the meaning of the foregoing sentence, but my principal opponents in this essay, whom I confront in Section 3 below, share my belief in its existence.

[3] It certainly sometimes has extrinsic value: slavery, which is an injustice, helped to build the (intrinsically valuable) pyramids.

[4] For a particularly (albeit predictably) intelligent elaboration of such skepticism about conservative factual assessments, see Bernard Williams, "Modernity and the Substance of Ethical Life."

new things are arriving—less than nonconservatives do.[5] In any case, there will be no defense of my conservative factual assessments in what follows.

Please bear in mind throughout that I am trying here to describe, in an attractive light, *one* kind of conservative disposition, that is, my own. It is indeed my own disposition, and if I did not have it I would not have been motivated to write this essay, but I think that this disposition of mine is not an eccentric one: I think that everyone who is sane has *something* of this disposition, even if the people that I call conservatives here have a sturdier form of the disposition than others do. But let me add that I do not claim that the *word* "conservative" is more closely associated with the particular disposition that I shall describe than it is with every other disposition. The only claim that I make about the *word* "conservative" is that it applies without strain to the attitude that I shall describe, whatever the relationship of that attitude may be to conservatism more broadly understood: there is some attention to that theme in Section 3(ii) below.

This is my first foray into this territory, and, if it seems to you that I am making some big mistake somewhere, or indeed throughout, then do not conclude that *you* are failing to see something. The probability is greater that it is *I* who am failing to see something. Making big mistakes is something that even the best philosophers do at early stages of research in philosophy. Therefore, *a fortiori*, it is something that I do, at *least* at early stages of my work on a theme.

A final preliminary remark. In this essay I seek to identify some conservative truths that bear on choice and that, so I think, are too often neglected in our practical deliberations and that are certainly widely neglected in our philosophical deliberations about our practical deliberations. But please do not expect me to say to what *extent* our practice should honor the truths that I hope to expose, in comparison with other truths the honoring of which sometimes conflicts with honoring what I perceive to be certain conservative truths.

Philosophers often have something novel to say about what, as it were, ingredients should go into the, as it were, cake even when they can say nothing about the proportions in which these ingredients, or values, are to be combined, across different cases: not because that is not important, but because the problem simply does not yield to general recipe making. Philosophers sometimes end their articles by saying this sort of thing: it is a task for future work to determine the *weight* of the consideration that I have exposed. Yet nobody ever gets around to that further work. Many wish they could, but nobody knows how to do it.

Although philosophers cannot produce the weighing that is necessary in any practical discussion, their disposition to notice things in ordinary experience that other people miss means that they can nevertheless make a contribution to

[5] Except insofar as the new things might crowd out the old: it is a shame when Wren's City churches are surrounded by ugly skyscrapers. But note, too, that new things sometimes (albeit more rarely) enhance the presentation of old things.

an immediately practical question. They can contribute by identifying a value that bears on choice and that is being neglected. Consider an analogy. A bunch of us are trying to decide which restaurant to choose. Suppose everybody talks a lot about how good the food is in various restaurants, how much it costs, and how long it takes to get there. Someone, hitherto silent, is uneasy. She feels that we have been leaving something out of account. Then she realizes what it is: "Like, nobody," she says, "is considering the decor!" This person has made a significant contribution to our practical discussion. But we should not expect her now also to say exactly how important a restaurant's decor is compared to the other things that matter when we are choosing a restaurant.

2. KEEPING VALUABLE AND VALUED THINGS AS THEY ARE, AND ACCEPTING THE GIVEN

It is a gross truth that my college, All Souls College, is a self-funding institution, which lives on its own endowment, and which is consequently unbeholden to any outside institutions.[6] For very much the most part, its Fellows, its member-scholars, rely on nothing but the college for the funding of their research and, indeed, of their lives. No money comes into the college,[7] and, apart from modest charitable donations, almost no money goes out of it to anybody other than its Fellows (including its Visiting Fellows).[8]

Some Fellows have challenged both sides of our practical insularity. They have proposed that the college should establish a relationship with outside sources of funding, such as the Ford Foundation, and also that it should create short-term research associations between Fellows and academics in other institutions, without admitting them to any sort of college Fellowship. These Fellows think that the chief aim of the college, which is the promotion of research, might be better realized under these less insular arrangements, in which we give more to and take more from the outside world.

My gut reaction to these proposals is negative on the Ford Foundation side and cautious on the institutional collaborations side. And my brain reaction, also negative, and/or cautious, is as follows. I do not *dis*believe that research

[6] The truth is thereby stated merely grossly, because, although not, strictly, a part of it, we have certain important relations with Oxford University. But, in our relation to Oxford University, we are, in Hegel's words, "at home with ourselves in our own otherness as such," and *that*, Hegel said, is when spirit is free.

[7] A semiexception to this generalization arises out of the fact that the college plays host to certain university posts: it quarters and feeds their occupants. Their salaries come from the university, but that does not count as *alien* money (see n. 6) funding a college activity.

[8] Once again, there is the semiexception created by a University of Oxford taxation scheme under which richer colleges subsidize poorer ones. The scheme makes us a bit less rich, but it does not prejudice our independence, and the money isn't exactly going *out*: see n. 6.

would be promoted by the proposed changes. Rather, I challenge a presupposition of the anti-insular argument, which is that everything that we justifiably decide to do may and must be justified as conducive to some good that our decision might produce. For, in addition to the consideration of what good we might do, which must of course affect our decisions, there is also the consideration of what we *are*, of our identity, and we may legitimately have regard to our desire to preserve that identity.[9] I believe that it belongs to the identity of All Souls, to *our central organizing self-conception*, that we are an independent institution that is governed by its members without any appreciable outside influence. And I believe that it is worth preserving that status not only because it satisfies the legitimate desires of many of us but also because All Souls is a valuable social creation, partly *because* of what makes it different from otherwise similar social creations. As a valuable social creation, it merits preservation, and a radical enough transformation would induce both deformation of our identity and, with that, a loss of (some of) the distinctive value that the college embodies. Vigorous engagement with external agents and agencies, on both the receiving and the giving ends, might cause or begin too radical a transformation.

Note, further, that to believe that All Souls should be preserved in its distinctiveness is not to believe that it is the only beautiful flower in the garden. It is not to believe that an academic institution that maximizes what is to be got from foundations does not also have its own distinctive value. On the contrary: the conservative attitude is at least de facto congenial to variety, because much variety reflects accident, and conservatism is constitutively friendly to the results of accidents (because of its tenderness towards already *existing* value and therefore to whatever value merely *happens* to exist: I shall say more about that in Section 3 below).

Two arguments are ingredient in what I have said in favor of All Souls keeping itself (more or less) as it is, in the stated respect. One is that it is the legitimate desire of its members to preserve their particular corporate identity. The other is that All Souls is a valuable creation that everyone, therefore, and not just the college's members with their particular desires, has reason to wish to see preserved, with its distinctive value intact.

The two arguments correspond to a distinction between two ways of valuing something other than as a pure function of the *amount* or *type* of value that re-

[9] That is, not who we are, which is our identity in the austerely metaphysical sense, but what we are, which is our identity in the vaguer but very important sociocultural sense that I try to formulate in the italicized words in the next sentence of the main text above.

I do not say that anything that has an identity has a reason to preserve it: I am happy to accept that if All Souls were a bad thing, there would be no good reason for anyone, including its members, to keep it going in its present state. And there was no case for preserving that (no longer extant) aspect of its identity which was that it excluded women. But none of that implies that the whole reason to keep the college going is the good that it produces.

sides in it. In the first way of valuing that I have in mind, a person values something because of the special relation of the thing to that person.[10] In the second way, a person values something *as* the *particular* valuable thing that it is, and not merely for the value that resides in it, but not, in this second case, because of her own special relationship to the thing in question. "Particular valuing" is discussed in Section 3, and "personal valuing" in Section 4.

As I said, both of these valuings, valuing the personal and valuing the particular, as such, value a thing other than solely on account of the amount and type of value that resides in the thing. But that is so for contrasting reasons in the two cases. It is true of valuing the personal, because what is then valued need not have *any* intrinsic value,[11] or, if it does have intrinsic value, it need have only little, in comparison to the amount of personal value that it has. And it is true of valuing the particular because, even though the particular indeed *gets* its value, in the first instance, from the intrinsic value that it has, our valuing of it, the particular, is not merely a valuing of the intrinsic value that it has, but also a valuing of *it*, the particular itself.

Its personal value for us and its particular value for anyone are not the only considerations that should govern our decisions about the future direction of All Souls. But it must be wrong to omit them from consideration. Because the college is a valuable human creation, it is not right to treat it as a mere means for the production of good results, as we do if we ask *only* what is the best that can be got out of it, or the best that can be made of it,[12] just as that is not the only question that we should ask about a human being; and there is additional reason for it not to be the only question when the human being is oneself (or when one is part of the human creation in question).

Just as you may love people because of who and what they are, rather than *just* for the value of what they produce and for the value of what they instantiate, so you may love a lovable institution because it is the institution that it is and it possesses the character that it has. So if you seek to set the agenda for an institution, you must ask not only what its goals are and should be, and how it may best achieve them, but also what it, the institution, *is*. And you have, once again, additional personal reason to do so, reasons of specifically personal value, when you, collectively, constitute the institution in question.

[10] The importance of personal valuing, in the stated sense, was brought to my attention by David Lloyd-Thomas. In a number of unpublished writings that were the original stimulus to the present reflections, he called what I am calling "personal value" *particular* value: I think "personal value" is a more appropriate name for it.

[11] See the eraser example at the beginning of Section 4 below.

[12] The second disjunct in that alternation is added because I mean to reject not only the treatment of the college as merely an instrument for certain purposes but also the treatment of it as merely a vehicle of (even noninstrumental) value, as opposed to something that is also *itself* valuable. See, further, Section 3(i), below.

Conservative conviction, as I understand it, thereby exhibits a bias in favor of retaining what is of value, even in the face of replacing it by something of greater value (though not, therefore, in the face of replacing it by something of greater value no matter how *much* greater its value would be). But there is a third idea, beyond preservation of the (intrinsically) valuable and the (personally) valued, in conservatism that warrants notice here, namely, the idea that some things must[13] be accepted as *given,* that not everything can, or should, be shaped to *our* aims and requirements; the attitude that goes with seeking to shape everything to *our* requirements both violates intrinsic value and contradicts our own spiritual requirements.[14] Given things that are of value ought to be retained, but, beyond that, we need some things to be given quite apart from whether they have value other than *because* they are given. It is essential that some things should be *taken* as given: the attitude of universal mastery over everything is repugnant, and, at the limit, insane. (Note that the idea that some givens warrant preservation *other* than because they are (otherwise) valuable is consonant with what is said in the penultimate paragraph of this section about keeping bad human features.)

That we must accept some givens, not any and all givens, but plenty of givens, was well illustrated by my daughter Sarah Cohen's wise reaction to the title of Jonathan Glover's book of 1984, *What Sort of People Should There Be?* Sarah, then ten years old, noticed the book and its title on my desk and exclaimed: "That's div![15] They should be like us." Certain things are to be accepted from nature, and that includes aspects of ourselves. That wisdom is part of the wider conservative thought that certain things are to be taken as they come: they are not to be shaped or controlled.[16]

[13] The constraint is normative, not causal: I do not mean that the given is immovable, that we must accept it in the way that we must accept the law of gravity, or (as some think) the Laffer curve. For another case in which a conservative normative truth might tend not to be discerned because it gets conflated with a structurally similar causal truth, see the second paragraph of Section 6 below.

[14] For a sensitive treatment of how unchoosing acceptance of the specifically *cultural* given may be reconciled with the liberal valuation of autonomy and choice, see Samuel Scheffler, "Conceptions of Cosmopolitanism," esp. pp. 126ff. As Scheffler says, the liberal "state merely disallows the coercive enforcement of cultural affiliations; it does not offer a voluntaristic theory of their ultimate moral import" (p. 128).

[15] I think this word is obsolete. So far as I was able to tell, it meant "doltish."

[16] As the point is sometimes expressed: we should not "play God." Jonathan Glover is mistaken when he opines that "[w]hen the objection to playing God is separated from the idea that intervening in this aspect of the natural world is a kind of blasphemy [against God himself—GAC], it is a protest against a particular group of people, necessarily fallible and limited, taking decisions so important to our future" (*What Sort of People,* p. 47). But one may also object on a ground more fundamental than the latter and at which I gesture in the sentence to which the present note is attached. To be sure, many, and almost certainly Glover, will regard that "ground" as obscure and confused, but let us acknowledge that impasse, and not obliterate the distinctive conservative view of the given, which is expressed eloquently enough by David Wiggins:

Consider this allegory. Quite far along a certain continuum there sits a man who is surveying his own fleshly parts, that is, those of his parts which are *still* made of flesh, which includes some of his brain-flesh parts, and he is replacing defective bits of his flesh by perfect artificial substitutes, made out of whatever best serves, such as silicon, tungsten, reprocessed dung, and so forth. The man has been doing this for some time, and a lot of him is already artificial. That is surely a ghastly scenario. But it conveys the attitude that many people manifest towards human frailty and deficiency, or, more accurately, the attitude that they defend. That phrasing is more accurate because no one really has the artificial man's attitude in practice: in practice, everybody is conservative to *some* degree.

One commentator on the foregoing objected that the example is biased, because the deficient fleshly parts are replaced in the example by undeficient, *un*-fleshly, artificial parts, and, to test for the presence of the conservative attitude that I extol, we should consider the replacement of bits of our bodies by artificially produced bits of *flesh* in particular, which have been genetically modified to match our own, save for the elimination of the undesired imperfections.

I reply that it is hard to see why, in the absence of any conservative impulse, we should prefer flesh to other materials that *ex hypothesi* do whatever we had expected flesh to do.[17] The alternative scenario is indeed less ghastly, but precisely because it at least retains the medium (i.e., flesh) in which our capacities have traditionally been embodied. The given flesh is indeed replaced, but the attitude of preserving the given is more satisfied when flesh, rather than silicon, does the replacing: thereby the given *form* of embodiment is retained.

There is a particular kind of slippery slope in these matters that commands attention, and I do not mean one that relates to the difficulty of drawing a line between what *we* (now) find acceptable and what *we* (now) find unacceptable. Suppose we face no such difficulty at all, and we think that the right limit to plasticization is given by precisely this amount and type of plasticization. But we also know that, once thus plasticized, people would favor more plasticization, and, perhaps, unending plasticization, as each successive plasticization renders

---

If we cannot recognize our own given natures and the natural world as setting any limit at all upon the desires that we contemplate taking seriously; if we will not listen to the anticipations and suspicions of the artefactual conception of human beings that sound in half-forgotten moral denunciations of the impulse to see people or human beings as things, as tools, as bearers of military numerals, as cannon-fodder, or as fungibles; if we are not ready to scrutinize with any hesitation or perplexity at all the conviction (as passionate as it is groundless, surely, for no larger conception is available that could validate it) that everything in the world is in principle ours or there for the taking; then what will befall us? Will a new disquiet assail our desires themselves, in a world no less denuded of meaning by our sense of our own omnipotence than ravaged by our self-righteous insatiability? (Wiggins, *Sameness and Substance Renewed*, p. 242)

[17] I allow here, what might be challenged, that the manufactured flesh is flesh. Nicer minds than mine might protest that it ain't flesh if it didn't come to be the way (natural) flesh does.

people insensitive to the extra plasticness of the next one. Then we have strong reason to bring about less plasticization than we think optimal (though not, of course, than we think it optimal for us to bring about, all things considered). The problem that we face is not that we do not know where the line should be, but that, if we draw it at that point, then *they,* or, for that matter, we, later, will draw the line improperly elsewhere, given what their, or our, desires and tolerances will consequently have come to be.[18]

Partly because of fear of such a slippery slope, I am wary of certain forms of stem-cell research even as a means of finding a cure for horrible diseases. A culture in which such research is routine practice will smile on the *next* stage of the use of living beings for research in the way we, who may find current forms of stem-cell research acceptable, do not. We then have strong reason to prevent that successor culture from supervening. We have reason not to bring into being people for whom what we regard as acceptable practice is the accept*ed* practice because they may go beyond us in what *they* find acceptable, perhaps beyond *their* existing practice to just the extent that *we* went beyond *our* once existing practice, and, therefore, further than we would have gone and than we think anyone should go. If there is such a propensity in human nature, to go just that bit beyond where we are now in a dangerous direction, then we might owe it to the future of humanity, though not to the desires of what threaten to be future humans and superhumans, not to start the journey.[19]

And do not say, "If *your* child's life depended on it. …" There are all kinds of awful things that I would not otherwise dream of doing that I might do if my child's life depended on it. When people say: "If *you* had cancer … ," one can sometimes reply: "Yes, of course, that might unbalance my judgment." Making people imagine that they are in dire straits in order to cause them to agree with something is an attractive resort for those whose arguments are not (otherwise) strong.

I said that I was wary of certain forms of stem-cell research: I did not say that I would prohibit them. My philosophical opponent is not one who says, "Yes, there's something unattractive about using human life like this, but when you consider the gains …" My philosophical opponent is rather one who says, "There's *nothing* wrong with using these life-forms in this way, and, since the gains are so great …" The word "that" is subject to different interpretations when it appears in the protest, "How can you deny us a cure for *x* for the sake of *that?*" "*That,*" here, might be thought by the speaker to denote something that is nothing, but it might also be thought by her to denote not nothing but something

[18] A slippery slope of this structure can also give nonconservatives pause. If, for example, such a slope in respect of judgments about the time after which abortion should be permitted leads to tolerance of infanticide, then it leads to an evil on which conservatives have no monopoly of aversion.

[19] See, further, Section 6, below.

that is not enough. Although we exhibit a difference of judgment, I might have no *philosophical* quarrel with the speaker who means the latter.

If I want us to continue as we are, do I want us to retain our negative features? What if a genetic manipulation could, for example, eliminate envy? One might fear, of course, that with the elimination of envy there would also disappear certain possibilities of virtue: most straightforwardly, the virtue of rising above one's own envy, but also, perhaps, less evident ones, that are more secretly tied to envy, or to its possibility, in the economy of the human psyche. But even once we have set such collateral considerations aside, I would not want to eliminate all of our bad features. I conjecture that that is partly because the negative traits are part of the package that makes human beings the *particular* valuable creatures that we *personally* cherish, and are therefore worth preserving as part of that package, but it is also partly because we court vertigo if we seek to place everything within our control.

I proceed to distinguish between particular valuing (Section 3) and personal valuing (Section 4). Correspondingly, one might distinguish between *the* reason to preserve human beings—that they are creatures that exhibit a certain form of value, and *our* (additional) reason to do so, which is that they are *us.*[20] But beyond those two themes, which we can call preserving the valuable and preserving the valued, a third has obtruded, which will not be revisited in the sequel, and that we can call *preserving the given* (as such). I set it aside not because it is unimportant but because it is too deep to explore here.[21]

3. CONSERVING THE VALUABLE VERSUS CONSERVING VALUE

(i) Conserving What Has Value: The Nature of the Thesis

The conservative propensity that I defend in this section is to preserve particular intrinsically valuable things, as such. There is a distinct and relatively well-known case for preserving things that are personally valuable, and I pursue that case in Section 4. That well-known case has strong sociopsychological components, but they play no role in the more metaphysically phrased defense of preserving what is valuable that I offer in the present section.

The recommended solicitous attitude to existing valuable things (precisely) does not reduce to endorsing the purposes that the things serve, or the principles that they exemplify, which might be better served or exemplified by things that

[20] Franklin Roosevelt once said about right-wing Latin American dictators: "Well, yes, they're bastards, but they're *our* bastards." And I say, *ad* (some of) our negative characteristics: "Well, yes, we're bastards, but we're *our* bastards."

[21] For highly suggestive remarks about the given in general, see Michael Sandel, *The Case against Perfection*, pp. 26ff. *et passim*.

do not exist and which could be created at little cost, but by which we should nevertheless not replace existing valuable things. (I do not mean that we should not replace them *no matter what* the cost of forgoing a superior alternative may be: the bias that I assert in favor of existing value is not absolute.) Note that, even if it is worth keeping something only if it satisfies some purpose or principle, it does not follow that the weight of the reason for keeping it is limited to the extent to which it satisfies that purpose or principle.

The conservative impulse is to conserve what is valuable, that is, the particular things that are valuable. I claim that we devalue the valuable things we have if we keep them only so long as nothing even slightly more valuable comes along. Valuable things command a certain loyalty. If an existing thing[22] has intrinsic value, then we have reason to regret its destruction *as such*, a reason that we would not have if we cared only about the value that the thing carries or instantiates. My thesis is that it is rational and right to have such a bias in favor of existing value, that, for example, if you happily replace a fine statue by a merely somewhat better one, the production of which requires destruction of the original statue, then you mistreat the now destroyed work as (so to speak) having had the merely instrumental value of being a vessel of aesthetic value.

A salient, though not the only, alternative to conserving what is valuable is to maximize value, but conservatives are resolved to conserve the valuable at the *expense* of maximizing value: what we distinctively value are the particular *bearers* of value. The conservative attitude that I seek to describe is a commitment to the conservation of *what has value.*

"Conservation of what has value" is, indeed, the canonical phrase here, and not "conservation of value." For if we take the phrase "conservation of value" in the standard way, on the model, that is, of "conservation of energy," or "of matter," a conservation of value policy is entirely *un*conservative (in the present sense of "conservative"). Conservation of what has value is not in that sense, in the conservation of energy sense, conservation of value, for you lose no value, value *itself* is conserved, when you destroy something valuable and replace it by a thing of the same value.[23] The conservative disposition is not to keep the value rating high but to keep the things that now contribute to that rating.

Valuing something is in some respects like loving it, whether or not either is a species of the other. Consider, then, two old popular songs about love, here

[22] That is, anything at all, whether or not it counts as a thing in the narrow sense in which, e.g., a process, or a feature, does not. See Section 3(vi), below, for some remarks on valuable processes.

[23] The value/what has value distinction is a generalization of the distinction between exchange-value and what has it that I use in the course of my (so I believe it to be) demolition both of the labor theory of value and of the claim that the said theory supports a charge of exploitation. In some contexts, "value" and "what has value" are just different stylistic variants. In the present context the difference between them makes all the difference. (See Cohen, "The Labor Theory of Value and the Concept of Exploitation.")

used as means to make the distinction I need, or one structurally parallel to it. First, there is "You, You, You," an Ames Brothers' hit of 1953:

> You, you, you
> I'm in love with you, you, you,
> I could be so true, true, true,
> To a girl like you, you, you.

If I were the girl addressed by the Ames Brothers, I would beam during the first three lines of their stanza but my beam would give way to a frown when I heard the fourth line. Sure, I want to be loved because of my qualities, because of what I'm "like," but once my lover makes that move from my attractive qualities to me, I want it to be me that he loves, and not just the qualities. I do not want to think that, if someone with the same qualities now came along, then he would be indifferent between staying with me and switching to her, or that he would be even truer to someone who had even better qualities than I have. I do not want it to be inscribed in my lover's love for me that I am a good illustration of my particular virtues, and if my qualities decline, then I want love not to alter when it such alteration finds. I want to be loved not as *a* good bearer of my virtues, but as *the* bearer of them that I am, or, indeed was.

By contrast with the Ames Brothers, Olivia Newton-John starts and finishes in the right way. She does not go from "you" to "*a* girl": she makes the necessary move from "a" to "the." She begins with, "You better shape up, because I need *a* man," but, when she finds one who has shaped up, he becomes "*the* one that I want, *the* one that I wa-ant (ooo, ooo, ooo)."

You might think that it does not distinguish conservatives that they want to conserve what has value, because everybody wants to conserve what has value. I have two responses to that objection. First, although, so I would myself insist, it is *indeed* true that everybody has some desire to conserve what has value, it distinguishes conservatives of the present stripe that they want to conserve what has value *more* than other people do. Second, and more importantly, and, even though it is true that everyone wants to conserve what has value, not all who reflect on value and our relation to it notice the truth that I am defending: many philosophers, and most nonphilosophers when they philosophize, ignore the truth in conservatism that *everyone* who is sane recognizes and honors in practice, to some degree.

Among the philosophers that I have in mind are utilitarians, who purport to see *nothing* wrong with *destroying* value, if *more* value results. To seek to maximize value is to see nothing wrong in the destruction of valuable things, as long as there is no reduction in the total amount of value as a result. Unlike the conservative, the utilitarian is indifferent between adding to what we have now got, at no cost, something that has five units of value, and adding something worth ten units of value at the expense of destroying something worth five. The utilitarian says: "Let us have as much value as possible, regardless of what happens, as a result of that policy, to existing bearers of value: they do not matter, *as such.*" Conservatism sets itself against that maximizing attitude, according to which the things that possess value, by contrast with the value they possess, do not matter at all.[24] My hostility to a radical change in the nature of All Souls does not *depend* on a belief that what would thereby supervene would be less valuable than what would thereby be lost. Conservatism is an expensive taste, because conservatives sacrifice value in order not to sacrifice things that have value. We keep the existing *particular* valuable things at the expense of not making things in *general* as valuable as they could be made to be. Value, one might provocatively say, is not the only thing that is valuable: so are particular valuable things. And the two desiderata sometimes need to be traded off against each other.

A nonutilitarian pluralist value-maximizing consequentialist, who believes in maximizing the aggregate of irreducibly different kinds of value, might regret destroying one kind of value as part of a project which produces more value overall. But, once again, and given that she is indeed a value-maximizing consequentialist, she cannot regret its destruction *as such,* as opposed to the nonappearance of anything that has *that* kind of value within the set of things that are there when day is done: she has no more reason to regret the *destruction* of something which has a specific kind of value than she has to regret no such thing *being there* now, and/or no such thing *having been there* in the first place.

Value-maximizing consequentialism stands in especially sharp contrast with conservatism as I have defined it, but a view need not be maximizing to be unconservative. Maximizing consequentialism, as understood here, is only one species of conception in which *the bearers of value, as opposed to the value they bear, do not count as such, but matter only because of the value that they bear, and are therefore, in a deep sense, dispensable.* That is the essential, and canonical, contrast: all such conceptions are rejected by the principle that valuable things warrant conservation. Thus, *if* one may be a "sufficientarian" with respect to the promotion of value (as opposed to, very differently, with respect to distributive justice), if, that is, it is possible to think that all that matters is that the world be made good *enough*, then conservatism in the present sense opposes that, too, as a sole normative principle about value.

[24] It follows that, unless we are to say that utilitarians have no values, we must interpret what Samuel Scheffler says here creatively, in order not to judge it to be false: "[I]t is difficult to understand how human beings could have values at all if they did not have conservative impulses. What would it mean to value things but, in general, to see no reason of any kind to sustain them or retain them or preserve them or extend them into the future?" If we take Scheffler literally, the answer to his question is easy: it would mean, for example, to be a utilitarian. (The passage appears in Scheffler's magnificent essay "Immigration and the Significance of Culture," p. 105.)

It follows from the essential contrast that, as Michael Otsuka has shrewdly observed, a Cohen-conservative, although not a (comprehensive) value-maximizer, might yet be a maximizer, in a certain local sense:

> [W]e might have a [Cohen-]conservative who thinks we should, above all else, maximize the quantity of preserved value by, for example, destructively throwing one of Michelangelo's Slaves into the path of the oncoming trolley so that it causes the trolley to come to a halt before it builds up enough speed to run over and destroy the other five Slaves.[25]

Indeed, what reason could he have *not* to do it? The doctrines of doing and allowing and of double effect have purchase with respect to the treatment of human beings, but maybe not to the treatment of things. Or if, as I contemplate in subsection (v) below, there are deontic obligations not to destroy things that have no rights (i.e., obligations that carry no corresponding obligation to *prevent* their destruction), then, even so, my argument does not stand on such deontic ground, as is, I hope, made clear in the said subsection.

The conservative propensity is to conserve, to not destroy, and, therefore, to not replace, even (within limits) by something more valuable. But it is not a propensity against creation of new things, save, perforce, when their creation requires or causes a destruction of existing value. There is no conservative objection, in my sense of "conservative," to things of new kinds, as long as they leave the old things intact. A conservative is not against the creation of a Hockney painting, but she resists destroying a mediocre Filippo Lippi to make the creation of a Hockney possible, artistically superior though she might think the Hockney is bound to be. I said in Section 1 that the mark of a conservative is that she laments the loss of existing good things more than a nonconservative does. It does not follow, and it is not necessarily true, that a nonconservative welcomes the good new things more than a conservative does. You can consistently adore Byzantine icons partly *because* of their oldness[26] *and* Frank Gehry architecture partly *because* of its newness.

When conservatives lament what has been lost, say, for example, traditional craftsmanship, when they lament, William Morris–like, that now everything is made by machines, then some anticonservatives scornfully reply that the world we have lost was a world of poverty and toil, and that conservatives are irresponsible romantics. But the proposition, which I have no reason, here, to deny, that humankind is a net beneficiary of modernization, is not a reason for not lamenting what has been lost, unless you are a nonconservative evaluator. A

[25] Michael Otsuka, private communication, August 2005.

[26] To be sure, a thing's being especially valuable because it is *old* is not the same as its being especially valuable because it *exists*. I acknowledge the important distinction between oldness and existence three paragraphs hence.

conservative can believe that what rises from the ashes is the greatest building ever and that it was right to build it, yet still feel distraught that the old building was destroyed. A conservative can also believe that the culture of a people would be much richer if its present culture were replaced by a different one, and yet resist that destruction, not only because the people are attached to their culture (a matter on which the discussion in Section 4 below bears), but also just because of the culture's existing value.

(ii) Some Limitations of My Thesis

Let me now state some limitations of my thesis, considered as an attempt to formulate *a* central conservative thought.

Note, first that the thesis does not *manifestly* endorse longevity as such. The special claim that I have defended is of the value that exists, regardless of how long it has been around. Even if the picture was painted only five minutes ago, there's a reason not to destroy it in order to use its pigment to produce a better one. Richard Christian[27] characterizes a preference for what I call, here, "longevity," as embodying a thesis about the *behavior* of value, which says that it increases over time. He says that the stated thesis is wholly independent of my own central claim that existing value is to be favored, which, he illuminatingly says, is a thesis not, like the longevity thesis, about the *behavior* of value, but about the correct *response* to value. If Christian's independence claim were true without qualification, then that would be a pity, because it would mean that there is a lack of connection between the conservatism defended here and more traditional conservative ideas, and that would make my distinctive claim less interesting than it would otherwise be. The question of whether the two themes are in some way connected requires further study. (To be sure, we have reason, if I am right, to keep on retaining what is valuable, and longevity will be a *by-product* of doing so, but that does not stamp value on longevity itself.)[28]

Let me note a further limitation (beyond its possible indifference to longevity) of the position that I am defending.[29] Consider the second epigraph to this essay: "It's not like it was." The remark expresses a familiar attitude that we would normally call "conservative," namely, a certain bias in favor of reversing recent change. The position that I defend in the present section cannot account for that bias, and indeed it rather runs against it, because reversing recent change means destroying what now exists.

[27] Private communication.

[28] Something might first be valuable because it is new, gradually lose *that* value, and *pari passu* gain the value of longevity. Its peak value would depend on the sort of thing that it is. (Maybe it is possible for me to be delighted both that the Seagram Building is only forty years old and that it is as much as forty years old.)

[29] This paragraph was inspired by astute comments from Patrick Tomlin.

It may, of course, be metaphysically impossible to reverse recent change by (literally) bringing back into existence a particular thing that has gone out of existence.[30] But you can sometimes bring into existence a true replica of what existed, or a feature or set of features that used to obtain but no longer do. And some desire to do so is certainly part of what we should normally consider the conservative attitude. The desire can be defended on grounds related to the theme of Section 4, which is that familiar things and usages that are lodged in our lives have a personal value for us that makes them worth keeping, and worth "restoring," through a replication of their features, when they have been destroyed recently, and when we are therefore still oriented to a life that includes them. But the conservatism defended in *this* section seems to offer no reason for restoring recently disappeared features.

(iii) Objections

a. The Regret Objection. I say that if, despite the gain in value that necessitated its destruction, we regret destroying the old building, that is because we have a certain bias in its favor: we are, up to a point, disposed to retain it rather than replace it by something better. But, so it might plausibly be said, we also regret not building the new more valuable building when we decide to retain the existing one, so why should we not *also* infer that we have a *bias* in *its* favor? Reply: it does not follow *logically* from the first regret that we have the stated bias. But I say that it is impossible to make sense of the first regret unless we value what exists "beyond its intrinsic value," unless, so to speak, we "overvalue" it, in the relevant sense. By contrast, the best explanation of the second regret requires positing no *bias* in favor of the unrealized future more valuable thing: the regret is simply explained by the increase forgone in intrinsic value itself. There is no "overvaluing" bias here.

b. Lippi-Hockney. Return to the Lippi-Hockney example. I said that a conservative does not oppose new creation, as long as the new creation leaves the old creation intact. But someone might object: if people look at a Hockney, there is that much time spent not looking at a Lippi. So new creation can imply replacement, and my conservatism therefore cannot be so sanguine about new creation. But then I am in trouble, because I surely do not want to prohibit or restrict access to Hockneys.

But the propounder of that argument mistakes the nature of my conservatism with respect to valuing the particular. For I do not celebrate, in the first

[30] I am, indeed, inclined to doubt, in all prephilosophical innocence, that this describes a metaphysical possibility, but Calvin Normore advises me that there is a controversy in the philosophical literature as to whether a particular can go out of existence and then come back into it.

instance, our *experience* of the valuable things, but, instead, the valuable things themselves. And the only way that the value inherent in the Lippi can be destroyed, the particular value that *I* have in mind, is by destroying the Lippi. Surrounding it by a distraction of Hockneys does not do that.[31]

Someone might protest: if it has value independently of its contribution to our experience, doesn't it follow that it would be good to preserve a work of art even if it were no longer to be perceived, and even in a perceiverless world? And aren't those consequences absurd?

In order to address that pair of questions, let us distinguish between the case of a world of blind people and the case of a world of no people, or other relevant perceivers. In the first case I think the blind people could value the fact that their world *contained* such beauty, even though no one could appreciate it. So it might indeed follow from my position that it is good that unperceived aesthetic value exists. But I do not find that embarrassing. And if it also follows from my position that something could have aesthetic value even in a *wholly* perceiverless and conceiverless world, then some will no doubt want to get off the bus there, but I would ride on even then.

If we had one thousand paintings and we knew that one hundred will never be looked at again, but we did not know which ones they were, would we say: "If only we knew which are the hundred that no one will ever look at. Then we could harmlessly destroy them, and use the space that they now occupy for something useful"? If more space were imperative, would we just as soon throw those never-again-to-be-experienced hundred paintings into the fire as we would some nondescript logs of wood?[32]

Note that the questions that were posed for my view three paragraphs back may also be posed, *mutatis mutandis*, for a subset of my opponents, namely, those who believe that value (itself) is as intrinsic as I believe it to be, but not that existing bearers of value enjoy a special status. And the answers to those questions will be essentially comparable to the ones that I gave. It is, accordingly,

[31] I adverted earlier (see n. 5) to the negative effect of surrounding Wren's churches by ugly skyscrapers. Michael Otsuka, whose example that is, suggests that "surrounding a Wren church with skyscrapers *does* seem to devalue the value inherent in the Wren church and not merely our experience of that value." But I do not agree that it does that, unless we conceive Wren's creation not as the church itself but as the church-within-a-particular-context, with some motifs in it that are intended to resonate well with its surroundings. Nothing that I want to claim would be affected by that expansive reading of what the church is.

Although—so I insist—the Hockneys circumscribing the Lippi do not devalue *it*, I need not deny that new things *can* devalue existing valuable things. As Marx asked, what is "Jupiter compared with the lightning conductor, and Hermes compared with the Crédit Mobilier?" And new things can also enhance the value of, or even confer value on, existing things.

[32] The position defended above, that aesthetic value is inherent in aesthetically valuable things, is consistent with an account of aesthetic value as a secondary quality, one, therefore, which is constitutively apt to stimulate or enable experiences of certain kinds. I here neither endorse nor reject that account.

inappropriate to press skepticism about intrinsic value in the particular context of this essay's polemic.

c. The Irrationality Objection. Many would say that attachment to the value of particular things, in opposition to maximizing value, or, indeed, to value satisficing, or to any view that fails to put a premium on existing value, is *irrational.*[33] Why have less value (or, for example, less than enough) when you can have more (or at least enough)?

Well, *ex hypothesi*, the attachment is not justified by the contribution that the thing makes to the general value account. But it does not follow that the antimaximizing (anti-etc.) stance is irrational, and I do not believe that it is: it is an error nourished by much academic work, especially in economics, but no doubt the error is of deeper than merely academic origin—it is an error to think that being rational about value requires the merely abstract accounting of it that denies the value of particular things as such. And even if you think that I am wrong to call that an error, even if you think that there is never a reason to honor an embodiment of value, as such, I am sure that you cannot think of a noncircular *argument* for that conclusion: for to what could you appeal, to judge between the claims of abstract value and the claims of particular value? (Some are quick to suppose that favoring existing value must reflect a fear that what would replace it would be less good, in universal terms. I cannot refute that hypothesis. But I see no reason to believe it, unless it has already been groundlessly decided that a preference for existing value is irrational and therefore in need of some such explanation as that the preference reflects anxiety about loss of abstract value.)

d. Wiggins's Rosebush. David Wiggins has proposed a counterexample to my view, namely, a rosebush that stood in his garden, which served no external purpose, and which he therefore valued intrinsically, but one towards which, he says, he did not exhibit the bias that I say goes with valuing something intrinsically. When Wiggins was dismayed to see that his gardener had cut down the rosebush, he was fully assuaged when the gardener said that she would shortly replace it by a more beautiful one.

I can think of three saving responses to the Wiggins counterexample, but I am not sure which, if any, is sound. First, one might conclude that Wiggins must have valued the bush not for its intrinsic value but merely for the pleasure it gave him. But I think he would protest that the stated response is untrue to the phenomenology of his experience: he would say that it gave him pleasure

[33] In their interesting article on "The Reversal Test," Nick Bostrom and Toby Ord scout what they call the "status quo bias." Caveats in the second paragraph of their article exclude its application against this one.

because he recognized its value. Second, one might conjecture that, despite his protest to the contrary, Wiggins *did* have a bias in favor of his rosebush, but not a very strong one, so that any regret at its destruction was swamped by the good news that a better one was coming. And, third, one might hold that the bias that I argue for is appropriate only once a certain threshold of intrinsic value has been passed, and that the value of a single rosebush falls below that threshold. The second and third responses might be said to gain a certain plausibility from the reflection that Wiggins's rosebush example is more arresting than would be an otherwise parallel one in which a complete and luxuriant garden is replaced by an even better one.

e. McHose's Blocks of Wood. I wish to notice an interesting counterexample to my thesis that is due to Brad McHose.[34]

A sculptor contemplates producing a wooden statue, one that he can fashion in either one of two ways. One way involves assembling unpainted wooden blocks into the form of the statue and then painting them. Prior to being painted, the block formation, let us suppose, is a statue that has intrinsic value. Thus painting it "destroys" something of intrinsic value, albeit in order to create something of (we can suppose) greater intrinsic value (the painted statue). But the sculptor can also produce the same painted statue without destroying anything of intrinsic value by painting the blocks prior to assembling them, because in this different case she does not (we may stipulate) produce anything of intrinsic value until the painted statue has been assembled. If there is a reason to preserve things that have intrinsic value, and to regret destroying such things, then the sculptor has a reason, if she is going to produce a painted statue, to paint the blocks in advance of assembling them. But it seems odd to think that she has such a reason, that is, to paint the blocks first for the sake of avoiding the (production and) destruction of something of intrinsic value in the course of producing the painted statue. Thus it seems that there is not a general reason to preserve things that have value.

Perhaps the right reply is to identify a concept of *privileged value creation*, in which valuable things that are created *for the sake* of creating things of greater value are exempt from the normal protection of valuable things. Consider what we should say if the sculptor dies before she has painted the assembled objects. Would it be good, would it be permissible, to paint them fifty years later, when the work in question could not so readily be regarded as merely provisional?

A more radical reply to McHose challenges his example. One might conjecture that the equanimity with which we view the "destruction" of the midprocess work of art is that we do not really accept the stipulation that it is a *complete*

[34] It was presented at Stanford University on November 12, 2007.

and (fine) work of art. Suppose, contrastingly, an elegant miniature version of a projected building for some reason needs to be destroyed in order that we may produce the (much more valuable) building itself. Would that not be a pity, or certainly more of a pity than the "destruction" of the unpainted blocks? And the aptness of the scare quotes in that last sentence points to a further weakness in the McHose case: do we really believe that to paint a statue is to *destroy* it, especially when, as is *ex hypothesi* true here, its value is thereby enhanced?

But many more distinctions have to be made. One might, for example, distinguish different ways of destroying a Tintoretto and, correspondingly, different attitudes to its destruction: by burning it in order to keep Picasso warm enough to do his painting, or by cutting it up and incorporating it into a Picasso, with the Tintoretto pigments still discernible.

(iv) Valuing the Particular and Incommensurability

Notice that the irreplaceability of which I have spoken of some valuable thing *A* by some more valuable thing *B* does not reflect incommensurability between the value of the *A* thing and the value of the *B* thing. Irreplaceability and incommensurability are manifestly different things, but in some of the literature on incommensurability the two are routinely conflated.

So, for example, it is said to show the incommensurability of friendship and money that one would not *give up* a friendship for money.[35] But although it may be true that one should not give up a particular *existing* friendship for money, it does not follow, and it is not in all respects and in all contexts true, that the values of money and friendship are incommensurable. I might have to choose between a job in Tulsa and a job in Milwaukee, and I might reason that in Tulsa I will make more money but in Milwaukee I will make more friends, and I might, noncorruptly, with my soul intact, consider those desiderata on some sort of common scale and decide which is more important to me. But no one without moral defect gives up an existing friendship for money, or, indeed, and with no hesitation, for another friendship that promises to be more valuable even from the point of view of what is deepest in the value of friendship.

To be sure, I may have good reason to move to another city, and I may anticipate that it will then be difficult to continue to interact with a certain current friend, but that is not (quite) *giving up* a friendship for money: I would not say to that friend, "I am sorry, but we cannot (in any sense) be friends any more, since I am moving to Tulsa." What I *can* say is: "It is unfortunately likely that our friendship will come to an end," and that is different. Predicting the demise of a friendship is not choosing to conclude it (e.g., for a gain in money).

[35] Joseph Raz, *The Morality of Freedom*, pp. 346–53.

(v) Valuing the Particular and Deontology

Is my thesis "just" a generalization of the familiar deontological truth, which is, pressed by critics of utilitarianism, that it is wrong to kill a sad person if a happy person can thereby be produced? There is, of course, a structural affinity here. But the stated familiar point is normatively overdetermined. For there is, first, the point that human beings have a *right* not to be destroyed, by contrast, perhaps, with cathedrals, sunsets (and colleges?). So binding is that right that there is, as it were, little room left on the normative billboard for the undeniable truth, which is indeed a special case of my claim, that the value embodied in a human being warrants protection *in* that embodiment. Nor would one happily say, in respect of the more familiar point, that it justifies a mere *bias* in favor of existing human value.

Now, restrictive deontological obligations might not reflect *rights* on the part of the items whose treatment they govern. A deontological bar on destroying something of value need not acknowledge a right that the thing in question possesses. Tom Hurka has helped me to see that the bias that I defend against destroying what is of value must nevertheless be distinguished from deontological constraints, in the contemplated wide sense of "deontological." The paragraphs that close this subsection are an edited version of his remarks.[36]

The view under defense here gives priority to the preservation of existing goods over the creation of new ones. A familiar deontological view gives priority to not *oneself* destroying goods, or more generally, to not *oneself* choosing against them, over promoting goods. (Causing evils gets a treatment analogous to that of destroying goods.)

These views yield the same verdict in the principal case that I have discussed, where one has the option of destroying one good in order to replace it with another slightly better good. But the views come apart in more complex cases.

Imagine that you can either prevent an existing good from being destroyed by natural forces or create another slightly better good. My view says that you should preserve the existing good, but the deontological view does not: it treats preserving and creating as two forms of promoting and allows you to create the new good. It may do this even when the first good is threatened with destruction by some other person's wrongful act, because what it prioritizes is *your* not destroying goods, not not destroying in general.

For a possible case on the other side, imagine that someone else is in the process of creating a new good and that I could intervene to sabotage his project, preventing his good from being created and thereafter creating another and greater good myself. My view does not forbid this, because I am not thereby

[36] In a letter to me dated May 23, 2007.

destroying an existing good that has priority. But the deontological view may forbid it, because the sabotage is aimed directly at preventing a good from being realized.

(vi) Unanswered Questions

Here are some good questions that were raised by Kimberley Brownlee and that I do not address: Might conserving something require repairing it, or even modifying it? What is more conservative, to repair the old pot with new clay, or to let it crumble? Does Cohen-conservatism permit cultivation and development of that which has value?[37]

Also neglected here is the truth that (sometimes?) cultural values can persist only if they are allowed to change: the matter is discussed with great subtlety by Samuel Scheffler in his "Immigration and the Significance of Culture" (pp. 106 *et seq.*).

The last two paragraphs raise issues that require more investigation than they get in this essay, regarding the question of what categories of things can qualify as vessels of value. Two examples of such different categories are, I think, material objects, such as trees, and processes, such as a tree's growth, decay, and death. And note that there can be conflicts not only, as in Otsuka's Slaves case (see Section 3(i) above), between saving some particular material objects and saving other ones, but also between protecting a process, like the self-renewing activity of a forest, and protecting objects, like trees, that the process operates on, and destroys. At the moment, I see no problems specific to such conflicts, problems, that is, that make the conflicts relevantly different from conflicts between preserving different valuable things within a single category of things.

Consider, in this context, deliberately ephemeral works of art. Consider, further, that it is in the nature of some valuable things to disappear, and it is therefore impossible to say that they should be preserved because of their intrinsic value: examples would be bonfires, and maybe shooting stars. But there is an application of my conservatism even to such things: for one would not destroy a bonfire before its time (to fizzle out) has come, in favor of what one knew would be a better bonfire.

Tim Scanlon has observed

> that the degree of bias toward the existing, and regret that is not assuaged by replacement by another thing of the same kind (another friendship or another [college] or whatever), depends on and derives from considerations internal to the value in question. That is, it depends on the particular attitudes and intentions that valuing such a thing requires us to have and respect (= take seriously).[38]

[37] Cf. the discussion of the McHose example, at Section 3(iii)(e), above.

[38] Private communication, March 2008.

And, at the limit, the value of something might be of such a sort that the bias, although more or less strong in other cases, quite disappears.

If that is right, then perhaps the most that one can say is that some things warrant the bias, and that the bias means rejecting maximization and its cognates. The reduced claim is: there exist valuable things in respect of which a conservative bias is apt. This existentially quantified claim is, of course, less interesting than the universally quantified one that I have tried to defend, albeit with an openness towards qualification and modification. But one cannot say that the residual point is of no, or of little, interest. For it is equivalent to a denial of the following inference: *A* would be better than *B*, therefore we should replace *A* by *B*. And many take that inference for granted, and apply it in practice, and, so I have argued, it is an importantly mistaken inference. Also, the reduced claim invites what might be an interesting research program, into what forms of value demand preservation and what forms do not.

(vii) Beyond Existing Particulars

I wish to notice a pregnant observation on a draft of the present essay that is due to Anca Gheaus.[39] Her observation promises and threatens (if I may lapse, temporarily—I assure you—into Hegelian) to *heb auf* the main theme of the present section.

Gheaus suggests that, just as one may "recognize the special importance of particular embodiments of value and thus resist change in order to preserve these embodiments," so one may sometimes "welcome change for the sake of change" and thus "accept the loss of some value in order to create something new. Like the conservative attitude, this one is at odds with" value maximization. Fashion (things being in and out of it, that is) seems to illustrate the point.

As Gheaus observes, "the two attitudes can co-exist in the same person, at the same time, with respect to different things." One can want (to keep) something because it exists, but one can also want (to get) something because it does not exist, and in both cases the focus is on the particular, *whether it be actual or prospective*, and against a merely abstract accounting of value.

If Gheaus is right, my defense of what I call conservatism is not impeached, but that which I defend is now seen to be an instance of something more general, namely, of the claims of particular valuable things over value in general. So, for example, we see the bias in valuing particular things over abstract value in the typical (not universal, to be sure) aspiration of the artist, who is aiming not to produce a certain mass or type of value but a particular valuable thing. In a post-Gheaus reworking of the theme of this essay, the emphasis on particular valuable things *that now exist* would be relaxed.

[39] Private communication, July 11, 2008.

Needless to say, the whole matter requires further study. And that further study must address a case put by Michael Otsuka.

Otsuka first argues that I am committed to a bias in favor of things that *will* exist over things that could be brought into existence. Suppose, he says, that you know that some wonderful thing will come into existence in the future, and you also know that you could set in train a process that will lead to its destruction and replacement by something superior the like of which could not be created without the said destruction. If you indeed set the "improving" process in train, then you would be "mistreat[ing] the [to-be-]destroyed [thing] as having the merely instrumental value of being a vessel of aesthetic value" (see the third paragraph of Section 3(i) above). So future existents, and not just present ones, can, on my view, be subject to the same abuse, and the same respect, now, as present ones. The distinction between the mass and type of value and particular value still obtains, but the present/future distinction disaligns with the distinction between particular and abstract value.

But this unavoidable (if Otsuka is right) application of my view to future particulars is strongly challenged by Otsuka's *asteroids example*:

> Note that the bias in favor of actually existing things that you defend has the following implication regarding future things that are not yet actual: Suppose that you come to learn that, after the extinction of human beings (and any other creature capable of enjoying beauty), a most beautiful patch of wilderness (far more beautiful than Yosemite or anywhere else in the world) will come into existence. It will, however, not last long, as a small asteroid will land on it, thereby transforming it into a nondescript, barren crater. I agree with you that you would have reason to ensure that this beautiful patch is preserved by now destroying this asteroid. Now suppose that you come to learn, in a variant of the above scenario, that the asteroid will hit this spot on earth before the beautiful patch would have begun to emerge, thereby rendering this spot inhospitable to the emergence of anything beautiful. If, however, you destroy this asteroid, then the beautiful patch will come into existence. It is an implication of your view that you would have less reason to destroy this asteroid in this scenario, as such destruction would not preserve an actually existing thing of value. Rather, it would instead allow for the coming into existence of a thing of such value. I do not find the thought that you would have less reason a compelling one.[40]

This brilliant example must serve, for the time being, as a springboard for further reflection.

[40] Private communication, July 18, 2008. Otsuka adds: "Since I don't find it a compelling thought, I'm led to wonder whether there is any justified bias in favour of the preservation of existing value as such. Perhaps the lesson we should take away from reflection on this case is that any such bias must be explained in terms of a less interesting claim regarding the personal value that existing things tend to have."

4. PERSONAL VALUE

I have a pencil eraser (or, in British English, a "rubber") that I have used ever since I became a lecturer forty-six years ago. When I got it, it was a cube, but now it is a sort of sphere, and although it is small, most of it is still there. It is not because I make very few mistakes that most of my eraser is still there, but because (a) I do not use pencils very much; (b) it takes only a little bit of rubbing to eliminate a mistake; and (c) I do not notice all of my mistakes. I would hate to lose this eraser. I would hate that even if I knew it could be readily replaced, not only, if I so wished, by a pristine cubical one, but even by one of precisely the same off-round shape and the same dingy color that my eraser has now acquired. There is no feature that stands apart from its history that makes me want to keep this eraser. I want *my* eraser, with *its* history. What could be more human than that?

If I had a paintbrush that once belonged to Monet, I would value it as such, that is, *because* it once belonged to Monet, and if it were removed and replaced by a more elegant brush, one that belonged to Manet, by a well-wisher who knew that I think Manet a greater painter than Monet, and that I care about elegance in brushes, then I would know that the well-wisher would have failed to understand something, and I do not mean that he would have failed to understand the sanctity of private property. He would have failed to understand that wanting to *keep* what one (already) has is a special sort of wanting.

It is not true that I am attached to the particular thing because I value attachments, and *this* particular old thing serves well as something to be attached to. Rather, I am attached to the thing itself, as such, and not for any general reason, such as the general reason that it is good to have attachments (which it certainly is). Thus, if my would-be benefactor had said: Oh, but I know that in time you will grow even more attached to the Manet brush, I should remain unmoved. It is the Monet brush that I want, not some quantity of attachment to something or other.

Consider the resistance to suburban supermarketization, on behalf of urban neighborhood shops. People who seek to protect neighborhood shops point to their many advantages, to the many purposes that they serve so well: local effects like providing access to provisions for old and infirm people, a meeting place that stimulates community, eccentric product lines, and also wider effects like reducing motor traffic, and opening up opportunities for people from deprived minorities to rise on the social scale, through self-, and even other-, employment.

But we deceive ourselves if we think that it is only because they deliver specifiable economic and social benefits that we cherish our local shops. It is not only the purposes that they serve that justify our resistance to their destruction. It is also because in all their vagariously caused uniqueness they are part of a social and cultural landscape to which we belong. I do not want you or, for that matter, me, to knock down part of my house and replace it by something bigger and better, even if it truly *is* bigger and better. I want my home to remain what it is and I want my neighborhood to remain what *it* is. (Of course, if either were really lousy, I would welcome, I might crave, something new. But if each is quite good, or good enough, then I may want them substantially as they are, despite their deficiencies on a generalization of the criteria that would make me judge them to be unacceptable if they were a *lot* less good, by those criteria, than they actually are.)

Both the economic market and state planning tend towards the destruction of the particular, and therefore towards the destruction of things that are both impersonally and personally valuable. (By "tend" I mean "tend," not "always do.") To be sure, some people are happy to pay over the odds, that is, to pay more than what they buy is worth to them, for stuff from the local shop, in order to help keep it going. But that's clearly countermarket behavior: game-theoretically speaking, these benign buyers are suckers. And some planners might accept its *being* there as a reason to *keep* something there.[41] But usually they will prefer a general consideration, something that the thing does well, or even the general consideration that a majority want it kept there—which is not, of course, the reason for keeping it there that the members of that majority *themselves* have.

The logics of the market and of planning tend against the truth that people want *particular* valuable things, not just satisfaction of *general* desiderata. If everything is added to or subtracted from the environment in neglect of the value of particularity and variety as such, then everything will tend to be the same everywhere, because serving the same requirements: every quarter will have its Starbucks.[42] But market choice is relentlessly general in the grounds of its preference, so market mania is deeply *anti*conservative and Thatcherite Toryism is a great betrayal of conservatism (about which I shall say more in Section 7). If you want everything to be optimal, nothing will be good. And some things have to just *be,* they have to just be *there,* if anything is to be good.

We are attached to particular things because we need to *belong* to something, and we therefore need some things to belong to us. We cannot belong to something abstract. We do not keep the cathedrals just because they are beautiful, but also because they are part of our past. We want the past to be present among us. We do not want to be cut off from it. We rejoice in our contact with the culture of *our* past. We of course value our particular past in the respectful way that

[41] People sometimes ask whether the present essay has any practical relevance. Well, it has at least this much: politicians and planners who are persuaded by it would realize that it is not enough to justify a replacement for something that it would be better than what it replaces.

[42] And every conservative diatribe like this one will badmouth Starbucks. In fact, Starbucks has things that recommend it, but I am regretting sameness, which is to say, lack of variety, not how bad each of the members of the repetitive set is. To regret that there's only one kind of flower in the garden is to say nothing about how beautiful that flower is.

we value any past culture, but we also value it in a more personal way. We want to be part of what Edmund Burke (famously) called the "partnership not only between those who are living, but between those who are living, those who are dead, and those who are to be born."[43] When people ask me how I can bear to think of my destiny, which is death, I tell them that I find great consolation in the American poet Carl Sandburg's lines: "Something began me and it had no beginning: / something will end me and it has no end."

Does its possession of personal value give us a reason not to destroy some thing, other than the reason that doing so would distress the person or people for whom it has that value? I am inclined to say "yes," but that is not so evident as it is where the value is not (merely) personal but intrinsic.

5. IDENTITY AND TRADITION

In Section 2, I contrasted using All Souls to produce independently desirable goods with the different aim of ensuring that All Souls remains what (but not therefore exactly *as*) it is. There is a conceptual complication about that second aim, that is, the preservation of identity, that I now want to explore.

Our identity[44] is not the sort of value that is characteristically preserved as a result of a successful attempt to preserve it. Our identity is characteristically preserved not as a result of our *aiming* to preserve it but simply as a result of our *not* aiming to change it, and of lack of exogenous convulsion in our lives. And when it is *necessary* to do something to preserve our identity, then our identity is in question. The preservation of identity is for the most part essentially a by-product, in Jon Elster's sense, something that won't be achieved by someone who strives to achieve it.[45] One can certainly say: "I'm attached to it *because* it's part of my tradition." But the more you have to say that, the more you have to *reaffirm* the tradition, the more likely it is that the grip of tradition is relaxing. Tradition is such a fellow that you have to hold on to *it* only when *it* has relaxed its hold on *you*.

When the All Souls Fellows who favored change made their recommendations, they were not only recommending what could contribute to a change in the identity of the college, but also manifesting a transformation of its identity: that their suggestions were not immediately greeted with derision says something about how the identity of the college had changed. In an earlier age no one would have raised such suggestions, and no one, moreover, would have re-

[43] Edmund Burke, *Reflections on the Revolution in France*, p. 96. I know that everybody quotes that: I'm not trying to be original here, just trying to hit the nail on the head, which Burke did.

[44] For what I mean by "identity," please see n. 9 above.

[45] See his *Sour Grapes*, ch. 2.

frained from raising them as a result of some reasoning about the identity of All Souls.

That our identity represents something that we mostly live rather than conceive nourishes noxious politically big-C Conservative and even big-F Fascist conceptions. The lived nature of identity connects with the Conservative celebration of the unsayable that is said to underlie social existence. Indulging his tendency to put truth in the service of antidemocratic reaction, Michael Oakeshott presented the depth that defies articulation as a reason for having a hereditary ruling class, one that is capable of transmitting the inarticulable wisdom about what we are to the next generation of rulers. I'm saying that there's *something* in the thought that Oakeshott perverted to his reactionary purpose. (Just as there is something in his thought that any sound proposal for social change is the "pursuit of an intimation," that is, of something already *in* the society. I agree with that, but I don't think that it disqualifies the Russian Revolution, which is the sort of thing that it is supposed to disqualify.) And the fact that our identity represents something that we live rather than conceive also nourishes Fascist conceptions, because thinking with the blood, valuing passion over reason, are perversions of truths about the impossibility of bringing everything to the ratiocinative surface.

6. PARADOXES OF CHANGE

If we are conservatives in my sense, then we have reason to change slowly because we have reason to be what we are and to carry on with what we have: we cannot simply erase our background and replace it by something better. A conservative regulation gives life continuity. We cannot reinvent ourselves, or our language, or anything that really matters, every day according to what our resources now are and what our opportunities now are. We cannot keep everything "under review."[46]

Conservatives often make a point about the unforeseeable consequences of large and rapid change, a point about looking before leaping, and about the difficulty of seeing what's coming, and so forth. But that *l'imprévu* point is not my point:[47] I recommend changing slowly for no such strategic reason. We have reason to change slowly even when we know very well what is coming next (and after that).

[46] This is not the Neurath-like idea that, at any given time, some things must be taken for granted whereas others are evaluated against the stable background that the accepted things provide. Within that idea, one *chooses* what the stable background will be, just as, in Neurath's analogy, one chooses which parts of the boat to replace and/or repair and which to keep as they are for the time being. I am saying the different thing that, at any given time, some matters are beyond our power to reconsider, *salva stabilitate*.

[47] For a fine treatment of it, see Geoffrey Brennan and Alan Hamlin, "Analytic Conservatism."

In the brilliant climax of his 1980 critical notice of two books by Anthony Kenny (*Will, Freedom and Power* and *Freewill and Responsibility*), Ted Honderich wrote:

> There is also the sad fact that our author, who might be thought to have an obligation in these matters, has joined those users of English who take concepts to include some that are voted for, driven, lived in, and installed. You can't do any of that to a concept, and you can't morally justify one either. ... No doubt the time will come when you can, but we needn't rush toward it.[48]

I have ruminated on the implications of that wise remark many times in the nearly thirty years that have passed since I read it. They include these: that (1) the first stage of linguistic evolution, or, rather, of one pervasive kind of linguistic evolution, is linguistic error; but that (2) once the error has become common enough, it ceases to be an error, and it may become even *required* usage, so that an older usage now qualifies as merely fussy, or at any rate quaint; but that (3) we who are attached to what is now correct usage may reasonably seek to decelerate the process of change, by avoiding deviation ourselves, which we ought to do anyway, quite apart from our particular tastes, because deviations *are* errors. (Maybe, because deviations are errors, there should not be *any* linguistic change of this type, even when it is beneficial in the end. Maybe, if it is wrong for it to start happening, it is wrong for it to happen.)

There are, of course, parallels in nonlinguistic behavior and style, in what is "the done thing." Do the thing that is not done often enough, and it becomes the done thing.

But, returning to language, we must here remember the point made in Section 3 above, which is that the disposition to protect the old can coexist, as it does in my own case, with a welcoming attitude to those new things that do not displace the old things. There is nothing wrong with expansion of the vocabulary stock, or with neologisms, like "like," as such. (Like, I really, like, *like*, "like.") The Honderich resistance that I endorse is against making errors that are in time self-legitimating and that thereby destroy old meanings.

[48] P. 133. I make no comment on whether Honderich is right, or was right in 1980, about the word "concept." I praise not the substance but the form of his admonition of Kenny.

It might seem ironical that an intransigent opponent of conservatism (see his *Conservatism*) should have given so powerful a formulation to an essential conservative thought. But maybe it is not really ironical, because, so Honderich says on pp. 1–2 of the book, his topic is not small-c conservatism.

On the other hand, Honderich might indeed be thought to be taking a swipe against small-c conservatism when he writes that "if Conservatism were at bottom a defence of *the familiar*, in the plain meaning of the term, we should have a mystery on our hands, the mystery of how an egregious idiocy could have become a large political tradition" (*Conservatism*, p. 2). To be sure, it would be an egregious idiocy to defend *everything* that is familiar, but it would also be an egregious idiocy to reject, for that reason, a characterization of conservatism according to which a conservative is *more* disposed to defend the familiar than others are.

7. CONSERVATISM AND THE POLITICAL RIGHT

Wanting to conserve what has value does not imply wanting to conserve exploitation and injustice, since they lack value. Wanting to conserve what has value is consistent with wanting to destroy disvalue.

Of course, something that is unjust can have value, and even in a fashion that is linked to the very thing that makes it unjust. Certain practices of deference, for example, which embody injustice, also facilitate forms of exchange that are deeply mutual in a distinctive way. But you can be both egalitarian and conservative by putting justice lexically prior to (other) value (whether or not—a further question—one could say that something that merits destruction because it is unjust might nevertheless be of great value, all things considered). (Lack of in-) justice, such egalitarians might say, is the first virtue of things.

This deference to justice does not trivialize the "we want to conserve what is valuable" thought. For conservation of the valuable *still* sometimes trumps value maximization (and so forth) and it needs something as momentous as justice to trump the (nonjustice) value that we seek to conserve.

I do not say that I am myself so uncompromising an egalitarian, so lexically projustice. I am not sure that we should regret the production of all the wonderful material culture that we have inherited and that was produced at the expense of gross injustice. Of course we regret that it was produced in that way, but would we be happier if it had not been produced, on the assumption that there would have been no nonunjust way of producing it?[49]

To be sure, if one is prepared to compromise justice, then one will be more prepared to do so, *ceteris paribus*, if one has the conservative attitude that I recommend. For the bias towards existing value will render an injustice more tolerable (than it is for a nonconservative compromiser) when this injustice cannot be eliminated without eliminating intrinsically good things.[50]

Note, further, that wanting to conserve the valuable, even wanting to keep things that have increased in value as a result of tradition, is not "wanting to keep things as they are," as such, where that means "wanting to preserve the status quo, the existing social and political situation." That is too undiscriminating a characterization to be the name of a proper object of conservative concern. And, in order to preserve valuable things in the status quo, we might have to revolutionize our situation. To keep the pictures safe, we might have to tear down the charming but damp and drafty old museum and build a new one.[51] One

[49] I propose a resolution of the tension between the Marxist commitment to advancement of productive power and the Marxist commitment to those at whose expense that advancement occurs in section V of "Peter Mew on Justice and Capitalism," which uses materials assembled in my *History, Labour, and Freedom*, pp. 303–4.

[50] I owe that point to Michael Otsuka.

[51] Compare the questions raised by Brownlee that are reported in the first paragraph of Section 3(vi), above.

thing Karl Marx said about the socialist revolution was that that revolution was necessary to preserve the fruits of civilization against the ravages of capitalism.[52]

Classical British Conservatism combined conservatism with a small "c" with preservation of wealth and inequality:

> The rich man in his castle
> The poor man at his gate
> God made them, high or lowly,
> And ordered their estate.
>
> ("All Things Bright and Beautiful," 1848, by Cecil Alexander)

The combination of conservatism with wealth and inequality was relatively easy to sustain in a precapitalist society, but, when inequality became capitalist inequality, the combination of conservatism with wealth and inequality became untenable, among other reasons because capitalism so comprehensively transforms everything, including itself: in the phrase of the *Communist Manifesto,*[53] under capitalism, "all that is solid melts into air." As Marx also said, "all earlier modes of production were essentially conservative,"[54] by contrast with capitalism. When the rich morphed, fully, into capitalists, the British Conservative Party became the anticonservative market party. As a matter of history, the bottom line of Conservatism with a capital "C" turned out to be not conservatism with a small "c" but preservation of wealth and inequality. With fierce international competition, conserving old ways is too costly to the maintenance of wealth. And with historical working-class gains in place, small-c conservatism becomes a buffer against *in*equality. For the sake of protecting and extending the powers of wealth, big-C Conservatives regularly sacrifice the small c-conservatism that many of them genuinely cherish. They blather on (as Prime Minister John Major did) about warm beer and sturdy spinsters cycling to church and then they hand Wal-Mart the keys to the kingdom. They are thereby in tune with the propensity of capitalism, which is to maximize a certain kind of value, in sovereign disregard of the value of any *things.*[55]

[52] As John McMurtry points out to me, my comment here may represent a misappropriation of Marx, because Marx might have meant that what was to be preserved was the *level* of development of the productive forces, and that is a nonconservative desideratum, because of its indifference to the value of the particular.

[53] Which Marshall Berman has made more famous by using it as the title of his magnificent book.

[54] *Capital,* vol. 1, ch. 15, section 9.

[55] Aristotle distinguished between the usefulness of things and their abstract economic value, and he disparaged the desire to accumulate the latter, a desire that has no shape and therefore no limit: see his remarks in *Politics*, bk. I, chs. 8–10. If I were more Continental, and therefore less continent, than I am, I would speculate that the maximizing stance in axiology is a projection onto the realm of value in general of the capitalist attitude to value, which is "Accumulate! Accumulate! That is Moses and the prophets" (Karl Marx, *Capital,* vol. 1, ch. 24, section 3).

APOLOGY

I have been working on this essay (intermittently) for a few years, and I have received an abundance of excellent criticism of it, some of which has been reported above. The essay was initially bold and simple, but it soon lost its pristine character. Incorporating criticisms, and my responses to them, turned it into a patchwork product.

Forty-five years ago I heard Bernard Williams praise a philosopher's book because its text revealed that the author "did his best thinking off the page." Well, much of my own thinking on the present topic, be it best (the thinking, that is) or otherwise, has been set here before you, on the page. In the Popperian terms that Bernard Williams might have accepted[56] to express the point, there has here been too much context of (would-be)-discovery and not enough context of justification. But that is because festschrifts have deadlines, and this one is upon me, and what you have before you is simply what I have been able to do so far. I would have liked to give Tim something more finished, but I know that he will, with his usual ample generosity, understand.[57]

[56] Or rejected: I think Bernard Williams did not admire Popper.

[57] I have a large debt to David Lloyd-Thomas, whose fascinating unpublished writing on particular value nudged me towards the present topic, and who has commented helpfully on drafts of this essay. I also thank John Baker, Annette Barnes, Marshall Berman, Chris Bertram, Akeel Bilgrami, Michael Bratman, Geoff Brennan, Harry Brighouse, Kimberley Brownlee, Richard Christian, Josh Cohen, Michael Cohen, Michèle Cohen, Angela Cummine, Paul David, Jon Elster, Cécile Fabre, Jeremy Farris, Dov Fox, Michael Freeden, Michael L. Friedman, Anca Gheaus, Kerah Gordon-Solmon, Kent Greenawalt, Alan Hamlin, Barbara Herman, Tom Hurka, David Kaplan, Tsehai Khemet, Rahul Kumar, Brad McHose, Alistair Macleod, John McMurtry, José Luis Martí, Mike Martin, Calvin Normore, Kieran Oberman, Michael Otsuka, Avia Pasternak, Piero Pinzauti, Amelie Rorty, Michael Rosen, Tim Scanlon, Sam Scheffler, Shlomi Segall, Seana Shiffrin, Lucas Stanczyk, Hillel Steiner, Jenny Szende, Patrick Tomlin, Jeremy Waldron, David Wiggins, Andrew Williams, Susan Wolf, Chris Woodard, and Arnold Zuboff.

Chapter Nine

VALEDICTORY LECTURE: MY PHILOSOPHICAL DEVELOPMENT (AND IMPRESSIONS OF PHILOSOPHERS WHOM I MET ALONG THE WAY)

Editor's Note: Before reading this chapter, please consult the Editor's Preface to this book, which explains why the lecture should, and how it can, be heard and read simultaneously.

Isaiah Berlin has made famous the statement by Immanuel Kant that "out of the crooked timber of humanity no straight thing is ever made." And I believe that's true. I can tell from my own case. So many of the things that we do and that matter so much to us we do both for good and for bad reasons. And sometimes we're too self-critical, I think. We think that the good reasons really don't make what we're doing good. But they do. And we're too self-critical of the fact that there's this admixture of the old additive responding to bad reasons in our makeup.[1]

I want to talk about how I came to study philosophy. I became a philosophy student for several good reasons, and also for one *bad* reason. The bad reason might be the most interesting one, but I'll start with the good reasons, which began to form in the 1940s.

I lived the first eight years of my life, until 1949, in a small apartment with my parents on Park Avenue in Montreal. Park Avenue was the Broadway of Montreal, in the Upper West Side *Jewish* sense of Broadway. It was not Park Avenue in the Park Avenue sense of Park Avenue. Our apartment sat above a jewelry store called "Shiveck's" and Mr. Shiveck was our landlord. I did not like Mr. Shiveck. I did not like him *because* he was our landlord. There was one apartment above ours, where Mr. and Mrs. Stein lived. They had a son called Boris Stein, and he was a student at McGill University, and, on the not very frequent occasions when my parents went out for the evening, Boris was my babysitter. One evening Boris came down to babysit and he brought one of his McGill textbooks with him. I read its title: phi—lo—so—phy. I loved the word, I reveled in the *sound* of the *word*: phi—lo-so-phy. It was like a lollipop, a luscious lollipop drink-your-fill-osophy of a tongue-loving word. I asked Boris what the word 'philosophy' meant. I don't remember what Boris said in reply, but I'm

[1] [This first paragraph was impromptu rather than part of the prepared text and has been transcribed from the audio recording.—Ed.]

sure his reply didn't teach me what philosophy was. One reason why I'm sure that it didn't is that I still don't know, for sure, what philosophy is, any more than anybody else does. Nobody knows for sure what makes a problem or a thought philosophical, but that doesn't prevent anybody from having a strong opinion about the answer to the question.

We have no clear shared understanding of what philosophy is, yet we manage to practice it together. That is very intriguing. And there are many other intriguing questions both about and within the subject, and they have an allure for me, and one big reason why I was drawn to philosophy is because it was wonderful to be able to think about those intriguing questions.

I turn to the bad reason. But, before I expose it, I must provide some background.

As many of you know, because I have not hidden the fact, I had an unusually ideological childhood, and the ideology that I learned, and that I learned to love, was Marxism. Initially, it was a kiddies' form of Marxism, a Marxism for tiny tots. I learned kiddies' Marxism at my first school, which was a pro-Soviet communist private Jewish school that taught in Yiddish in the mornings and in English in the afternoons. One of our subjects in the Yiddish morning was *geschichte fun klassenkampf*, or the history of the class struggle. I can neither remember nor imagine now what we were taught under that heading in 1949, when I was eight years old.

Now a key tenet of kiddies' Marxism, and also, come to think of it, a key tenet of adult Marxism, was that, as my mother used to say, "everything is economic," by which she meant that "everything is economically explained," or anyway everything social, or anyway everything social that's important, so maybe not why the fork goes on the left of the plate, but certainly why liberalism replaced conservative monarchism across the course of the nineteenth and twentieth centuries. The belief that everything is economic was still with me when I embarked upon the B.A. at McGill University, in 1957.

In those days the Arts degree at McGill was a four-year course. In the first year you took a salad of subjects. You more or less had to do Latin, French, Mathematics, and English Literature, but the fifth course was your choice, and, under the influence of the "everything is economic" tenet, I chose economic history: that was the only economic offering for first-year students. The course was taught by the vice-chancellor of the university, an Englishman called Frank Cyril James. He lectured in an elevated English accent, indeed too elevated an accent to be accepted as genuine, for he had, after all, been educated at the LSE, and not at Oxford or Cambridge.

James lectured on the economic history of the world, from its semiscrutable beginnings up to whatever year he was lecturing in, which, in my case, was 1958. Now, because of my background convictions, I was stunned by something that James said about a certain economic period, some particular modern quarter century or so: I am sorry to say that I cannot remember which one it was. James said, referring to the years in question, "These were excellent times economically. Prices were high, wages were low …"—and he went on, but I did not hear the back part of his sentence because I was stunned by its first part. I wondered whether he had meant what he said, or, perhaps, had put the words "high" and "low" in the wrong places. For although I had not yet *studied* economics, I was convinced that high prices and low wages made for hard times, not good ones. In due course I realized that James had *indeed* meant what he said, and that what he meant when he said that times were good because prices were high and wages were low was that times were good for the employing classes, since when wages are low and prices are high you can make a lot of money out of wageworkers. James, a spokesperson for the employing classes, spoke of human labor the way the capitalist system treats it in reality: as a resource for the enhancement of the wealth and power of those who do not have to labor, because they have so *much* wealth and power. The experience of listening to James's lectures did not diminish my childhood belief in the centrality of class war to social existence.

In the second year of the B.A. at McGill you could begin to specialize, and, given my faith in the omniexplanatory power of economics, I decided to do an honors degree in that subject. You could not, however, do economics on its own. You had to do it together with political science, and you couldn't do it together with anything else. So I was about to enroll in the Economics and Political Science course. But then I discovered—and here I come to the bad reason that helped to push me towards philosophy—that Economics and Political Science was the course of choice for a certain species of person that was well represented at McGill, a species consisting of suit-wearing bourgeois Zionistic middle-class Jewish boys, a species to which, incidentally, my nonrelative *Leonard* Cohen then belonged, and one from which, as you may know, he later escaped. It was a species to which *I* did not belong and one to which, in my shameful vanity, I wished to be *seen* not to belong.

I was in a dilemma. Economics was to be my subject, but I didn't want to be associated in people's perception with the bourgeois Jewish boys. I was Jewish, that bit I couldn't help, and that was also the bit that I liked, but I was not bourgeois or suit-wearing or Zionistic or middle-class and I didn't want people to think I was because of the subjects I was studying. Then, while rummaging ruefully through the McGill course book, I noticed that if I enrolled not in Economics and Political Science but in Philosophy and Political Science, I would be required in my second year of the B.A. to take exactly the same courses in economics and political science as the bourgeois boys would take, and I would then have the further requirement of a philosophy course. As a student of the nonbourgeois or less bourgeois course in *Philosophy* and Political Science I would take exactly the courses that I would have taken under Economics and Political Science, and I could switch back to Economics and Political Science in the third year, if I didn't like philosophy. By going for *Philosophy* and Political Science, I wouldn't be burning any boats.

So that is what I did. And, in the event, I fell in love with philosophy, and I dropped economics. Marx and Engels rolled over in their graves. I dropped economics because I couldn't do philosophy *and* economics. But I kept political science, so that I might retain *some* sort of connection with the real world (at least with the superstructure, since by doing philosophy I was depriving myself of the economic base).

But I found that I didn't *like* the real world very much. I liked the *ideal* world of philosophy more than I did the earthy, gritty world of political science. There were too many facts in political science: political science was *stuffed* with facts, it was fact-*engorged*, and, as some of you know, I am hostile to facts. Consider, for example, December 1958, when I had just been dropped by what had been my semigirlfriend, and I was miserable, and I had to write an essay on the differences among the committee systems of the British, American, and Canadian legislatures. Imagine having to learn all those facts while suffering the miserable yearning of thwarted love. I thought then how much nicer it would have been to fly with Plato into the heavenly world of immaterial forms. That would have been a better antidote to my yearning for the semigirlfriend's material form, which might not have been as beautiful as the pure form of beauty of Plato's dialogue the *Symposium*, but which was certainly beautiful enough.

In that Platonic dialogue, the *Symposium*, we begin with "the beauties of the earth," its "beautiful forms," and we go from those "beautiful forms to beautiful practices, and from beautiful practices to beautiful notions," and then we ascend from beautiful notions to pure beauty itself, in all its beautiful purity, in a wild and wonderful act of the mind. What I loved about philosophy is that there were no parliamentary committees to study and your imagination could soar: you, not the textbooks, were in charge of what you thought, and you were entitled to think whatever, in full and sober concentration, you were inclined to think. I got into philosophy because it seemed to have no rules or boundaries, because in philosophy one could fly free. And now I love philosophy for the opposite reason, namely, that the rules are clear and everything is to be scrutinized using the most stringent standards of intellectual acceptability.

Analytical philosophy has taught me to scrutinize rigorously in that uncompromising way. But we didn't *do* analytical philosophy at McGill. Instead, we studied great texts, and in that first philosophy course the texts were by Plato, Descartes, Hume, and William James. William James was a lightweight in that company, but he was on the syllabus because he was liked by our principal teacher, a Virginian called James Wilkinson Miller, who looked like Mark Twain, and who spoke as I would have expected Mark Twain to speak, at least when Mark Twain was in a genial mood. Miller walked back and forth on the stage as he lectured, and he had an endearing habit of patting his tummy, in the area of his appendix, while lecturing. Miller expounded Descartes's ontological argument for the existence of God, which went like this. God is by definition perfect, he wouldn't be perfect if he didn't exist, therefore he exists. But Miller was concerned that some students might think that Descartes thought that he was only proving the *idea* of God, whatever that might mean. So Miller explained: "Did Descartes believe in a God that was alive? Well, what kind of a God would it be that wasn't alive? It would be one hell of a God."

Our most charismatic teacher was called Raymond Klibansky, who had a certain presence in Oxford, both before and after McGill. Klibansky was a Paris-born Polish Jew with a great shock of salt-and-pepper colored hair. I remember seeing him through the open door of the academic staff men's lavatory mussing up his mane five minutes before the Hegel and Marx seminar that he was about to conduct. I felt critical of him for doing that. Thirty years later I found myself doing something similar in my private All Souls bathroom, just before I was going to lecture, maybe with less commitment than Klibansky showed, and then I suddenly remembered how I had disapproved of Klibansky when I had seen *him* doing what *I* was more or less now doing. I had to choose between exonerating Klibansky and condemning myself. I chose to exonerate Klibansky.

Klibansky wanted us to be in awe of Hegel and Marx. He taught us to approach them with caution. Suppose somebody said at the seminar, "Professor Klibansky, how come Hegel says that consciousness wraps itself around itself and returns to itself in order to find itself not being at home? How could consciousness be so, uh, so *snake*-like?" Klibansky would admonish the student, thus: "Your question shows lack of understanding, Mr. Shapiro, but we must understand Hegel before we criticize him." But that exciting transition, moving from understanding Hegel to criticizing him, never actually happened. In fact, I'm not sure that the *understanding* Hegel part *itself* ever happened.

When, in due course, I had done my final exams at McGill, and I was destined for the B.Phil. in Philosophy at Oxford, Klibansky summoned me to his office, which was not in the Philosophy Department itself but in a little house, called Duggan House, up a steep hill, which was the foothill of Mount Royal, which is the mountain, or hillock, that gives Montreal its name. (I should say as an aside that I once bumped into Klibansky when I was walking up the steep hill in question and he was walking down that hill, and I cheekily said to Klibansky, "If Heraclitus's office had been in Duggan House, he could not have said that the way up and the way down are one and the same." And Klibansky replied, with the beginnings of a sneer: "Heraclitus would have said that Mr. Cohen is a very *superficial* philosopher.")

Anyway, Klibansky sat me down to talk about Oxford in his office, which was also his large and impressive library, with many ancient books in it, for Klibansky was an expert in medieval philosophy and a collector of rare texts. Once I was sitting comfortably, Klibansky proceeded to describe the position of his library in space, and, I assure you, I'm not making this up. There will be some invented sketches this evening, but the following is from real life. So, as I said, Klibansky proceeded to describe the position of his library in space. "To the west," he said, "we have the vast expanse of Canada, through the Great Lakes and the rolling prairie and across the majestic rivers to the Pacific Ocean. To the south, there is the massive territory of the United States and of the other Americas, carrying the marks of British and Spanish and other European civilization. And to the east, across the Atlantic, we have the great panorama of Europe itself, the cradle of all that is precious in Western culture and thought. But now look to the north! Look to the north, Mr. Cohen." (I looked to the north.) "To the north, you have only mountain and ice and snow and forest and nothing, until you reach the Arctic tundra. And along all that way north, if you draw a straight line from here to the polar ice cap, you will not find a single library! This library is the final library! Farther than this no mind can go! Mine is the last outpost of learning!"

Klibansky then proceeded to offer me advice about how I should conduct myself at Oxford. "There," he said, "you will learn this new form of philosophy, which is talk about talk." (He really said that.) "You will neither reject it completely nor accept it completely. You will respond to it with proper balance. And at Oxford there will be distractions. There will be the Labour Club, and the so-called Campaign for Nuclear Disarmament. These you will cast aside." I didn't cast them aside.

When I left McGill, I had a choice of going to Harvard or Oxford or Paris for graduate work, Oxford and Harvard because I had duly applied to them and been accepted, and Paris because McGill awarded me a special scholarship that was tenable only at the University of Paris. I rejected Paris because my French wasn't good enough for me to need to think up any other reason to reject Paris. I don't know what would have happened to me had I gone to Paris. A great deal of what I have described as French bullshit in a partly unpublished paper available free from me called "Deeper into Bullshit, and Why One Kind of Bullshit Flourishes in France" was beginning to flourish in Paris.[2] If I had gone to Paris, would I have sunk into a sea of bullshit, and become a bullshitter myself? We shall probably never know.

Because my French wasn't, as I judged, good enough, because I couldn't contemplate doing graduate work with a linguistic impediment, the real choice was between Oxford and Harvard. I inclined towards Oxford, because Europe was nearby, and I wasn't rich, so Oxford offered Europe in a way that Harvard couldn't. When I told James Wilkinson Miller, who was a Harvard man, that I intended to go to Oxford, he disparaged the quality of philosophy at Oxford. So I said what about A. J. Ayer? And Miller replied, "Quine could put Ayer in his pocket."

So I came to Oxford, and, in particular, to New College.

[2] [Now wholly published as Chapter 5 ("Complete Bullshit") of this volume.—Ed.]

I arrived at New College a couple of weeks before term began and I was allocated what must still be the highest college rooms in Oxford, at the top of Robinson Tower overlooking Holywell. The nearest *toilet* was five stories down in the adjacent staircase, and that led to certain difficulties at certain times, but I do not go into detail here because the relevant difficulties belong to my *non*-philosophical development.

During those two preterm weeks nobody told me what I was supposed to do when the term began, and then term duly began, it was the first day of Michaelmas, and I still didn't know what I was supposed to do. I didn't know who was supposed to supervise me, but I did know who was supposed to *guide* me, because I had a *moral* tutor at New College, a person who was supposed to oversee my general welfare. *My* moral tutor was the philosopher Anthony Quinton, who was mostly called *Tony* Quinton. Or at least that's what he was called *then*. Now he's called *Lord* Quinton, the *Baron* Quinton, or, sometimes, just, the *Baron*. In Britain they have these amazing changes of personal identity: a person starts out Tony and he ends up—Baron. You know in Montreal, when I was growing up, there *were* also some Barons, … *and* some Earls. I knew quite a few Earls. There was Earl Goldstein, Earl Shapiro, e.g., there was even an Earl *Baron*, Sam and Sadie Baron's little boy. But these guys were *always* barons and earls: they were born earls and they'll die earls—the exact same rabbi that circumcised them will eventually bury them. In Montreal, once an Earl always an Earl … But in the UK you could be born a Nigel or a Neville or a Nedgley but one day … ping … you've become Earl.

Anyway, I happened to bump into Quinton in the New College front quadrangle, on that first day of term, and I questioned him, I questioned Quinton in the quadrangle. I asked him what I was supposed to do. And he said, and I quote: "I should have thought you would have got in touch with Gilbert Ryle."

"I should have thought you would have got in touch with Gilbert Ryle." I was thrown by the syntax. We don't *have* tenses and *moods* like that in Yiddish. Either you think or you don't think. I thought: "Whaddya mean you *should* have thought? So why *didn't* you? It would have cost you something to *think* it? And it wouldn't have killed you to volunteer that information to me. I should have thought I shouldn't have had to ask you."

In any case, I took Quinton's advice. I rang Professor Ryle, at Magdalen College. "Ryle" was what he said when he picked up the phone. That's all. *Ryle*. I assumed he was naming himself. So I said: "Er, Sir, my name is Jerry Cohen, and I was ringing …" "Ah, Cohen!" "I was ringing to ask whether I could come and see you?" "Certainly!" "Er, when, Sir?" "Pretty well anywhen. What about Thursday, crack of dawn? That's ten o'clock?" That's really what Ryle said.

Ryle became my supervisor. I want to try to convey to you how wonderful he was, in the literal sense of "wonderful" meaning by "wonderful" not "terrific," although he *also* was terrific, but meaning by "wonderful" "worthy of being wondered at." I shall report a few incidents that occurred in our supervision sessions.

I shall then offer an invented extrapolation of Ryle, an imaginary extension of his already ample actuality.

Ryle was very forthright in speech, very no-nonsense, very much the army major that he was in the Second World War. Once when I was still under the René Descartes Cartesian spell that Ryle's book *The Concept of Mind* was supposed to *dis*pel, I said to Ryle, who thought all mental phenomena were tractable and sortable and in general pinnable-down, so I said to Ryle: "Surely, Professor Ryle, emotions are ineffable?" To which Ryle replied, "Well, I've never known anyone who was any good at effing them." Which taught me that there was no such thing as ineffability in the relevant ghostly Cartesian sense.

Ryle would introduce certain topics in a most abrupt fashion. Everything about him was abrupt, including his highly abruptable short name. Ryle once began to make a philosophical point by saying: "A medical brother of mine, now dead, used to take a great interest in pain. One day he applied a burning cigarette to the back of his hand, and he noticed …" I don't remember what Ryle's brother was said to have noticed. I just remember feeling moved to say something caring and kind about Gilbert's loss of his brother, but I was unable to do so, because there was no gap in the regimented flow of words where it would have been possible to intervene.

On another occasion, the name of the philosopher W. T. Stace came up. Ryle had had some sort of communication from Stace. I was surprised, because I knew that Stace had published a book called *Hegel* in 1927, and it seemed to me like an old man's book, so I was surprised that this person who was old in 1927 was still alive here in 1961, and I said, "Oh, is W. T. Stace still alive?" "Walter Stace?! Alive!? Certainly, both alive and flourishing. *Son* died last year in an airplane accident and his daughter was recently divorced. So *parentally* things are not going too well. But otherwise flourishing."

Ryle's eccentricity extended to the conduct of supervision. Much of the supervision took the following form. Ryle would have made some general claim in *The Concept of Mind*, or would make some general claim in the supervision session, and then I would produce what I thought was a counterexample to it. Sometimes the counterexample was pretty much on the mark, and then Ryle would say, "I don't know how to deal with *your* case, but I do know how to deal with the following halfway house case." And then a fairly innocuous example was presented and we'd argue about it, with Ryle calling it "my boring case," and *my* own more challenging case was never revisited. Ryle once averred that we only ask who is *responsible* for something if the something isn't good, or if it's at least fishy. So I said, "But Professor Ryle, I might return from the Continent after some years' absence and, on the boat train from Dover, I might say to a fellow passenger: 'I wonder who is *responsible* for the great improvement in British Railways.'" Ryle said: "Well, there is that sort of case, but I'm sure it's not an accident that it's a minority one." I didn't know what to say.

I once asked Ryle if we could do some aesthetics, to which he replied: "I'll talk to you about expression, but I won't talk to you about significant form." So we talked about expressing, evincing, enouncing, announcing, denouncing, Roget's thesaurus and so forth on until Ryle said, "Care for a glass of sherry, Cohen?" Which I did.

Now here is another conversation that actually occurred but that I shall embellish at a certain point, and I'll let you know when I reach that point, by raising my right arm.

Ryle once ventured, rather on the wavelength of his book *Concept of Mind*, that, as he put it, and I quote, verbatim, "Unlike pain, pleasure lacks a specific bodily location." It didn't take long to come up with a counterexample. "Er, Sir, what about sexual pleasure." "Ah, there is that, but I was thinking of something more interesting. There's a difference between agony and torture, but I'm not quite sure what it is. Do you have any thoughts about that?" "Well, I can agonize and I can torture, but I can also agonize about and I can't *torture about*." [At this point Cohen raises his right arm to indicate embellishment.—Ed.] "Except in the irrelevant sense in which I torture about a dozen natives, in my capacity as district officer. And I can *be* in agony but I can't be in torture, although I can be in torture instruments, if they happen to be the commodity that I'm selling. Musical instruments and instruments of torture are the same kind of thing, but they're not the same type of thing, since kinds and types are different sorts of things, even though they belong to the same category, because sorts and categories, while alike in nature, differ in character, since natures and characters, though identical in quality are different in hue or color."

Here is a Ryleism that was invented by Tony Skillen of the University of Canterbury, about forty years ago, but I present with further embellishments by me. "Adjectives are NOUN-hungry, but that doesn't mean that we should invite them to the officer's mess, or to Magdalen high table. The way in which an adjective is hungry for a noun is different from the way in which a starving schoolboy is hungry for a pork pie, and it's also different from the way in which a starving Jew is hungry for a pastrami sandwich. There's a difference between a pastrami sandwich and a nonpastrami sandwich, and there's a difference between a pastrami omelet and a pastrami nonomelet, but the difference between a pastrami sandwich and a nonpastrami sandwich is a different *kind* of difference from the difference between a salami omelet and a salami nonomelet. But, in addition to being entirely different, it's also entirely the same. There's a difference between sameness and difference and there's a sameness between difference and sameness, but, in the end, all things are the same, and also almost entirely different from each other."

Because I was unsure of how well I could cope with hard analytical philosophy, I sought permission from Ryle to tilt my examination choices in the direction of moral and political philosophy, which were less hard, at least then, than more central philosophy, and which in any case were the subjects that I was most interested in. I asked Ryle whether I could do the exams in Moral Philosophy, Political Philosophy, and, a novelty then for B.Phil. philosophers, the Politics paper on Political Theories of Hegel and Marx. I asked if I could do those exams, and a thesis on some aspect of Marxism.[3] "All right," Ryle said, "As long as you keep your ears open for other noises." I made (and kept) a promise to do so.

[The next seven paragraphs of the text of this lecture recount Cohen's first meeting with Isaiah Berlin, whom Ryle had arranged to supervise his studies of Hegel and Marx. These paragraphs are not included here, since they are a slightly edited version of Section 2 of "Isaiah's Marx, and Mine," which has been reprinted as Chapter 1 of this volume.—Ed.]

There was, as I shall shortly illustrate, a lot of pedantry in the Oxford of 1961, but Isaiah was not pedantic. He was simply precise, and he demanded precision from others. Students could be victims of that demand. So for example, and as Steven Lukes relates, there was this American student who asked a question following one of Isaiah's lectures on Marx: "Sir Isaiah, where would you locate the concept of alienation in the galaxy of Marx's thought?" "In the what? In the what? In the what of Marx's thought? Please repeat the question." (Repeats it, this time a bit hesitantly): "Sir Isaiah, where would you locate the concept of alienation in the … uh, galaxy of Marx's thought?" "Ah, the galaxy! Yes, very good, the galaxy, the galaxy, yes the galaxy." And that, I think, was the whole of Isaiah's answer to the question.

Isaiah was visited by rich Jewish businessmen who wanted to discuss deep questions.[4] One such Middle European I remember asking: "Sir Isaiah, don't you agree that modern man has lost his way?" "His way? Modern man? Yes, indeed, why not? Quite lost. Quite irretrievably lost."

And here is an exchange between Isaiah and an American student that I do not know happened but I know that it could have happened.

"And where did you study?"

"At Wesleyan University. You may know one of my teachers, Norman O. Brown, the author of *Life against Death*."

"Oh, yes, Brown, *Life against Death*, yes, a charlatan's book, full of vague speculation … Norman O. Brown is a rogue, a complete rogue."

"Well, yes, but he's a marvelous teacher, Sir Isaiah."

[3] [At this point, there is a gap in the audio recording. The point in this text at which the audio recording resumes is indicated by n. 4 below.—Ed.]

[4] [The audio recording resumes in the midst of some ad-libbed remarks and then returns to the text at this point.—Ed.]

"I have no doubt, he's probably a splendid teacher. But nevertheless a rogue, a consummate rogue."

"But how could a man who is a total scoundrel also be a great teacher?"

"A scoundrel? Who's a scoundrel? Which scoundrel do you mean?"

"Why, the man we're talking about, Norman O. Brown."

"Norman O. Brown, of Wesleyan a *scoundrel*? No, not at all! A *rogue* yes, but not at *all* a scoundrel, no one could be *less* of a scoundrel."

The rogue/scoundrel story is essentially due to Richard Wollheim, from whom you will hear towards the end of this lecture. But then a real-life exchange between Isaiah and me occurred that had the same amusing structure. We were gossiping following one of my first All Souls Stated General meetings, and I said about one Fellow that I thought he was very oily. I shall not reveal who the Fellow was. So I said, "*X* was oily, wasn't he?" And Isaiah replied. "*X*, oily? No, not at all. Smooth yes, but not at all oily."

It is a lovely structure. Isaiah willingly applies a certain description, and then denies the application of a semantically neighboring description that we less precise folk would think entailed by the description that Isaiah applied. Or the other way around, whatever that may be. And at first it sounds pedantic to the point of ludicrousness. And then, when you think about it, Isaiah turns out to be right. "Good, no. Not at all good. Excellent, yes." "Not at all cold, just a distinct lack of warmth." "More than five, no. More than a hundred, yes, of course."

Partly because of such tropes, Isaiah was a famous conversationalist. But it tended to be a one-way conversation. If I hadn't seen him for a few days, he might begin:

"Tell me what you've been doing, bring me up to date, I want to know what you've been thinking about, what you've been writing, where you are heading."

"Well, the …"

"The Babylonians did not have the word 'the.' They abhorred the definite article. Not so the Sumerians …"

He was also a famous lecturer, and I should now like to simulate one of his lectures, on one of his favorite subjects, namely, nineteenth-century European Romanticism:

> Why do men need a conception of the good, of what is valuable, or worthwhile, why can't we dispense with the good, dispose of it, dispatch it, disregard it, in a word, or in several words, or in very many words, why can't we turn our backs on the good and leave it behind, why do we so desperately *need* a conception of the good? Because men face choices, and the good guides them in their choices. Every man, when he comes of age, whether he be called Archibald or Aziz, Basil or Bobby, Malcolm or Moishe, every man must choose. He must choose, for example, whether to believe in a God, in a deity, in a divine power, and if so, which one. He asks himself: shall I be a Buddhist, or a Hindu? Shall I follow in the steps of Jesus or shall I crawl behind

Zoroaster? Shall I worship Mohammed, or the true, *Jewish* God? And he faces other choices too: where shall I live? Shall I live in the country or in the city, and if in the city shall I live in the pulsating heart of town, or in the sleepy suburbs; in a safe part of the city with no cafés or restaurants, or in a part full of bars and nightclubs but where thieves and cutpurses and cutthroats lurk and threaten, where pickpockets may take my pocketbook, where there are desperate men, men without values, without principles, men bereft of norms, without virtue or morals, desperate men who would take my life for a ha'penny?

Women are more fortunate, because they are less burdened. They do not have to answer questions about the good life, but they too must make choices. They must ask themselves: what sort of man shall I *marry*? Do I want a Muslim or a pagan? Perhaps I should pick a Sikh? Do I want a city slicker or a country bumpkin, a Thomas Hardy farm laborer or a stamp collector or an acrobat, a Dodger or a Yankee fan? Do I desire a Hindu or a thin Jew, someone brahminical or something more rabbinical? And then, when she has formed her ideal conception of the mate to which she aspires, the woman must stride into town or mount her horse and ride through the country to seek him, scanning all the highways and byways, the mountains and the valleys and the bens and the glens, in her energetic search.

And in all *their* choices men need a conception of the good. And these conceptions change over time. They are not the same at all times, or, indeed, in all places. Take, for example, Europe around the beginning of the nineteenth century, in the high Romantic period, indeed, in the colossally High Romantic period, higher than Everest, higher than a kite, higher than a gentile peasant on cider. Take that high period. Suppose you were to go somewhere in Europe, at that very romantic time, say Amsterdam, say Antwerp, say Athens, or Andorra, say Arnhem, or Assisi, say Birmingham, or Bristol, say Berlin or Bologna or Baloney, say Biarritz, say Brussels, say Baden-Baden, say Baden Baden Baden, say any number of Badens you like, say Cologne, say Düsseldorf, say Essen, say delicatessen, say anywhere up to and including Zermatt and Zurich. Suppose you were to go to some such place, what would you find, what would you experience, what would you encounter, what would capture your attention, what would strike you, what would you find salient? What did men think good, desirable, worthy of their affection, what commanded their admiration, what did they think wholesome, nourishing, supportive, enabling, helpful, fine and graceful … and what did they think *bad*, evil, bad *and* evil, what did they think unworthy, contemptible … ?

At this time, at this point in European history, men said that the good was: energy! assertion, power, vitality, zip, exuberance, expressiveness, the rendering outward of the inner, the good, for them, were they in Moscow or in Marseilles, were they in Baden-Baden or in Brussels Brussels, or in Aix-en-Provence or in Aix-la-Chapelle or in Aix-Les-Bains, or Minsk or Pinsk or Akmolinsk, the good for men was, in a word, activity, agency, acting, being engaged in activity, being an agent, *doing* something, instead of just hanging around or lounging or loitering or lolling about. And what was the bad thing, what was bad? Bad was passivity, bottling everything up, passionlessness, oomphlessness, indeed, *lack* of energy, lack of assertion, lack of power, lack of vitality leading to tiredness, ennui, drowsiness, perpetual napfulness, the death of the spirit.

This is what you would hear in the cafés of Vienna, in the pubs of Newcastle, in the trattorias of Venice and Naples. In Paris women would call out to women in the Luxemburg Gardens and explain that, for men, the good was the positive, the strong, the effective and the bad was under*going*, underneathness, underneathitude, indeed belowness of every hood and underkind.

And it was at this *point*, at this *moment* in European intellectual history that Herman Von Supine wrote his work *Towards Passivity*.[5] And what did Von Supine say? What was his message, as it fell upon the tables of the bookshops from Cologne to Colchester, from Berlin to Birmingham, from Novgorod to Nizhny Novgorod, among the Norwegian fjords, or in the forest of the Ardennes? Von Supine's message, his teaching, his doctrine, his insistence was that there had been *too* much activity, there had been *too* much energy, *too* much assertion, that the age called for a certain degree of passivity, a modicum of calming down, people should be more laid back. Von Supine said that the time had come for *some* peace and quiet.

But Von Supine was not in favor of *total*, unalloyed, passivity. In this way he distinguished himself from his predecessor Samuel Von Pooped, who, fifty years earlier, had written *Towards Unalloyed Passivity*.[6] Von Pooped was in favor of absolute, total passivity, Von Pooped's famous watchword was: everybody should lie down and shut up, maybe not forever, but at least for a century or two.

Von Supine was deeply influenced by Von Pooped but he modified Von Pooped's doctrine. Von Supine was indeed in favor of passivity, but not of unalloyed passivity, he was in favor of moderated, tempered passivity, passivity within limits, a slightly active passivity. *Some* activity was still desirable, but less, much less, not as much, very much not as much as then prevailed.

And how was Von Supine's doctrine received? What was the response to it? It was ignored. Carlyle never read it. For Chateaubriand it was as though it had never been published. Tocqueville set it aside. For Hegel, it did not exist. If you read any novel by any Brontë, the doctrine of moderated passivity is not mentioned. You could sit all day in a café in Vienna or a beer hall in Prague or a brothel in Rome, or a vaudeville house in New Orleans, and no one would discuss it. Fifty years later it seemed for a time as though Von Supine's doctrine would have *some* impact. But even then it was totally ignored. Why then was it so important? I shall explain why in the ensuing twenty-five lectures.

[5] [At this point, Cohen writes the names of the author and book on the whiteboard.—Ed.]

[6] [At this point, Cohen writes the names of the author and book on the whiteboard.—Ed.]

As I said, I do not think it would be right to call Isaiah a pedant. But there was plenty of pedantry at philosophy seminars in the early nineteen-sixties, and I enjoyed it very much. I say there was plenty of pedantry at the seminars, or perhaps I should say plenty of pedanticness: what, you don't know the difference between pedantry and pedanticness?! Let me explain.

Here are some examples of seminar pedantry:

> "I'd like to make a point here, but the difficulty is, I can't think of one."
>
> "Then why did you say that? I don't get your point."
>
> "Because it's true, I really would like to make a point. In fact, I would like to make a point very much (that is, if I had a point to make). I've been wanting to make a point for *years*. But there's always this obstacle, which is that I can't think of one. I've never been able to think of a point."
>
> "Oh, I see your point."
>
> "No, no, no, I don't *have* a point. That's the whole point."

[The next few minutes of the lecture are delivered extemporaneously and are not reproduced here.]

I do not want to give the impression that only the Brits were pedantic. There was an American pedantry too, of a rather more aggressive kind. Let me offer some examples:

> Two American philosophers are listening to Judy Garland: "*If little bluebirds fly across the rainbow, why can't I?*"
>
> "I don't see why it follows from the fact that *bluebirds* can fly across the rainbow that *Judy Garland* should be able to fly across the rainbow."
>
> "She didn't say that."
>
> "No, but she implied it."
>
> "I didn't deny that she implied it."
>
> "I didn't say that you denied that she implied it."

And here's a true story, or anyway my friend Arnold Zuboff said he heard this, at a meeting of the American Philosophical Association, sometime in the seventies. It was a plenary session, and a certain hermeneutically inclined philosopher was delivering a keynote address:

> "You know, for a long time us phenomenologists have been talking about the hermeneutic circle, and people always say they don't know what we mean. And I'm beginning to see that maybe they're right. So I'm not going to talk about the hermeneutic circle any more. From now on I'm going to talk about the hermeneutic spiral."
>
> And, from the back of the room, a little guy shouted: "Now I get it!"

It was interesting when a British pedant confronted an American pedant. Here is my representation of such an occasion.

"Well, we're very happy to have with us today here at Eastern Southern Arizona College Professor Neville Cutfine, of the University of Great England …"

"Actually, I'm not a professor."

"Well, we're very happy to have Dr. Neville Cutfine."

"Actually I have no doctorate …"

"OK. Well, we're very happy to have our speaker, this person here, whatever he should be called, and he will be giving a talk about dyadic sets. At any rate, 'Dyadic Sets' is the *title* of his talk."

NC:[7] "Thank you very much. This paper, or as Professor Laibowitz said, this talk, and of course there's a close relationship between the paper and the talk, since the talk, so to speak, is a *reading* of the paper. In any case, this talk, or paper, is entitled 'Dyadic Sets,' and the talk is indeed *about* dyadic sets, or using a phrase that I shall sometimes also use to designate the sets in question, the paper is about sets with two and only two members. I use these phrases, 'dyadic set' and 'set with two and only two members,' interchangeably: I don't mean anything different by the one from what I mean by the other. You might now ask yourself, or indeed, you might ask me, why, then, I nevertheless use both phrases and the answer is that I alternate the phrases in order to avoid … monotony.

"Now the first point I'd like to make about any such set, that is, a dyadic set—I'm not making any points about sets quite generally, or at least not at this very early point in what is after all a very *long* paper—the first point I'd like to make about any set with two and only two members—is that if we take either member of such a set, we can say of it, that member, the one we took, that it, the member, is not the only member of the set in question, but that, over and above that member, paradoxically or otherwise, there is, within the very same set, yet another member, a further or different or *second* member (of course it might in turn have been the one we first took, but on this particular occasion I began with what one could call the *other* one). In any case it is in virtue of that *other* member, or, looking at it in the other way around, the first one, that it, the set *qualifies* or *counts* as a dyadic set, or, as one might also say …"

A: "Now, wait a minute, OK, so, I know it's rude to interrupt when somebody's giving a talk …"

NC: "… or a paper …"

A: "… OK or a paper, I mean it's rude, like near the very beginning, especially when it's a guest from Britain …"

NC: "… or as one might prefer to say: *Great* Britain …"

A: "… but how much longer is this going to go on? I mean, this is driving me nuts! What you said about CLASSES is just so pedantic I don't know if I can sit here and listen to more in the same vein going on and on constantly repeating variations in your phrasings, and so on and so on … Are you gonna say anything *substantive*

[7] [From this point, Cohen inserts the bold letters "**NC**" for Neville Cutfine and "**A**" for the American pedant in order to indicate the speaker.—Ed.]

about classes? I mean something with a little beef or some sort of flesh, with blood and sinew in it?"

NC: "I don't recall making any remarks about *classes*. I offered certain reflections about sets, and, as I was at pains to indicate, not about sets quite generally, but about dyadic sets, that is …"

A: "… SETS WITH TWO AND ONLY TWO MEMBERS. Sets! Classes! Classes! Sets! Dyadic! Dy(ai)shmadic! We're getting bogged down in this semantic crap, I mean, you know, I don't care if you call them sets or classes, I wanna hear something substantial … so far you've just been playing around with the words, and repeating and repeating and repeating …"

NC: "I think it can be quite dangerous to suppose that a philosopher, or even a lay person, of more or less either gender, it can be dangerous to suppose that when such a person is speaking about sets he or, if necessary, she is *eo ipso*, that is, *in* so speaking, offering reflections about classes. There are a *number* of philosophers who use the terms 'set' and 'class' quite differently. To be sure it's a small number, very few of whom are still alive and none of whom are still actively thinking, nevertheless …

"Now it is true that as I use the terms 'set' and 'class,' they're perfectly synonymous. Therefore anything which I say about sets, for example dyadic ones, is something that I would be *prepared* to say about classes. Nevertheless, I didn't *actually* say anything about classes …"

… and so forth. I am unwilling to endow Neville Cutfine with a punch line.

While waiting for the results of my B.Phil. examinations, it was my intention to proceed the following year to Harvard, to do a philosophy doctorate. But when Ryle told me that the American institution Kalamazoo College had a branch in Aix-en-Provence, where its students could do a junior year abroad, and that Kalamazoo needed somebody to teach a course on existentialism in 1963–64, that the pay was £300 for the year, with free accommodation, I leapt at the chance. It sounded rather a doddle and I looked forward to teaching especially the undergraduettes. I was only twenty-two years old, and I was allowed to look forward to the undergraduettes, according to the morals of the time.

But then a week later Isaiah said, "There's a job in philosophy at University College London. I want you to apply for it."

"There's no point in doing so, Isaiah," I said. "As philosophers go, I'm not good enough."

"Nonsense," he replied, "Of course you're good enough."

"You think that because I'm your student, but you don't know the other B.Phil. students."

"Richard Wollheim is interviewing candidates next week in my room, and I want you to apply."

Well, my ears pricked up when he said that, because I figured that if Richard Wollheim was interviewing in Isaiah's room, then Isaiah must have some influence on him, and if Isaiah had influence on him, then maybe contrary to my expectations, I had a chance.

So I agreed to be interviewed, and I turned up in my three-piece suit bought from Walters of the Turl and Wollheim asked me how I would introduce beginning students to the subject, and I said that I would do a seminar on the mind-body problem and Wollheim asked me what I would ask the students to read and I said Descartes and I mentioned a few others and after I left the interview I kicked myself for forgetting to mention Strawson on persons and I was sure I wouldn't get the job, but I did get it. Having been offered the job, I asked if it could be postponed for a year, because I still wanted to meet the undergraduettes in Aix-en-Provence but Richard said "No" so I forsook Kalamazoo, who were very kind about that, and in October 1963 I pitched up at University College London and a marvelous twenty-one and a half years ensued.

At Oxford, it had been the prevailing notion that there were in philosophy plainly right and plainly wrong answers, that a hardheaded clear-mindedness would without too much ado generate the right ones, and that the right answers were likely to be not surprising but already familiar.

Things were different at UCL. There, every Wednesday afternoon Richard Wollheim presided over a staff discussion group, in which the prevailing notion was different from at Oxford, and one that I experienced as liberating. It was that on any large philosophical question there were bound to be different *views* (that was the operative word), that it could be hard to tell which one was right, and that there was no reason to suppose that the right one was comfortable or long since known. I remember how Richard would restore a sense of perspective, when one of us had rehearsed some accepted wisdom. He would utter a corrective sentence which began "Well, there *is*, of course, the *other* view, that …" And I also remember the thrill I felt, listening to Richard's beautiful inaugural lecture called "On Drawing an Object," when he said of his predecessors A. J. Ayer and Stuart Hampshire that, and I quote, "they did not encourage the desire to agree."

Richard himself was an extraordinarily eccentric person, as you will see if you allow yourself the pleasure of reading his wonderful posthumous description of his childhood in his book *Germs*.

[The next few minutes of the lecture are more extemporaneously delivered from more fragmentary and abbreviated notes, which have not been reproduced here.—Ed.]

And there I must end the story of my journey, which is incomplete. We have not left the nineteen-sixties. But, if you all promise to come back next year, I shall deliver a sequel, a postvaledictory lecture, in which I present impressions of philosophers that I have met in the forty years that ensued.[8] I wish to close

[8] [Cohen did not deliver this sequel during the remaining fifteen months of his life.—Ed.]

by addressing the graduate students and especially the doctoral students in this audience: you are the future of our profession, and you suffer a lot of anxiety. You have not yet arrived, as the permanent academic staff have, and you will be judged make or break, you will either succeed or fail: you will not be judged in the more gentle differentiated way that undergraduates are, and these judgments that you face will determine your future. It is a considerable struggle, for most graduate students, to be graduate students, and I think we teachers don't always acknowledge that as much as we should: we do not show enough compassion. Some of you may sometimes feel like giving up, and some of you do, but I say press on, press on under all the burdens financial and administrative that government has placed upon us, press on, because the prize is a job where you are paid to seek the truth, and to reveal it to others, and for many of us that is the best job we could possibly have. Certainly it is the best job that I could have had, and I want to express my gratitude for having had it. I thank McGill University, and Oxford, and University College London, for the wonderful working life that I have had, and I thank you, everybody here, for sharing this closing celebration of it with me.[9]

[9] I thank Mike Otsuka for invaluable criticism and suggestions.

Chapter Ten

NOTES ON REGARDING PEOPLE AS EQUALS

Editor's Note: Before reading this chapter, please consult the Editor's Preface to this book for an indication of the provisional and unfinished status of what follows.

> Is there for honest Poverty
> That hings his head, an' a' that;
> The coward slave, we pass him by,
> We dare be poor for a' that!
> For a' that, an' a' that.
> Our toils obscure an' a' that,
> The rank is but the guinea's stamp,
> The Man's the gowd for a' that.[1]

> Cuba is particularly enjoyable because of the equality of personhood there based on the fact that the government-state, whatever its claimed faults, stands for the poor and provision for their most basic human needs above all. Persons filling the most lowly functions relate as equals, kid you around, dance on the job, laugh a lot with—just a great breath of fresh air to be around.
>
> —John McMurtry[2]

1. I had hoped to retire with no new writing projects on my plate. But now this big question looms, one to which I have never given the attention that a person of my views should have done. The question is: what is it to regard people as equals? What is it to conceive of them in that way?[3] This question threatens my prospect of a leisurely retirement.

What follow are preliminary reflections, many of them barely half-baked. (If you don't think I really think they're half-baked, do read on.)

[1] Robert Burns, "A Man's a Man for A' That," 1795. I hesitated before including this great poem here, thinking many would think it a cliché, but then I remembered that it is one of the tasks of old people to pass on the wisdom of the ages to the young. [Cohen reproduced the entire poem in his manuscript, whereas only the first stanza is included here. The young will be able, and are hereby exhorted, to read the rest on the Internet.—Ed.]

[2] In private correspondence, 2009.

[3] Note that the question can be asked both by those who think such conceptions are beliefs and by those who understand conceptions less cognitively. I mean to be neutral across those alternatives, unless and until I am forced to be otherwise.

The question that the paper addresses is "What is it for me (or *X*) to regard another as my (or his or her) equal?", and not, at least immediately, "What is it for *X* to regard *Y* and *Z* as equals (as equal, that is, to each other)?" I say "not, at least immediately," because the answer to either of those two questions must surely have implications for the answer to the other. I need to explore the relations between the questions, and I have not done so yet. One conjecture is that "I treat them as equals because …" and "I treat you as an equal because …" might have different appropriate continuations: the pressure to find something in common across persons might be greater with respect to the third-person question.

There is a literature devoted to the following questions:[4] What, exactly, *is* it to regard all people as equal? And what *justifies* the equality of regard? What are the minimal features *f* that chimpanzees lack that make the required regard (perhaps?) unwarranted in their case?

But those might not be our questions. They were not Hegel's questions when he defended a kind of equality, that is, absence of servitude and mastery, on the grounds of its enabling self-realization for each party to the relationship.[5] To be sure, you can't have that with baboons, so there still must be qualifying features. But we look for them in the context of the requirements of mutual recognition, and then they're less important.

This line of thinking says that you treat the other as an equal as a necessary condition of your own self-realization: but only as a necessary condition, because self-realization is not achieved unless she reciprocates, in her own quest for self-realization.[6] To be rude to a waitress is to commit the sin of demeaning your own humanity.

If my wife and I treat each other as equals, that is not because of some features common to us that we perceive, but rather it is because of the nature of the relationship that we seek, and value. To be sure, not any being, with just any features, could enter such a relationship: there are features, capacities, perhaps even motivations, that are conditions of entry. But they aren't of the *first* importance, which belongs to the relationship itself.

So we can distinguish between the view that you regard them as equal to you because that is how you wish to treat them, where the goal is primary, and the standard view that you treat them as equals *because* you regard them as equals, which is the view that prompts the wild-goose chase for defining characteristics.

[4] The finest contemporary contribution to which, to my knowledge, is Ian Carter's unpublished "Respect and the Basis of Equality" [subsequently published in *Ethics*—Ed.].

[5] Ed Skidelsky made this important point at a conference on equality in Exeter in June 2009. I do not know whether he would endorse my development of it.

[6] It would, incidentally, appear to follow, on this line, that if she does not reciprocate, you have no reason to continue to treat her as an equal, and, if that not only follows but is true, then it is hard to explain on the "I treat him as an equal because, like me, he has crucial feature *f*" view.

2. All Souls College is an institution in which different people fulfill contrasting roles. One of those roles is the role of what is called a "Fellow," and another is the role of what is called a "scout," or, as he or she used to be known, in the embarrassingly recent past, a "staircase servant." The Fellows do academic work, and the scouts do menial work, cleaning the rooms, bringing the post, and so forth. And scouts are regarded by Fellows in two contrasting ways, depending on who the Fellow is, and maybe also, sometimes, on who the scout is.

Some Fellows regard scouts as, precisely, servants, that is, as people who do not serve others merely as a matter of fact and circumstance, but as people whose *status* is such that it is *appropriate* that their lot in life is to serve others. That sort of regard might show itself, for example, in a certain brusqueness in the instructions as to desired service that these Fellows give to scouts, and in the nature of the response that the scouts get when they serve well, or badly.

But by some Fellows, at least some of the time, scouts are regarded as equals, as people who, despite their low social status (which is conferred partly by those who regard them in the *first* sort of way) are as much deserving of respect as Fellows are themselves. In this way of regarding them, scouts merely *happen* to be carrying out a service role—they are not thought of as people for whom service is *appropriate*. Fellows show that they regard scouts in that way when they pitch their requests to them nonbrusquely, without conveying that, because of their *own* contrasting status, they are *entitled* to the scouts' service. Of course, they are entitled to that service in a certain sense: it is, after all, the job that the scouts have contracted to perform. So one needs to specify in what deeper sense the less egalitarian Fellows feel not unentitled to the service, by contrast with the more egalitarian ones, who feel that they are merely the lucky beneficiaries of that service.[7]

Do the egalitarian Fellows regard the low status of the scouts as a mere accident *because* they think they merit equal regard, or do they think of them as equal partly *because* they think their low status is an accident? Surely the first: for only by inferring in that direction does the "accident" judgment possess the appropriate meaning. The idea of the accidentality of their station therefore doesn't *explain*, but just *expresses*, the egalitarian thought (or sentiment: see n. 3 above).

To be sure, a person who had thought that differential merit explained her being in a good job, and another not, might think in a more egalitarian way upon discovering that it was sheer accident, in a sense that doesn't presuppose some norm of equality, that explains their different stations: it was the roll of the dice.

[7] Male Fellows who engage in the first, inegalitarian, sort of treatment may think it appropriate that scouts address them as "Sir." (So far as I am aware, there is no equivalent form of address that scouts use when they address female Fellows.) Those Fellows who treat scouts in the more egalitarian way cannot think of "Sir" as justified by anything but convenience, that is, the convenience, for scouts, of not having to remember every male Fellow's name. But one might think that "Mate," or "Bub," or the very interesting "Guv" and "Squire" would be just as convenient.

She might then say, "There, but for the grace of God, go I." But "merit" here does not mean what it meant in the paragraph above. For egalitarians believe not that people's (descriptive) merits are equal, but that people merit equal regard even though their descriptive merits are unequal. It is hard to see how an experience of straightforward accident could support the relevant egalitarian thought.

Andrew Williams suggests the following account of the contrast between the attitudes of the two groups of Fellows:[8]

> Both groups [might] agree that All Souls should have a division of labour with various positions involving different and unequal levels of authority and influence, and both [might] agree upon something like the present division in which the authority tends to correlate with academic rather than non-academic skills.
>
> The more egalitarian fellows, however, realise that under different background conditions an alternative division would be justified, and their endowment of skills would have conferred less authority upon them. Since the conditions lie outside their control but are beneficial to them, the more egalitarian fellows view their greater authority as a happy (for them) accident. More positively, the egalitarians believe that whether the present division is justified depends, at least in part, on how it serves the interests of all the participants and that nobody's interests count more than those of anyone else.
>
> In sharp contrast, the less egalitarian fellows think that the more intellectually able *deserve* [or are otherwise entitled] to rule over the less able in virtue their greater gifts rather than merely because of the effects of their rule. Their greater authority, therefore, is not contingent on local background conditions but is generally desirable, and so should not be viewed as happy accident. Insofar as they believe that individuals' interests matter when justifying the division of labour, the less egalitarian fellows do not assume that everyone's interests are equally important but might instead think that the interests of the intellectually gifted matter more than those of the less gifted.

I agree with Williams's second paragraph but I have a question about his first one. For I think that the more egalitarian Fellows could regard the staff as equals even if they thought that they would remain subordinate no matter *what* the background conditions were. But does it follow that they could then *not* regard their subordination as an accident?

3. One may also regard a person's station as appropriate even if one does not think that it matches some nonsocial[9] feature(s) of that person. One may think of the person's occupancy of the station as a wholly social circumstance, yet one that is now fit and meet. I once had occasion to plead the case for improved liv-

[8] Personal communication, November 23, 2008. I have modified (in square brackets) Williams's words in ways that he would, I believe, endorse.

[9] In the sense of "social" that is explained in chapter 4 of my *Karl Marx's Theory of History*.

ing accommodation for a low-status college worker. The resisting college official said that the worker's existing accommodation was fine for a person of her place in society. That's the attitude that I'm trying to characterize, in general terms, in this paragraph. The ungiving official need not believe some improbable claim about how it is appropriate to her nature that the menial is in that station. He might simply believe that society *creates* upper and lower stations (and a good thing too!).

4. One might think that to regard someone as an equal is to be disposed to treat her as an equal. But that isn't so. I can say, "I regard him as an equal, but I'm too selfish (or biased) to treat him as one." And someone might regard someone as an equal but not treat him as an equal, because he doesn't know how to do so, because he lacks the capacity to bridge a social distance. Some progressively minded public school boys at Oxbridge want to treat college staff as equals, but they don't know how, or just can't.

Contrariwise, some Fellows may treat scouts with politeness and even deference but nevertheless regard them as servants. That treatment would be patronizing: it would embody a pretense that you think that scouts have a higher status than you really think they have. And I can treat a war criminal as an equal in court, without regarding him as an equal.

More generally and more deeply, the identification of regarding as equal and treating as equal fails because the regarding is a *reason* for the treating, which it could not be if it were not distinct from the latter. Regarding people as equals implies (trivially?) believing that they should be so treated, but even if the regarding is identical with the normative belief that people ought to be treated equally, the regarding remains distinct from the treating.

Might regarding, rather than being a normative belief, be a belief in some sort of factual proposition about people? But it is elusive what the content of such a proposition might be. Certainly not that we are equal in natural gifts. It is often said that we are equal in our capacity to feel pain. But is that really true? Suppose someone was not particularly sensitive to pain.[10] Would you therefore not regard her as an equal?

5. Whatever its relation may be to regarding people as equals, what, exactly, is *treating* people as equals?

People sometimes say that treating people as equals is applying the same standards to everyone. If I apply the same standard, then I might give the bigger child more food: the standard is sufficient calories for nourishment. But I also apply the same standard if I distribute money according to height. It is the standard itself that may or may not treat people as equals.[11]

[10] Or not particularly prone to affection: see Bernard Williams, "The Idea of Equality," p. 112.

[11] Cf. ibid., p. 111.

May we infer that *treating people as equals* is just *behaving in the right way towards them*, that the two are conceptually identical?[12] No, because you can believe you're behaving towards people in the right way without regarding them as equals. The italicized phrases therefore express different concepts (at least on a view about the relationship between beliefs and concepts that I hereby manifestly embrace).

6. Perhaps we regard everyone as an equal when and because we *respect* them equally: that is certainly a familiar thought. But do egalitarians[13] *really* respect people exactly, or even roughly, equally? You can't respect a baby in the full-blown way in which you respect an adult, and there are surely appropriate degrees of respect *between* those due to babies and those due to adults, and, therefore, different degrees of respect are appropriate for different adults (even ones of the same age). It looks as though respect can't be something that every (adult) person merits equally.

But perhaps that conclusion is hasty because respect is what everyone merits equally when whatever the features are that justify respect reach a certain threshold of presence. The thought is that, although the features that warrant respect can come in different strengths, when certain minima are present, then the selfsame respect is warranted in all cases.[14]

But might not a supremely moral person be worthy of more respect than the respect everyone above any such threshold merits? It is easier to deny that low-placed people merit less respect than to deny that highly meritorious people merit more.

You might think that Darwall's distinction between recognition respect and appraisal respect,[15] with the former connecting within what might count as regarding people as equal, and the latter not, would dissolve the puzzles of this section. I think that would be hasty. I mean to be speaking near the "recognition" pole.

[12] This would be an example of what Bernard Williams calls a "much too weak" interpretation of equality:

> The idea of equality is used in political discussion both in statements of fact, or what purport to be statements of fact—that men *are* equal—and in statements of political principles or aims—that men *should be* equal, as at present they are not. … In both these uses, the idea of equality notoriously encounters the same difficulty: that on one kind of interpretation the statements in which it figures are much too strong, and on another kind much too weak, and it is hard to find a satisfactory interpretation that lies between the two. (ibid., p. 110)

[13] For the purposes of the present scientific communication, egalitarians are people who regard people as equals.

[14] See Rawls on "range property" in *A Theory of Justice*, p. 508, and Ian Carter's critique of Rawls in "Respect and the Basis of Equality."

[15] [See Stephen Darwall, "Two Kinds of Respect."—Ed.]

7. At first I thought what I wanted to understand was *treating*, rather than *regarding*, as equals, and I interrogated one or two people about treating people as equals: was it, I wondered, respecting them equally? At that stage of my research my brother suggested to me that there might be a person whom he (my brother) did not respect, because he's a bastard, but whom he would still treat as an equal. But Joseph Raz said the opposite about the bastard: that he would not treat him as an equal but that he would respect him. Perhaps there was no difference of opinion between Raz and my brother. Perhaps they were using words differently to make the same distinction. Perhaps, *inter alia*, my brother was using "respect" in what Darwall calls the appraisal sense and Raz was using "respect" in the recognition sense of the word.

8. For a long time Ronald Dworkin thought that *government* must treat everyone with equal respect and concern, but he restricted that obligation to government.[16] I think individuals must treat everyone with equal respect but, unlike government, not with equal concern. That he is not part of my family is a reason for me not to treat him with equal concern. It is not a reason for not treating him with equal respect.

9. Maybe respect is dimensional. I don't regard the waiter as an equal in philosophy but I care about his caring about his children just as I do about that caring on the part of more highly placed people.[17]

10. A serious anxiety: Perhaps I am being too much of a philosopher here, seeking *the* meaning of regarding people as equals? Maybe there is no such unitary or even multiform thing as "regarding as an equal." Maybe there are just various thoughts and attitudes, some of which suggest more regarding as an equal than others do. "To the extent that she … she regards everyone as an equal. … To the extent that she … she does not."

11. What, if any, are the consequences for distributive justice of the equality of regard and/or respect that I am trying to describe here? One might think that they are quite modest. One might think that regard and respect are consistent with any stance on distributive justice, including pure let-them-die-if-that's-how-things-happen-to-turn-out laissez-faire. Or one might think that respect implies a belief that scouts merit a decent salary, but nothing more in the direction of equality.

[16] He dropped *respect* in "What Is Equality: Part III."

[17] Cécile Fabre asks: would you care about a bastard's caring about his children—assume that his being a bastard has nothing to do with his relationship with his children—just as you would care about the same caring on the part of a morally decent person? Fabre thinks she would.

On the other hand, one might think that respect is inconsistent with thinking it OK that there is a large inequality of salary between Fellows and scouts.[18] A scout might cynically say, "He claims to regard us as equals, but he sees nothing wrong with making three times as much as we do: so much for his saying that he regards us as equals." Is the scout saying, "He doesn't really regard us as equals," or, rather, "Who cares about being regarded as an equal? It doesn't amount to much."? I think what the scout is saying is false under either interpretation of his words.

Note how much more solid the scouts' cynicism would be if, in those remarks, what was at issue was not making money but making the scouts do subservient work, or even just accepting subservient service. "He claims to regard us as equals, but he sees nothing wrong with me cleaning his toilet and him not cleaning mine." Here it is more plausible that he does not regard the scout as an equal and that, if he does, then that regard doesn't amount to much. If I employ a rickshaw driver—not just hire one from time to time for particular reasons—I'll have to have a pretty special story about why I nevertheless regard him as an equal.[19]

12. Perhaps the right principle is: nobody is anybody's better. "The rank is but the guinea's stamp." And we move towards equal regard when we treat socially (as opposed to specifically legally) constructed status as mere guinea's stamp.

13. What do we acknowledge when we nod at a stranger in the street, without smiling? Can we represent that as a case of respecting without *any* friendliness? Is what's acknowledged when we acknowledge a stranger the answer to what it is to regard people as equals?[20]

[18] But why do the large disparities of salary among football players not make us think that they belong to different classes?

[19] I thank Dan Butt for the important point that casting people in certain sorts of subordinate roles is inconsistent with equal regard.

[20] I thank Michael Cohen, Michèle Cohen, Sarah Cohen, Cécile Fabre, Natalie Jacottet, Kasper Lippert-Rasmussen, John McMurtry, Michael Otsuka, Michael Pratt, Joseph Raz, John Roemer, Andrew Williams, and Lea Ypi for criticisms and suggestions.

Chapter Eleven

ONE KIND OF SPIRITUALITY: COME BACK, FEUERBACH, ALL IS FORGIVEN!

Editor's note: Before reading this chapter, please consult the Editor's Preface to this book for an indication of the provisional and unfinished status of what follows.

1. I retired from my Oxford professorship and, therefore, from my (full) membership of All Souls College at the end of September, 2008. But the real transition occurred on August 15, because it was on that day that I moved out of the remarkable set of rooms at the heart of the college that I had occupied throughout the twenty-three years of my professorship. I moved into a very nice but simply single room some twenty minutes' walk from the college, in a house once occupied by Herbert and Jennifer Hart, in which the college has been willing to keep me, for four or five years.

In the two or three weeks that preceded the August 15 departure, I was busy packing books and other things, for various new destinations. This was physically quite hard work, about ninety cardboard boxes being involved, each packed to just below hernia-inducing (that is, Cohen-relative hernia-inducing) level. It was actually OK to do some physical work for a change, but what wasn't at all OK was the spirit in which I did it. I was mournful and morose. I was losing a fifteenth-century apartment that had a very big study lined with Jacobean (that is, early seventeenth-century) paneling, a serviceable bedroom for naps and other lie-downs, with a wardrobe and a table, my own private bathroom with toilet and bath and shower, a large corridor with lots of sturdy bookshelf space, and also a little corridor leading to a different college staircase from the one from which one would normally enter and leave the set. I was mournful and morose to be losing all that: a "that" which had given me such rich comfort over the years and which had helped to make my twenty-three All Souls years ones of great happiness. I dreaded August 15.

Then August 15 arrived, and the movers were to come in the morning, a morning graced by brilliant sunshine. And when I got to college, to prepare for the move, I was suddenly filled with a deep sense of well-being: I felt enormous gratitude for the great good of having had those rooms for twenty-three years. I was now without any regret at all about leaving them, and that feeling of fulfillment has persisted to this day. I felt, and feel, blessed that I should have had such a boon for so long. And on that day, for the first time, I saw the wisdom in an old saw that I had always dismissed as banal, the idea that you can look at the glass as half-full or as half-empty. I saw that the glass was twenty-three-years-full, and that it just didn't matter that this particular glass would not have anything added to it in the future. (I had had a merely analytical response to the glass image in the past, the smart-ass response of noting that a glass is half-empty if and only if it is half-full, a philosopher's response that misses the difference of *attitude* between the two thoughts.)[1]

When I got home after the move I told my wife that I felt this enormous gratitude, and that I felt blessed. My wife is skeptical of such things. She said, "Oh, you're just happy that you were so lucky." I protested that that was not what I had said, or meant. But she claimed that only a person who believed in a deity could feel gratitude and feel blessed: for otherwise there was no being to be grateful to and no being to do the blessing. And she did not have to add that I don't believe in a deity: we both know that I don't.

There are at least two different ways of taking the descriptions of my condition which I felt it natural to describe in terms of gratitude and blessedness. One is as a mere metaphor for the form in which my wife would express what, in this first interpretation of the gratitude/blessedness language, is the same thought. You could put it prosaically, as she did, or poetically, as, apparently, I had been moved to do: my wife would not have reacted as she did had she thought that mere (and as she might also have thought, cheesy) poetry was in question.

But a second way of understanding my description of my condition on that day would be to take it nonmetaphorically, in which what is said is that there is a deity by whom I feel blessed and to whom I feel gratitude.

The present essay is a search which, at the point of embarkation, I do not feel sure will be successful, for an interpretation of the language that I was disposed to use that treats it neither as deity-affirming nor, as in my wife's fashion, reductively as (at best) *merely* metaphorical. I do not say, of course, that to speak, nontheistically, of being blessed is not to use a metaphor. Much of the religious language that is employed in this paper is transparently metaphorical. But to suggest that, if God is not affirmed, then the language is *merely* metaphorical is, as the phrase "merely metaphorical" is used here, to imply that the metaphor conveys nothing that could not be put, as it were, in fully prosaic terms. And that is what I am inclined to deny.[2]

[1] [See Postscript.—Ed.]

[2] Editor's note: What follows are unrefined notes, in telegraphic form, written down for further reflection:

> Are there *degrees* of metaphoricality? Are the literal materialist and literal deity readings ends of a continuum? Jeremy W [Waldron—Ed.]: One might think that some spiritual discourse is metaphorical without thinking that we can get a literal way of saying it, and therefore without thinking that the discourse is *merely* metaphorical. That is very plausible for describing music. Might there not be certain human attitudes (etc.) that can be captured

2. I am going to give some other examples of what one might call "spiritual" experiences, but before I do so, let me acknowledge that I am aware that you might find the present exercise unattractively self-focused, and maybe that's a reasonable judgment. But I am genuinely puzzled as to whether a third interpretation of the language that I find natural is possible, and I don't know how to pursue this inquiry without reflecting on my own experience, as opposed to on the descriptions of their experiences by saints and visionaries and such. I want to see what kind of sense can be made of my own experience, although I of course expect the character of my experience not to be entirely different from that of those who have reported their experiences in religious traditions.

There are also thousands, maybe millions, of pages of relevant theology, in the tradition (if it does not show bumbling ignorance to juxtapose these names) of Ludwig Feuerbach and Rudolf Bultmann. Those many pages constitute, no doubt, a repository of insight and nuance from which I could benefit. But I am too slow a reader to *begin* by addressing all that, and I have to hope that you do not think me arrogant to seek to work out whatever I can from within.

3. Alastair McKinnon was one of my philosophy teachers when I was an undergraduate at McGill University. In 1959–60 he gave the Ethics 300 class, and he presided over it with commitment and earnestness: he was in no way expressly theological, but it was not hard to believe, what was true, that he was a non-practicing ordained minister in the United Church of Canada. He had had a radio program, in which he presented his thoughts, and—so I was told: I never heard the program myself, which was, I think, defunct by the time he was my teacher—he ended the program, each week, thus: "And remember, happiness is not too good to be true, but, if it's good, it's got to be true."

In the beautiful May of 1961, when I had just received my B.A. degree, McKinnon and I were walking on the McGill campus. At an inaudible distance

---

only by descriptions that mobilize religious discourse that isn't translatable into day-to-day talk?

Some might say that words like "blessed" and so forth are more decorous, that that's all there is to it. But why *should* they be more decorous? And here is a less sharp skepticism: what does "being blessed" add to "being lucky"? Does it add a nuance of attitude or feeling? How could we tell?

Consider: "God is within you." The same three possibilities (see [main text to this note—Ed.] above) obtain here too. Now some believers who place great emphasis on statements like that *effectively* reduce God to properties like the goodness that is within us. No deity, no *person*, is really affirmed. This is a kind of cop-out: they want to have their cake and not eat it, because it's too hard to swallow. I say that "God is within you" is worth saying literally only if God is literally also *not* within you.

But my daughter [Sarah—Ed.] responds to that skepticism about "God is within you" by saying that people are skeptical only because they haven't registered the true awesomeness of what is indeed within.

from us, and on a higher physical plane, there also walked Frank Cyril James, the soon-to-be-retired principal and vice-chancellor of the university. James had led McGill and, from that base, had played an important part in the educational policy of the Province of Quebec, for more than twenty years. Looking up at him, McKinnon said to me: "He's had the world, and now he has to work out his salvation."

I was intrigued and puzzled by what Alastair said. Because I had been brought up as a devout Marxist atheist, I should therefore have regarded what Alastair said as mystifying rubbish, or, again, at best, as a metaphorical way of saying: he has had great success in worldly affairs, and now he must come to peace with himself and find a less energetic way of living. But I didn't take it that way. It resonated more deeply with me. And it is an utterance that has come back to me many times over the years, and repeatedly, now, in my retired condition. *I*, too, have had the world, not exactly like James, but mutating a few *mutanda*, and now it is time for me to work out *my* salvation.

But I do not address a God who might be my savior. And, indeed it has never occurred to me that, when McKinnon said what he did, he meant me to accept that there is a God by whom James would now seek to be saved. McKinnon himself may have believed that—he was, after all, an ordained minister—but I think he thought, rightly, that I did not have to believe in any such Personage to accept what he said as he had intended it.

4. When I first read the Gospels, there were a number of passages that gripped me, and that still do. One of them is a well-known utterance of Jesus in the Garden of Gethsemane. He is waiting for the Roman soldiers to come and arrest him, and he foresees the torture and death that he will undergo. Kneeling at the top of a hillock which serves as an altar,[3] Jesus says, "Oh, Lord, take away this cup," and then rapidly adds, "but not my will, Lord, thine." This motif of the surrender of will appealed to me immediately, and the appeal has endured.

One afternoon in 2005 Tim Scanlon and I were walking through the Christianity-infested Isabella Stewart Gardner Museum in Boston, and I told Tim how impressed I was by the "not my will" part of Jesus's utterance. But Tim said that he disliked the passage, because it celebrates the submission of a person to the will of another. Yet I had never read the passage in that (plainly available!) way. I had thought of the surrender of will, the attitude of the lilies of the field who do not toil or spin, as just plain surrender, with no one being surrendered *to*. In that sense, I thought of the self-transforming surrender as parallel to the gratitude of Section 1 above, a gratitude that is just grateful, but to no one. Here,

[3] At least as the scene is depicted in the *Agony in the Garden* paintings by Andrea Mantegna and his brother-in-law Giovanni Bellini in the National Gallery in London.

again, a piece of discourse *seems* to presuppose a deity, yet much seems left when the deity is excised. (Perhaps it could be said that by surrendering my will as Jesus did in Gethsemane, I achieve humility, and humility is not so paradoxical as a nonrelation-to-anybody.)

5. On being healed, after a medical procedure, I was moved to say, "I feel touched by the hand of God." And, once again, the question put itself to me whether we can give substantial meaning to that utterance without treating it *either* as mere metaphor *or* as affirming the existence of a deity.

But I think that one may have been phony. I am writing this paper, and I am getting off on my own supposed spirituality. I have to let whatever may be there come, and not force anything. "Pride," Rawls rightly said, "extends itself into the highest reaches of the spiritual, into the best efforts of the personality. Even to cure oneself of pride is the occasion of pride."[4]

6. Certain poems that I first read forty-five and fifty years ago, and that I more or less know by heart (because I have read them and repeated them to myself so many times, and not because I have prodigious memory power), have been with me ever since, and have served as interpretations and crownings for me of various good and bad things that have happened. I am in some moods ashamed of how large a role these poems play in my emotional experience.

Let me explain the shame. When I was twenty I had a friend called Dorothie (she wanted to distance herself from the conventional spelling of her name that her parents had used) who lived in a dormitory for women at McGill University, called the Royal Victoria College. She had a friend, whom I'll call *A*, and, one day when she and *A* were together in *A*'s room, another girl, *B*, visited *A*. And *B* told Dorothie and *A* some sad story about something that had happened to her. And when *B* had left, *A* turned to Dorothie and said, "That was such a sad story. If I had seen it in a movie, I would have cried."

Well, I'm sometimes ashamed that I use poetry in the way *A* might have used films: to rouse the emotional self. Something poignant will happen to someone, and I'll be told, but the frisson or tear will come only after I have crowned the story with, for example, these pregnant words of T. S. Eliot: "And nothing happens but the wheel turns, and remains forever still."[5]

One of my very favorite poetic companions, one not summoned in for utilitarian emotion-rousing service, but actually loved for its own sake, is Tenny-

[4] *Brief Inquiry*, p. 201.

[5] [This is probably an imperfectly remembered concatenation of the following lines from Eliot's *Murder in the Cathedral*: "That nothing lasts, but the wheel turns" (p. 38) and "That the pattern may subsist, that the wheel may turn / and still / Be forever still" (p. 41).—Ed.]

son's "Ulysses," and especially its last long stanza which begins "There lies the port." The poem ends thus: it is the final part of the address by Ulysses to "My mariners":

> Though much is taken, much abides …
> To strive, to seek, to find, and not to yield.

I must have spoken those lines to myself more than a hundred times over the years. But, on a recent occasion, when I was engaged in rehearsing them, the last line changed by itself. This time the line said, "To strive, to seek, to find, and then to yield." For I am retired: the era of striving is over, and the era of the surrender of the will has begun.[6,7]

Postscript. When we say it's half-full, we celebrate what we have. Instead of measuring what we have by some ideal, which leads to half-empty, we measure it from base 0, and then all goods are boons.

A friend from abroad was visiting us in England and we were planning to go out to dinner. A number of us suggested a certain restaurant, because we thought it was good, but the friend from abroad did not immediately fall in with the recommended suggestion. Instead, she asked: "But is that the *best* place to go around here?" I was struck by the question. At the time, all that its inappositeness revealed to me was that what's good is, often anyway, good enough, that it was wiser, often, to satisfice than to maximize.[8] But I did not ask myself why it was wiser. Now I can add that it is because your life is at least half-empty if you measure what you've got by what you might have and more than half-full if you take every boon as a boon, as part of what some think of as God's bounty.

What one might call *true* religion celebrates life, and the world, and looks for the good in everything. Since there is no God for the relation of celebrating (or sacrificing and so on) to be in relation *to*, but it is a sentiment fraught with relationality, it can find its completion only in relation to the

[6] Some years ago my good friend Sholom Glouberman guyed Tennyson's last line in what I thought was a very funny way. Sholom said, "To strive, to seek, to find—perhaps to yield." That was already lodged in my consciousness, and its presence might have greased the rails along which the novel "and then to yield" ran. But certainly "then to yield" was no joke.

[7] [Cohen originally prepared these words on Tennyson's "Ulysses" as part of his closing comments for a conference in his honor at Oxford in January 2009. An audio recording of Cohen's remarks, the first and last few minutes of which are especially poignant, is currently posted at http://social-justice.politics.ox.ac.uk/events/Cohen/pcast.asp.—Ed.]

[8] Even if technically satisficing is reducible to (a form of) maximizing, as some claim, there is definitely a huge psychological difference between the attitudes that I've indicated, and if it can be proved that satisficing is a form of maximizing, then satisficing/maximizing simply fails to capture the important attitudinal difference.

world and to other human beings. Camille Pissarro said that "[e]verything is beautiful if you look at it in the right way," and the analytical-philosophical response to that is to reach for the counterexample machine. But I think Pissarro's statement is defensible. Hegel said that in old age we see the good in everything.[9] Old analytical philosophers should understand when not to use the counterexample machine.

[9] Editor's note: In private correspondence, Michael Rosen has written that Cohen probably had in mind the following passage from the introduction to Hegel's *Science of Logic* that is "not about seeing the good but about experience leading to a fuller comprehension":

> Only after a more profound acquaintance with the other sciences does logic rise for subjective spirit from a merely abstract universal to a universal that encompasses with itself the riches of the particular: in the same way a moral maxim does not possess in the mouth of a youngster who otherwise understands it quite well the meaning and scope that it has in the spirit of a man with a lifetime of experience, to whom therefore the weight of its content is expressed in full force. (p. 37)

Works Cited

Note: Unless otherwise indicated, all above page references in this volume are to the first version listed below of writings that have been reprinted.

Austin, J. L. *How to Do Things with Words*. Oxford: Oxford University Press, 1962.

Balibar, Étienne. *The Philosophy of Marx*. Chris Turner, trans. New York: Verso, 1995.

Berlin, Isaiah. "La théorie politique existe-t-elle?" *Revue française de science politique* 11 (1961): 309–37.

———. *Four Essays on Liberty*. London: Oxford University Press, 1969.

———. "Political Ideas in the Twentieth Century." In Berlin, *Four Essays on Liberty*.

———. "Two Concepts of Liberty." In Berlin, *Four Essays on Liberty*.

———. *Concepts and Categories*. London: Hogarth Press, 1978.

———. "Does Political Theory Still Exist?" In Berlin, *Concepts and Categories*.

———. *Karl Marx: His Life and Environment*. 4th edition. Oxford: Oxford University Press, 1978.

———. *Russian Thinkers*. London: Hogarth Press, 1978.

———. "Alexander Herzen." In Berlin, *Russian Thinkers*.

———. "Herzen and Bakunin on Individual Liberty." In Berlin, *Russian Thinkers*.

———. *Against the Current*. London: Hogarth Press, 1979.

———. "Benjamin Disraeli, Karl Marx, and the Search for Identity." In Berlin, *Against the Current*.

———. "The Counter-Enlightenment." In Berlin, *Against the Current*.

Berman, Marshall. *All That Is Solid Melts into Air*. New York: Simon & Schuster, 1982.

Bostrom, Nick, and Toby Ord. "The Reversal Test." *Ethics* 116 (2006): 656–79.

Brennan, Geoffrey, and Alan Hamlin. "Analytic Conservatism." *British Journal of Political Science* 34 (2004): 675–91.

Brown, Norman O. *Life against Death: The Psychoanalytical Meaning of History*. Middletown, Conn.: Wesleyan University Press, 1959.

Burke, Edmund. *Reflections on the Revolution in France*. Oxford: Oxford University Press, 1999.

Carter, Ian. "Respect and the Basis of Equality." *Ethics* 121 (2011): 538–71.

Cohen, G. A. "A Note on Values and Sacrifices." *Ethics* 79 (1969): 159–62.

———. *Karl Marx's Theory of History: A Defence*. Princeton: Princeton University Press, 1978; revised edition, 2000.

———. "Capitalism, Freedom, and the Proletariat." In Alan Ryan, ed. *The Idea of Freedom*. Oxford: Oxford University Press, 1979. Reprinted in extensively revised form in David Miller, ed. *Liberty*. Oxford: Oxford University Press, 1991; in David Miller, ed. *The Liberty Reader*. Edinburgh: Edinburgh University Press, 2006; and in Cohen, *On the Currency of Egalitarian Justice*.

Cohen, G. A. "The Labor Theory of Value and the Concept of Exploitation." *Philosophy & Public Affairs* 8 (1979): 338–60. Reprinted with revisions in Cohen, *History, Labour, and Freedom.*

———. Review of *Karl Marx* by Allen Wood. *Mind* 92 (1983): 440–45.

———. "Peter Mew on Justice and Capitalism." *Inquiry* 29 (1986): 315–23.

———. *History, Labour, and Freedom*. Oxford: Oxford University Press, 1988.

———. "Incentives, Inequality, and Community." In Grethe B. Peterson, ed. *The Tanner Lectures on Human Values*. Vol. 13. Salt Lake City: University of Utah Press, 1992. Reprinted as chapter 1 of Cohen, *Rescuing Justice and Equality*.

———. *If You're an Egalitarian, How Come You're So Rich?* Cambridge, Mass.: Harvard University Press, 2000.

———. "Why Not Socialism?" In Edward Broadbent, ed. *Democratic Equality*. Toronto: University of Toronto Press, 2001. Reprinted in revised and expanded form as Cohen, *Why Not Socialism?*

———. *Rescuing Justice and Equality*. Cambridge, Mass.: Harvard University Press, 2008.

———. *Why Not Socialism?* Princeton: Princeton University Press, 2009.

———. *On the Currency of Egalitarian Justice and Other Essays in Political Philosophy*. Michael Otsuka, ed. Princeton: Princeton University Press, 2011.

———. *Lectures on the History of Moral and Political Philosophy*. Jonathan Wolff, ed. Princeton: Princeton University Press, 2014.

Craven, Roy. *Indian Art: A Concise History*. London: Thames & Hudson, 1976.

Darwall, Stephen. "Two Kinds of Respect." *Ethics* 88 (1977): 36–49.

Dworkin, Gerald. "Morally Speaking." In Edna Ullmann-Margalit, ed. *Reasoning Practically*. New York: Oxford University Press, 2000.

Dworkin, Ronald. "What Is Equality? Part III: The Place of Liberty." *Iowa Law Review* 73 (1987): 1–54. Reprinted in Dworkin, *Sovereign Virtue*.

———. *Sovereign Virtue*. Cambridge, Mass.: Harvard University Press, 2000.

Eliot, T. S. *Murder in the Cathedral*. New York: Harcourt Brace & Company, 1935.

Elster, Jon. *Sour Grapes*. Cambridge: Cambridge University Press, 1983.

———. *Making Sense of Marx*. Cambridge: Cambridge University Press, 1985.

Frankfurt, Harry. "On Bullshit." In Frankfurt, *The Importance of What We Care About*. Cambridge: Cambridge University Press, 1988.

———. "Reply to G. A. Cohen." In Sarah Buss and Lee Overton, eds. *Contours of Agency: Essays on Themes from Harry Frankfurt*. Cambridge, Mass.: MIT Press, 2002.

———. *On Bullshit*. Princeton: Princeton University Press, 2005.

Freud, Sigmund. *Jokes and Their Relation to the Unconscious*. In *The Basic Writings of Sigmund Freud*. New York: Modern Library, 1955.

Gambetta, Diego. "'Claro': An Essay on Discursive Machismo." In Jon Elster, ed. *Deliberative Democracy*. Cambridge: Cambridge University Press, 1998.

Gellner, Ernest. *Words and Things: An Examination of, and an Attack on, Linguistic Philosophy*. London: Gollancz, 1959.

Glover, Jonathan. *What Sort of People Should There Be?* London: Penguin, 1984.

Hare, R. M. *Freedom and Reason*. Oxford: Oxford University Press, 1963.

Hegel, G.W.F. *The Phenomenology of Mind*. J. B. Baillie, trans. London: Allen & Unwin, 1949.

———. *The Science of Logic*. George di Giovanni, trans. Cambridge: Cambridge University Press, 2010.

Honderich, Ted. Critical Notice of *Will, Freedom and Power* and *Freewill and Responsibility* by Anthony Kenny. *Mind* 89 (1980): 121–33.

———. *Conservatism*. London: Penguin, 1991.

Marx, Karl. "The Future Results of British Rule in India" (1853). In Marx and Engels, *Collected Works*. Vol. 12. London: Lawrence & Wishart, 1979.

———. *The Grundrisse* (manuscript 1857–58). Harmondsworth: Penguin, 1973.

———. Preface to *A Contribution to the Critique of Political Economy* (1859). London: Lawrence & Wishart, 1971.

———. *Zur Kritik der Politischen Ökonomie* (manuscript 1861–63). Vol. 6. *Marx-Engels Gesamtausgabe*. Berlin: Dietz Verlag, 1982.

———. *Capital* (1867). Vol. 1. Harmondsworth: Penguin, 1976.

———. "Speech on the Hague Congress" (1872). In David Fernbach, ed. *The First International and After*. Harmondsworth: Penguin, 1974.

———. *The Critique of the Gotha Programme* (manuscript 1875). In *Marx/Engels Selected Works*. Vol. 2. Moscow: Foreign Languages Publishing House, 1958.

———. *Capital* (1894). Vol. 3. Harmondsworth: Penguin, 1981.

Mehta, Ved. *Fly and the Fly-Bottle*. Boston: Little Brown, 1962.

Nagel, Thomas. "Getting Personal: Why Don't Egalitarians Give Away Their Own Money?" *Times Literary Supplement*, June 23, 2000, pp. 5–6.

Naipaul, V. S. *An Area of Darkness*. London: Penguin, 1968.

Nehru, Jawaharlal. *The Discovery of India*. New Delhi: Oxford University Press, 1981.

Rawls, John. *A Theory of Justice*. Cambridge, Mass.: Harvard University Press, 1971.

———. *A Brief Inquiry into the Meaning of Sin and Faith*. Thomas Nagel, ed. Cambridge, Mass.: Harvard University Press, 2009.

Raz, Joseph. *The Morality of Freedom*. Oxford: Oxford University Press, 1986.

Ryle, Gilbert. Critical Notice of *Sein und Zeit* by Martin Heidegger. *Mind* 38 (1929): 355–70.

———. *The Concept of Mind*. London: Hutchinson, 1949.

Sandel, Michael. *The Case against Perfection*. Cambridge, Mass.: Harvard University Press, 2007.

Scanlon, T. M. *Moral Dimensions*. Cambridge, Mass.: Harvard University Press, 2008.

Scheffler, Samuel. *Boundaries and Allegiances*. Oxford: Oxford University Press, 2001.

———. "Conceptions of Cosmopolitanism." In Scheffler, *Boundaries and Allegiances*.

———. "Immigration and the Significance of Culture." *Philosophy & Public Affairs* 35 (2007): 93–125.

Sen, K. M. *Hinduism*. London: Penguin, 1991.

Sokal, Alan. "Transgressing the Boundaries: Towards a Transformative Hermeneutics of Quantum Gravity." *Social Text* 46 (1996): 217–52.

Sokal, Alan, and Jean Bricmont. *Intellectual Impostures*. London: Profile Books, 1998.

Tully, Mark. *No Full Stops in India*. London: Penguin, 1992.

Wallace, R. Jay, Rahul Kumar, and Samuel Freeman, eds. *Reasons and Recognition: Essays on the Philosophy of T. M. Scanlon*. New York: Oxford University Press, 2011.

Wiggins, David. *Sameness and Substance Renewed*. Cambridge: Cambridge University Press, 2001.

Williams, Bernard. "The Idea of Equality." In Peter Laslett and W. G. Runciman, eds. *Philosophy, Politics and Society*. 2nd series. Oxford: Blackwell, 1962.

———. *Shame and Necessity*. Berkeley: University of California Press, 1993.

———. *In the Beginning Was the Deed*. Geoffrey Hawthorn, ed. Princeton: Princeton University Press, 2005.

———. "Modernity and the Substance of Ethical Life." In Williams, *In the Beginning Was the Deed*.

Wittgenstein, Ludwig. *Philosophical Investigations*. 2nd edition. G.E.M. Anscombe and Rush Rhees, eds. Oxford: Blackwell, 1958.

Wollheim, Richard. *Germs: A Memoir of Childhood*. London: Waywiser Press, 2004.

Yu-lan, Fung. *A Short History of Chinese Philosophy*. New York: Macmillan, 1960.

Index

abortion, 151n18
academic boycott, 20–25
academic freedom, 20, 22–23
advertising, 100, 101, 102, 103
African National Congress, 21, 23
All Souls College, ix, 4, 146–47, 148, 155, 169–70, 185; Fellows and scouts in, 195–96, 197, 199, 200. *See also* Oxford University
Al-Qaeda, 117
Althusserian school, 94–95. *See also* philosophy, French
Ames Brothers, 154
Anderson, Malcolm, 113n43
Anglophone culture, 109, 110–11n36
anticonservatives, 144
apartheid, viii, 20–25
a priori truths, 6
Arafat, Yasser, 129n26
Aristotle, 3, 173n55
Ascherson, Neal, 25
Augustine, St., 100n13
Austin, J. L., *How to Do Things with Words*, 120n10
Ayer, A. J., 6, 114n46, 180, 191

Balibar, Etienne, *The Philosophy of Marx*, 108n29
Bengalis, 58
Berlin, Isaiah, vii, 1, 4–15, 175, 184–88, 190; character of, 4, 6; Cohen's parody of lecture by, 185–87; "The Counter-Enlightenment," 8n7; *The Hedgehog and the Fox*, 4; *Historical Inevitability*, 4; *Karl Marx*, 4, 7–8; and Marx, 6–15
Berman, Marshall, *All That Is Solid Melts into Air*, 173
Bernadotte, Count, 117n5
Black, Max, 98–99
Blue Tops terrorists, 115
Bostrom, Nick, "The Reversal Test," 160n33
Bricmont, Jean, *Intellectual Impostures*, 108n30
British Conservative Party, 173
Brown, Norman O., 184–85; *Life against Death*, 184
Brownlee, Kimberley, 164
bullshit, viii, 84, 94–114, 180; academic, 96, 97, 105, 106, 107n27; and advertising, 100, 101, 102, 103; as bluffing, 97, 98; and bullshitters, 108; and deception, 97; essence of, 96, 99, 100; everyday, 96, 107n27; in France, 105, 108–14; and goals vs. tactics, 103; as grossly deficient arguments, 105; and horseshit, 98; as insincere talk or writing, 97–98; and intention, 97, 104, 106, 107, 108; and irretrievably speculative comment, 105; and lying, 99, 100–102, 103; and negation, 105–6; as nonsense or rubbish, 96, 97, 98, 104; *OED* definition of, 96–97, 99; and reality, 102; and state of mind, 97; and style, 110; and suggestiveness, 106; as trivial or insincere talk or writing, 96; and truth, 99, 100, 102–3, 104, 105, 107n27, 108; as unclarifiable unclarity, 104–7, 108
bullshitters, 97, 99; and bullshit, 108; French, 112; goal of, 101–2; and intention, 106–7; paradigm, 100; and unclarifiability, 106–7
Bultmann, Rudolf, 203
Burke, Edmund, 169
Burns, Robert, "A Man's a Man for A' That," 193

Camp David accords, 129n26
Camus, Albert, 111
capitalism, 9, 10, 12, 18, 177; and bourgeois press, 19; and British Conservative Party, 173; and inequality, 173; and Marx, 11, 13–14
Carter, Ian, "Respect and the Basis of Equality," 198n14
Casal, Paula, 112n42, 114n47
change, 157–58, 169, 170–71
Charlton, Willie, 2
chimpanzees, 194
Christian, Richard, 157
class conflict, 12
class struggle, 176
Clinton, William Jefferson, 115
Cohen, G. A., *Karl Marx's Theory of History*, 7, 84, 111n40
Cohen, Gideon, 115, 132
Cohen, Maggie, 81
Cohen, Michael ("my brother"), 199

Cohen, Michèle, 26, 52, 54, 69, 75n11, 202
Cohen, Miriam, 81
Cohen, Morrie, 143
Cohen, Sarah, 50, 81, 115, 149, 203n
communism, vii; and Cohen's time in India, 78, 89; and Cohen's upbringing, 16, 17, 139, 176; and Czechoslovakia, 16; and Isaiah Berlin and Marx, 9, 12, 15; and McCarthyism, 103; and socialist ideals, 16, 17, 18–19
communist philosophers, 112
condemnation: compromised utterance of, 120; and criticism, 121; of disproportionate response, 127; moral capacity for, 121; as morally permissible or obligatory, 120; and motivated selection, 138; and negative moral belief, 121; right to, 119, 120–21, 125, 131; silencing of, 119–20. *See also* criticism; grievances; terrorism
condemnation, arguments against: "Do as I say, not as I do," 140; "I'm not in a position to criticize," 120–21; "It's your fault that I did it," 125; "Judge not, that ye be not judged," 122; "Let he who is without sin cast the first stone," 119, 122, 134; "Look who's talking," 121–22, 123, 126; "mote in my brother's eye," 122, 135; "That's the pot calling the kettle black," 122, 123, 134; "You caused our grievance," 129; "You forced us to use terrorist means," 129; "You helped me to do it," 125; "You made me do it," 123, 125; "You're involved in it yourself," 123, 125–31; "You started it," 123, 125. See also *tu quoque*
consequentialism, value-maximizing, 155
conservatism, ix, xi, 144–74; and acceptance of the given, 143, 149; capitalism and markets as antithetical to, 168, 173; and change, 170–71; and choice, 145; and existing value, 147; and fascism, 170; and intrinsic value, 144; and particular value, 152–66; and personal value, 144, 167–69; and political right, 144, 172–73; and preservation of the valuable, 149; and regret at destruction, 153, 155, 158; and restoration, 158; and Starbucks, 168; state planning as antithetical to, 168. *See also* valuable things; value
coresponsibility, 126, 129n23. *See also* responsibility
creation, 156, 158, 161–62, 163
critic: compromised utterance of, 120; good faith standing of, 119; right of, 120–21; silencing of, 119–20
criticism: compromised, 125; and condemnation, 121; moral capacity for, 121; and responsibility for thing criticized, 123. *See also* condemnation; grievances
Czechoslovakia, 16–18

Dante, 111
Darwall, Stephen, 198
Deleuze, Gilles, 108n32
Derrida, Jacques, 108n32
Descartes, René, 178, 179, 182
Disraeli, Benjamin, 5, 13
Dobb, Maurice, 58
double effect, 124, 156
Dworkin, Gerald, 135–36, 137–39; "Morally Speaking," 119n8
Dworkin, Ronald, xi, 199

Eastern Bloc, vii
Eastern Europe, 16–17
economic history, 7, 176–77
economic market, 168
economics, 176, 177, 178
ego, quoque (preemptive me), 139. See also *tu quoque*
Eliot, T. S.: and fascism, 122n14; *Murder in the Cathedral*, 47, 205; *The Waste Land*, 92
Elster, Jon, 169; *Making Sense of Marx*, 10n17, 84
emotion, 205
Engels, Friedrich, 9, 11, 178
English, the, 58, 83, 86, 176; compared with the Scots, Welsh, Irish, Bengali, and Jews, 58
Enlightenment, 11
equality, x, 19, 172, 193–200; and caste system, 87–88; of civic standing, 24; Hegelian conception of, as absence of servitude and mastery, 194; and Isaiah Berlin, 12–13
exchange-value, 153n23

Fabre, Cécile, 109n36, 111n39, 199n17
factual assessments, 144, 145
fascism: and Conservatism, 170; in India, 38, 39, 44, 49, 54; and T. S. Eliot, 122n14
faults/sins, 122, 125–26, 134; quality of, 135–36, 137–39, 140; quantity of, 135, 136, 140
Feuerbach, Ludwig, 203
Foot, Philippa, 3
Ford Foundation, 146
France: and authoritarian ethos of intellectual life, 112; bullshit in, 105, 108–14; cultural unipolarity of, 109–10, 112–13; lay audience in, 110–11; philosophical debate in, 113n43;

and philosophy, 108–14; political culture of, 113n43
Frankfurt, Harry, "On Bullshit," viii, 94, 95–107
Freed, Jenny, 17
Freed, Norman, 17, 18
freedom. *See* liberty/freedom
French Marxism, 94
Freud, Sigmund, 100–101
Fung, Yu-lan, *A Short History of Chinese Philosophy*, 106n25

Gambetta, Diego, 95n2, 109n35, 131n29; "Claro," 111n40
Gearty, Conor, 142
Gehry, Frank, 156
Gellner, Ernest, *Words and Things*, 6
Gheaus, Anca, 165
Glouberman, Sholom, 206n6
Glover, Jonathan, *What Sort of People Should There Be?*, 149
God, xi, 202, 204, 205, 206
Goethe, Johann Wolfgang von, 111
goods: deontological view of, 163–64; independently desirable, 169
gratitude and blessedness, 202, 204
grievances, 115, 116; constraints on response to, 127–28, 130; as disproportionate response, 127; involvement or implication in, 125–31; legitimate, 126–27. *See also* condemnation; criticism; terrorism
Grunzweig, Emil, 132, 133

Hampshire, Stuart, 191
Hare, R. M., 3; *Freedom and Reason*, 140n10
Harvard University, 180, 190
Hegel, G.W.F., x, xi, 146n6, 179, 207; and bullshit, 104, 105, 114; Cohen's study of, 3, 4, 5, 184; and conservatism, 143; on servitude and mastery, 194
Heidegger, Martin, 104
historical inevitability, 1, 4, 9
historical materialism, 6–7, 8, 12, 13
history, 9, 13, 14–15
Hockney, David, 156, 158–59
Holocaust survivors, 117n5
Honderich, Ted, 171
human beings, preservation of, 149–52
humbug, 98–99, 102, 103
Hume, David, 178; *Enquiry Concerning Human Understanding*, 45
Hurka, Tom, 163

icons, Byzantine, 156
identity: as lived vs. conceived, 170; metaphysical vs. sociocultural sense of, 147n9; preservation of, 147, 169–70
Ignatieff, Michael, 117n5
India, viii, 26–93; activity of the poor in vs. in the West, 33; Cohen's intense fascination with, viii, 28, 93; fascism in, 38, 39, 44, 49, 54; poverty and begging in, 29–30, 31, 32–34, 45–46, 51, 59–61, 71–73, 79, 80–81, 82, 89–90; terrorism in, 32, 46, 87. *See also* Bengalis
indignation, 134
inequality, 173
injustice: available means of fighting, 118, 127; as lacking intrinsic value, 144; and Marx, 12, 14, 15n50; responsibility for, ix. *See also* justice
innocent people, killing of, 115, 116, 124–25. *See also* terrorism
interpellation, of individual as subject, 95
Isabella Stewart Gardner Museum, 204
Islam, and suicide, 131n29
Israel, 117n5, 121, 129n26; as causing grievance, 131; founding of, 132; as implicated in terrorism it condemns, 127; oppressive policy of, 123–25; restriction of response by, 128–29, 131; and *tu quoque* challenge, 123–24; and "You're involved in it yourself" challenge, 126–31
Israeli-Palestinian conflict, 117, 118

James, Frank Cyril, 176–77, 204
James, William, 178
Jesus, 122, 134–35; prayer in Gethsemane of, 143, 204–5
Jews, 58, 175; and Isaiah Berlin, 5, 13; and Israeli-Palestinian conflict, 117; and Marx, 9; at McGill, 177
justice: and academic boycott, 24; and communism, 16; and conservatism, 144, 172; distributive, 15, 199; and double effect principle, 124; and lack of acceptable alternatives, 128; and legitimate grievance, 126–27; and Marx, 11, 12, 14–15. *See also* injustice

Kafka, Franz, 16
Kant, Immanuel, 3, 175
Kenny, Anthony, 171
Khartoum, 115
King David Hotel, 117n5
Klibansky, Raymond, 1, 179–80

Kristeva, Julia, 108n32
Kuhn, Thomas, 113n44

Lacan, Jacques, 108n32
liberal democracies, 140–42
liberalism, 176
liberty/freedom, 18; civil, 140–42; and Isaiah Berlin, 12–13; and Marx, 15; in South Africa, 22, 23; of South African academics, 20–21; of speech, 18–19
lies/liars, 99, 100–102, 103, 120n9. *See also* bullshit
Lippi, Filippo, 156, 158–59
Lloyd-Thomas, David, 148n10
love, 148, 153–54
Lukes, Steven, 184

Maistre, Joseph Marie, comte de, 8n7
Major, John, 173
Mann, Thomas, 111
Marx, Karl, xi, 3, 4, 5, 6, 178, 179, 184; anti-Semitism of, 9; *Capital*, 11; character/personality of, 9–11, 14; *Communist Manifesto*, 173; *Critique of the Gotha Programme*, 15; and inevitabilitarian view of history, 9; and Isaiah Berlin, 4, 6–15; and justice/injustice, 11, 12, 14–15; motivation of, 13–14; as person vs. set of writings, 8; Preface to *A Contribution to the Critique of Political Economy*, 51; and self-realization, 49; theory of history of, 6; and values, 11–13
Marxism, 172n49; and bullshit, 94–95; Cohen's study of, 3, 6, 184; and Cohen's time in India, 31, 36n4, 53, 57, 84–85, 89; and Cohen's upbringing, 17, 176, 204; Isaiah Berlin's skepticism regarding, 4, 7
maximizing vs. satisficing, 206
McCarthy, Joseph, 103
McGill University, 1, 6, 175, 176, 177, 178, 192
McHose, Brad, 161–62
McKinnon, Alastair, 203–4
McMurtry, John, 173n52, 193
merit, 195, 196, 198
metaphor, 202, 204, 205
Michelangelo, Slave series, 156
Miller, David, 105
Miller, James Wilkinson, 178–79, 180
modernization, 156
Montaigne, Michel de, 111
Montefiore, Alan, 3
Montreal, 16, 122, 175
morality: and academic freedom, 22; and condemnation, 121; and criticism, 121; and Isaiah Berlin, 5, 9; and Marx, 11, 15; and means of fighting injustice, 118; and oppressor, 118–19; and terrorism, 116
moral philosophy, 2, 3, 119n8
moral utterances, interpersonal dimension of, 119–20
Morris, William, 156
Moyne, Lord, 117n5

Nagel, Thomas, vii
Namier, Sir Lewis Bernstein, 5
Nazis, 123, 125–26
Nehru, Jawaharlal, 37; *The Discovery of India*, 38
Neurath, Otto, 170n46
New College, Oxford, 180–81; "Identity and Individuation" seminar, 1–2. *See also* Oxford University
New Deal, 13
New Testament, 143; Gospels, 204
Newton-John, Olivia, 154
Nietzsche, F. W., 122n14
9/11 attacks, 141, 142
Non-Bullshit Marxism Group, 95
Normore, Calvin, 158n30
Nozick, Robert, xi

Oakeshott, Michael, 170
orator, bullshitting, 102–3
Ord, Toby, "The Reversal Test," 160n33
Oslo agreement, 129n26
Otsuka, Michael, 106n26, 156, 159n31, 164, 166
overdetermination, 95
Oxford University, 2, 6, 146n6, 146n8, 180–81, 191, 192. *See also* All Souls College; New College, Oxford

Palestinians, 121, 123–25, 141; constraints on responses of, 128, 129, 130, 131; legitimate grievances of, 126–27, 128–29; sovereignty for, 129n26; and state, 118, 124–25, 129; terrorism of, 116, 117, 120, 123–24, 128; and *tu quoque* challenge, 124–25
Pascal, Blaise, 111
Pascal, Fania, 99
past times, 168–69
pedantry, British vs. American, 188–90
philosophy: analytical, 178, 183; British, 112; Cohen's study of, 175–76, 177–91; French, 108–14; lay audience for, 112–13; and litera-

ture, 111–12; moral and political, 183–84; at Oxford University, 2, 6; and passionate writing, 112; and practical deliberations, 145–46; and religion, 112; rhetorical style in, 112; rules and boundaries in, 178; style in, 112–13
Picasso, Pablo, 162
Pissarro, Camille, 207
plasticization, 150–51
Plato, 3, 59; *Symposium*, 178
poetry, 106, 202, 205–6
political philosophy, 2–3
political science, 177, 178
politics, 100, 102, 120, 134
postmodernism, 114
Prague, vii, 16, 17, 18
preservation: deontological view of, 163; of human beings, 149–52; of identity, 147, 169–70; of status quo, 172
pride, 205
principles, exemplification of, 152–53
production, 7
public relations, 100
purpose, 152–53

Quine, W. O., 180
Quinton, Anthony, 181

Rabin, Yitzhak, 132
Rao, P. V. Narasimha, 37, 87, 88, 91
Rawls, John, xi, 205; *A Theory of Justice*, 2–3, 198n14
Raz, Joseph, 199
reason, 11
reciprocity, 194n6
replacement, 158
replicas, 158
research, 146–47, 151
responsibility: and "Look who's talking," 126; for thing criticized, 123; and "You're involved in it yourself" challenge, 126–27. *See also* coresponsibility
Ricks, Christopher, 122n14
Roman Catholicism, 17, 112
Roosevelt, Franklin Delano, 13
Rousseau, Jean-Jacques, 111
Ryle, Gilbert, 3, 4, 104n22, 181–84, 190; *The Concept of Mind*, 182, 183

Sandburg, Carl, 47, 169
Sandel, Michael, *The Case against Perfection*, 152n21
Sartre, Jean-Paul, 111, 114n46
Scanlon, T. M. ("Tim"), 164–65, 204; "Blame," 132n30
Scheffler, Samuel: "Conceptions of Cosmopolitanism," 149n14; "Immigration and the Significance of Culture," 155, 164
security, 141–42
self-realization, 141, 194; and Marx, 49
self-transforming surrender, 204
Sen, Amartya, viii, 89
September Group, 95
servants, 195
servitude and mastery, 194. *See also* equality
Shaw, Thurstan, 24
Shtauber, Zvi, 121n11, 130, 131, 132; condemnation by, 115, 116, 117, 120; and Israeli restriction of response, 128–29; and *tu quoque* challenge, 123, 125; and "You're involved in it yourself" challenge, 126, 127
Skidelsky, Ed, 194n5
Skillen, Tony, 183
social division, 12
socialism, 16–19, 36n4, 37–41, 63, 78, 83–85, 89
social status/station, 195, 196–97
sociology, 7
Sokal, Alan, 106, 107; *Intellectual Impostures*, 108n30
South Africa, academic boycott of, viii, 20–25
South African National Students' Congress, 23
South West African People's Organization, 23
Soviet Union, vii, 16–17, 19, 132
speech, freedom of, 18–19
spirituality, x, 201–7
Sraffa, Piero, 58
Stace, W. T., 182
state, and Palestinians, 118, 124–25, 129
state planning, 168
status quo, 172
status quo bias, 160n33
Stein, Boris, 175
stem-cell research, 151–52
Strawson, Peter, 8
strikes, 19
Strong, Tracy, 113n45
suburban supermarketization, 167
suicide, 131n29

Tagore, Rabindranath, 4
Tennyson, Alfred Tennyson, Baron, "Ulysses," 205–6

terrorism, ix, 22, 115–33; aims of, 117; as always wrong, 128; as to be condemned, 131; as best course, 131; condemnation of Palestinian, 128; condemnations of, 116, 121; as counterproductive, 117; definition of, 116; as disproportionate response, 127; effectiveness of, 131; in India, 32, 46, 87; lack of acceptable alternative to, 125, 127, 128, 129, 130; and legitimate grievance, 126–27; and liberal democracies, 140–42; nonviolent unconventional alternatives to, 129n27; as only effective strategy, 127; and oppressive Israeli policy, 123–24; as productive, 117n5; as unsustainable, 128. *See also* condemnation; grievances
Thatcherism, 39, 62, 168
theory, 8, 11
Third World scholars, 20
Thomas, Norman, 78
Tintoretto, 162
tradition, 169, 172
truth, 122n14; and bullshit, 104, 108, 110; and freedom of speech, 18; and French bullshit, 112, 113–14; and moral capacity to criticize or condemn, 121; and moral condemnation, 120
Tully, Mark, *No Full Stops in India*, 29–30, 80
tu quoque, 123, 125, 131, 134–40; counterfactual, 123n16; and disproportionate response, 127; and double effect doctrine, 124; force of, 137–39, 140; and hypocrisy, 139; and Israel, 123–24; and Jesus, 122, 134–35; and respect, 137–38; scope of, 134–37. *See also* condemnation, arguments against; *ego, quoque* (preemptive me)
Tutu, Desmond, 23

Unamuno, Miguel de, 111
unclarity. *See* bullshit
United Democratic Front, 23
United States, 117
University College London, 6, 40, 56, 190–91, 192
utilitarianism, 154–55, 163

valuable things: and creation, 156, 158, 161–62, 163; cultivation and development of, 164; deontological bar on destroying, 163; destruction of, 153, 154–55, 156, 157, 158, 160, 161–62, 163, 166, 168, 169; as disappearing, 144; as disappearing by nature, 164; existing, 152, 153, 155, 156, 157, 158, 160, 162, 163, 164, 165, 166; experience of, 159; repair of, 164; as replaced by something of greater value, 149, 153, 156, 158, 162, 165, 166; replacement of, 153, 157, 160–61, 164; that will exist, 166
value: aesthetic, 159; amount or type of residing in thing, 147–48; bearers of, 153, 155, 159; behavior of, 157; bias in, 149, 153, 158, 160, 161, 163, 165, 172; categories of things qualifying as vessels of, 164; conservation of vs. conservation of what has value, 153–56; correct response to, 157; and deontology, 163–64; destruction of, 154–55; existing, 147, 157, 172; human, 163; and incommensurability, 162; injustice and exploitation as lacking, 144, 172; instrumental, 153, 166; intrinsic, 144, 148, 149, 152, 153, 159–60, 161, 172; labor theory of, 153n23; maximization of, 153, 154–55, 156, 160, 165, 172, 206; in old things, 156–57; particular, 152–66; and perception, 159; personal, 144, 167–69; for production of good results, 148; rationality about, 160; sacrifice of, 155; satisficing, 160, 206; sufficientarian promotion of, 155; total amount of, 154; of what merely happens to exist, 147
values: and Marx, 11–13
valuing: particular, 148, 152–66; personal, 148, 149, 152; of the valuable, 143; of the valued, 143
Van Leer Institute, 132
variety, 147
virtue, 152
Voltaire (François-Marie Arouet), 116n3

wageworkers, 177
Waldron, Jeremy, 202n2
Walzer, Michael, 87
weapons of mass destruction, 123n16, 128
Weizmann, Chaim, 5
welfare, 141
Wienerkreis tenet, 6
Wiggins, David, 1, 160–61; *Sameness and Substance Renewed*, 149–50n16
Williams, Andrew, 118n7, 196
Williams, Bernard, 8n11, 174, 197n10, 198n12; "Modernity and the Substance of Ethical Life," 144n4; *Shame and Necessity*, 49
Wittgenstein, Ludwig, 99, 105, 143; *Philosophical Investigations*, 140
Wollheim, Richard, 185, 190–91; *Germs*, 191; "On Drawing an Object," 191

Woods, Michael, 1–2
working class, 9, 13–14, 15, 16, 173
World Archaeological Congress (WAC), 20–21, 23, 24
World Marxist Review, 17
World War II, 108, 109n34
Wren, Christopher, churches of, 145n5, 159n31

"You, You, You" (song), 154

Zionism, 5, 177